The Way Successful
Fashion Designers
Use Fabrics

Fabrics in Fashion Design

Stefanella Sposito   **Photos: Gianni Pucci**

promopress

Fabrics in Fashion Design
The Way Successful Fashion Designers Use Fabrics

Original title:
Tessuti nella moda
Come i tessuti vengono usati dai grandi stilisti

Translator: Kevin Krell

ISBN: 978-84-15967-05-7

Copyright © 2014 Ikon Editrice srl
Copyright © 2014 Promopress for the English
language edition

Promopress is a brand of:
Promotora de prensa internacional S.A.
C/ Ausiàs March 124
08013 Barcelona, Spain
Tel.: +34 93 245 14 64
Fax: +34 93 265 48 83
Email: info@promopress.es
www.promopress.es
www.promopresseditions.com
Facebook: Promopress Editions
Twitter: Promopress Editions @PromopressEd

First published in English: 2014

Graphic design and layout: Pause Design
Text: Beata Sperczynska
Cover design: spread: David Lorente
Photographic stylist for the front cover
(Dior HC 2012 OR Lanvin 2012-13)

Printed in China

INTRODUCTION

This book arises out of the conviction that fabric, a necessary and irreplaceable material for our survival, is the essential element of clothes: this simple, ductile raw material conditions the receiving public as well as taste, style, price, aesthetics, ergonomics, functionality and durability. Experts know that fabric is "what makes the difference", granting garments an identity which accompanies them throughout their existence. It is therefore essential to discover the secrets of the suggestive and dazzling universe of fabrics, replete with references observable from different perspectives. The art of tailoring, a highly regarded professional specialty, increasingly attracts new talent devoted to producing capsule collections and highly innovative limited-edition series while at the same time allowing young fashion and textile design students to develop their inventiveness and creativity. Within the framework of fashion it is important to consider what fabric, the material that accompanies the fashion product in all its stages, contributes at the aesthetic, psychological, industrial production and commercial levels. From the creative concept to the production cycle culminating in shop windows, fabric requires broad attention, one ranging from the internal adjustment of garments to the sustainable ecological balance of the planet. Fabric is a flat, flexible surface made up of an assemblage of materials that form a three-dimensional structure. It is produced using different types of spun fibers, which pass through production processes on looms or other textile machinery to obtain a wide range of products. Knowing their specific characteristics and expressive possibilities is also necessary for consumers who wish to be informed about the quality of the clothes they choose to wear. To this end, we have gathered the identifying characteristics of each of the most commonly used fabrics in all market segments in a compendium that will be useful for recognizing their appearance and qualities. For easier reference, in this book fabric types are grouped in categories that meet common production technique criteria and an in-depth advanced educational standard. We begin with the most simple and linear fabric (flat-woven fabric) and conclude with the most complex and elaborate ones. Analyzing different textile structures, we see that they share common denominators, related to the general manufacturing system, and can be classified in large groups, which can be divided, in turn, into sub-groups whose secondary characteristics also differ. To get our bearings among the different manufacturing systems, a general classification of groups that share sector techniques will be useful. In the first group are orthogonal intersection fabrics consisting of one or more series of threads arranged perpendicularly that form a compact, stable and resistant surface. They are also called shuttle fabrics, after the instrument that carries the weft. The second group has a diagonal fabric surface involving at least three threads in the direction of the warp (braids), a system similar to bands of wo-

Salvatore Ferragamo ss12

M. Galante ss11

ven straw in bags and baskets. This technology is used in the production of passementerie, ribbons, shoelaces and hats. The third group consists of knit fabrics where the thread follows a curvilinear path and forms linked loops that cross the surface breadthways (weft stitch) and lengthways (chain stitch). This structure is elastic and flexible. The fourth group includes openwork fabrics: meshes, tulles, gauze and English lace, obtained with sinuous or mixtilinear fabrics, also called "triaxial fabrics" because the components cross at three different axes. The textile surface is also achieved by handling the fiber directly, uniting it using different systems, as in the case of nonwoven fabrics, felt and woven felt. These fabrics are light and insulating fabrics but easily lose their shape. This first classification leads us to consider fabric as a material in constant evolution that utilizes textile engineering for the development of industrial processes that offer polymers, fibers, yarns or threads in the planning and development of the management of textile, mechanical textile and chemical textile processes. The philosopher Arthur Schopenhauer wrote: "Life is like an embroidered fabric: we see its outside during the first half of existence and its reverse side during the second half. While the latter is not as beautiful, it is much more instructive, as it allows us to see how the threads intertwine in the weave." Orthogonal intersection fabric uses two types of thread: the warp, positioned vertically, and the weft, arranged horizontally. The warp is the element that supports the fabric: its threads are thinner, coarser and more twisted. The weft, made from less elegant material, has a more bulging appearance. The alternation and superimposition of both, according to a programmed order, determines the weaving of the material. The thread count is the number of threads and weft in a square centimeter of cloth. The higher the number, the thinner the threads and vice versa, and this determines the density of the fabric surface and its weight. The more or less smooth appearance of the material and the design of the texture depend on the type of fabric made from threads spun on the loom, according to a design called a weave. There are basic weaves – plain, serge and satin – on which more complex ones are constructed by varying their elements through the regular and systematic increase of connection points. The term "weave pattern" describes the minimum number of warp and weft threads needed to form the fabric weave; the pattern repeat, on the other hand, refers to the threads needed to create a decorative form; this can require several weaves and is repeated in accordance with the pattern articulated by the textile designer. The graphic representation of this design is called a "punched card" and it is carried out on special technical paper in such a way that the weaver receives all useful information regarding the choice of colors and the position of devices on the loom. The graphic representation consists of small filled-in and empty squares. For fabrics with more than one warp and weft, there are concordance representations of the different punched cards. The type of weave, the result of a detailed study, is determined by the possibilities of the loom, which can be equipped with a heddle system (for simple fabrics) or a jacquard system (for complex fabrics). Flat fabrics also require the representation of the diagram of the tuck, the pre-established order in which the warp threads are arranged in the heddle mesh, which lifts them when the weft is introduced. A third diagram represents the sequence in which the raising movement of the heddles occurs for the actual production of the fabric. In the case of fabrics manufactured with modern technologies, the first step is a sketch by hand of the design, which is then scanned and developed in a CAD/CAM machine with all its characteristics (number of threads and weft pattern, thread count per square centimeter, sizes, colors, etc.) until a design that serves as a punched card is obtained. The information is then transmitted to a loom controlled by a computer that reproduces the characteristics of the jacquard production. The lateral margins of the material are the most consistent, demarcated by the selvage (longitudinal border between 0.5 and 1 cm), which provides dimensional stability and protection to the extremes. The selvage is made with a different fabric than the background, or with a tighter thread (double thread) or striped thread. Valuable fabrics have text on the selvage that identifies the composition of fine yarn and/or the factory brand. The false selvage is made with leno yarn, a nearly invisible weave that blocks the weft laterally. For a more in-depth look at specific manufacturing processes, we recommend that the reader consult a good textile technology manual that illustrates all the different manufacturing phases of products. From the design point of view, we should be aware that through the combination of basic and derivative weaves, we have at our disposal instruments that offer vast expressive opportunities for creating new textile designs and recognizing existing types. If in addition to mixing textile and color effects, we occasionally select more diverse materials, we will be able to see that the variety of compositions is unlimited. The textile designer must be skillful in appreciating the different qualities of yarns in terms of appearance, consistency, thickness, smoothness, flexibility, durability and lightness. For guidance in the selection it is necessary to use a specific classification criterion that allows for systematic ordering of the different types of fibers. Weavers use a classification criterion according to the weave, which identifies the fabric based on its internal rather than external structure. Many textile theorists, technicians and scholars of diverse nationalities share this nomenclature. The classification of textiles that we propose in the following pages is accompanied by technical and product information, as well as aesthetic, historical, economic, cultural and traditional facts,

A. Ruiz De La Prada aw10

and is related to practical matters of use of interest to fashion designers. Each description includes: the origin and meaning of the name of the fabric, geographical origin, a brief description of the most common uses, material composition, typology of the threads and the fabric, production on the loom, the most frequent weights and colors and finishes applied. Fabrics are identified by their specific names, thus individualizing and distinguishing them. The use of technical language is indispensable for the exchange of information and helps focus the designs featured in collections, oriented in regard to combinations of available materials. The criterion for assigning names is governed by many factors: the nature of the fiber (e.g., byssus), the characteristics of the yarn (shantung), the arrangement of the threads in the weave (fil á fil) and the weave or design (houndstooth). The typology is also determined by textile technology (shearing), the effect of light (shot silk), consistency (matelassé), weight (voile) and feel (light wool). In another cases, the treatments (sizing), finishes (pleating) and performance of the fabric (impermeability) determine the name. Geographic origin can also be a determining factor, linking the fabric to the city (Oxford), region (Casentino) or place of manufacturing (jersey). Some names refer to how the material has been used (moleskin), while others allude to historical, economic or political events that might have had an effect on a fabric's success (Ottoman), to specific figures (Prince of Wales) or to significant events. To illustrate the symbolic value of each fabric, we also include curiosities related to literary, sports and music figures as well as actors and performers whose image is associated with certain clothing made with the fabric in question. The selection criterion that the consumer

adopts is not only tactile and visual but symbolic as well. It is a reflection of aspects at the heart of a person's individual and social identity, a physical expression and extension of who we are and how we see ourselves and how others see us. Fabric, assimilated to a second skin, contributes to the creation of emotional and affective implications that we associate with the clothes we wear at a given time. Its characteristics evoke feelings and perceptions connected to the memory of a particular object, such as a scarf we have received as a gift or the dress worn by a young debutante. In this way, tactile and visual sensations come to the surface of the mind, reinforced by the perception of smells, perfumes and sounds, generating powerful fascinations. "I, for one, seek to create with emotions and to transfer them to the smallest details... If I couldn't transmit emotions with my dresses, fashion wouldn't interest me... It is important that clothes be beautiful, but for me it is essential that mine be felt," Belgian avant-garde stylist Ann Demeulemeester once

stated in an interview. The descriptions are completed with notes concerning the use designers have made of fabric in contemporary fashion and are illustrated with the beautiful images of photographer Gianni Pucci, taken directly from his extraordinary features of prêt a porter and haute couture fashion shows. The selection of photographs shows possible uses according to the most recent proposals of fashion designers and reflects the expressive possibilities of the fabric, displayed in its multiple options on fashion runways across the world, similar to a small collection of samples in motion.

PLAIN WEAVE FABRICS

1

L I N E N

Linen is a compact fabric soft to the touch produced with linen threads. It has the same flat surface on both sides. The Italian word for cloth, *tela*, comes from the Latin verb *textere* (to weave), and in the past was synonymous with linen fabric, which was already being used in ancient Egypt. Linen comes in different weights, depending on the fineness of the thread and the fabric's intended use. Italian and Irish linens are the most suitable for summer. Lighter linens can have a coarse, weighty appearance, such as Dutch fabric, similar to batiste, or a fine transparent consistency, similar to gauze. Medium-weight linens have a uniform appearance, are light and particularly suitable for printing and embroidering. The heaviest linens have very visible threads, which can play a decorative role, and an almost irregular surface. Linen has a very wide range of uses, from shirts to household linens to clothes for women and children to classic men's suits. Linen fabric is easy to dye, and a vast array of colors is always available. Being both compact and rigid, it lends itself readily to scalloped embroidery, cross-knit geometric patterns and openwork.

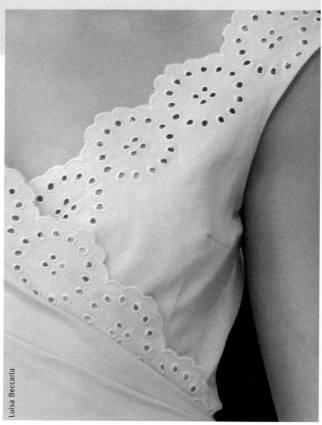

Luisa Beccaria

Dries Van Noten

Gianfranco Ferré

Alviero Martini

Ermenegildo Zegna

This robust, resistant fabric is the most used material in the world, for one because it withstands high-temperature treatments that guarantee maximum hygiene. Its surface is the same on the outside and the inside, with a simple base weave (the minimum interweaving of warp and weft threads that can be used), and has a dull appearance due to the use of short cellulose fibers from the pods of the plant. Cotton fabric was already known in the valley of the Indus River and among the Aztecs, and is referred to as "white gold" in an Egyptian document from the time of Nebuchadnezzar. The Arabs introduced cotton fiber to Europe (the word "cotton" comes from the Arabic word *katun*), and subsequent colonial conquests led to its intense cultivation starting at the beginning of the 17th century in Louisiana, an activity that increased the slave trade with Africa. The mechanization of cotton production played a significant role in the 18th century during the first Industrial Revolution. Thanks to its versatile textile characteristics, cotton has innumerable uses and is the ideal foundation for applying a series of finishes in the creation of complex fabrics used in fashion or in more general fields such as technology, sports and health. In clothing, we find cotton in solid colors and prints, in diverse weights and consistencies, always ready to lend itself to the fantasies of the most whimsical designers and the economic demands of the most competitive markets. Robust cotton cloth is used to produce espadrilles with soles made of esparto grass. Among the finishes applied, the most common is mercerized cotton, made from caustic soda in the form of hydroxide and an absorbing agent discovered in the mid 19th century by English chemist John Mercer and which can be applied to the thread and the piece. This treatment eliminates irregularities in the fiber and adds more thickness and dimensional stability vis-à-vis successive washes, while the colors remain unchanged over time. High-quality cotton yarn and fabrics, such as Egyptian Mako cotton, naturally take on an extreme sheen, better hygroscopic characteristics, compatibility with dyes, and anallergic and antibacterial qualities. In recent years, large fashion companies seemed to have discovered the ecological aspects of biological cotton, the fruit of farming methods that do not use pesticides in the cultivation of botanic species.

Ashish

Philosophy by Alberta Ferretti

Thierry Colson

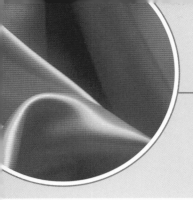

T A F F E T A

Compact fabric made with silk thread with a cloth or plain weave. The name comes from the Persian word tafta, which means twisted, interwoven, intertwined. Taffeta looks the same on both sides; its surface is light but rigid and crinkly, very tight, and makes a whispering sound when brushed up against. The fabric is lustrous and silky, though somewhat cool. Often it is made with added synthetic fiber to reduce the cost. Taffeta is a sculptural fabric, suitable for highlighting volumes, used in shirts with wide sleeves, pleated or puffed skirts, evening gowns with flounces and wraparound collars, stoles and wedding gowns. It was very much in fashion in women's clothes in the second half of the 19th century, in skirts almost always held together by wide crinolines. Shot silk versions are also popular thanks to the use of different color warp and weft threads. In addition, taffeta is used in the lining of clothes as well as in curtains and decorative accessories, granting these objects an air of luxury and opulence.

Marthé & François Girbaud

Blugirl

Marc Jacobs

Alexander McQueen

Louis Vuitton

Bottega Veneta

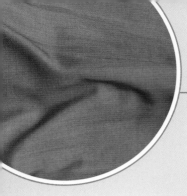

WOOL

Fabric with a regular surface, the same on both sides, made with woolen threads of varying types and thicknesses. It is soft to the touch and slightly elastic, though compact. Occasionally, wool fabric has a thin appearance, due to the low warp and woof thread counts, and lends itself easily to drape in a diagonal pattern and puffed designs, following the contours of the body in tight-fitting garments. It absorbs dye well, occurs frequently in prints, flare skirts, decorative panels, shawls, stoles and foulards. Wool material can have a smooth and fluid appearance when made with spun threads or a soft, hazy look if carding material is used. For classifying woolen cloths, the origin, species and length and quality of the fleece from which the fiber is obtained are taken into account. Options range from Australian merino wool to Yorkshire English wool, Irish wool (particularly warm) to springy and delicate mohair, from alpaca to the highly prized vicuna to New Zealand cashgora, a hybrid fiber obtained from crossing mohair goats with camels. A light, combed-wool fabric, called "tropical", is used in men's suits. A woven fabric cloth, rustic in appearance, made of wool and cotton or wool and other fibers is known as "cotton wool". For less expensive kinds, recycled wool threads are used. These threads are obtained by reusing leftover material or recycling old garments that, appropriately treated, take on a new life, resulting in a less resistant and elastic product that can be dyed, spun, woven or braided to adapt successfully to diverse market trends.

Bottega Veneta

Marni Diesel Black Gold Y3 Vivienne Westwood Red Label

Compact and resistant fabric with a plain or derivative weave, manufactured in different weights depending on its intended use. It preserves the appearance of a rough, unfinished material with a very tight thread count, robust and economical, once made with natural non-dyed hemp fibers and later substituted by cotton fibers. The Italian word for canvas, *Iona*, comes from the Olona River, on the outskirts of Milan, on whose banks windmills powered by water once used for bleaching fabric abound. In the past, canvas was used primarily in the nautical sector, as its resistance greatly increases when the fabric is wet. Canvas was used to make ships' cloths, hammocks for the crew and kit bags for provisions and clothing. The characteristic ecru-colored hemp sails of the *Amerigo Vespucci*, a historic vessel of the Italian navy, survive to this day. Soaked with linseed oil, canvas became waterproof and was used in calash and cart tops. For clothing, the fabric was used in nightshirts and work clothes. Today, canvas appears in tents, made from coarse cotton threads, and in big tops, made with hemp warp and burlap weft often waterproofed as the result of successive treatments. In its lighter versions, always made from cotton, canvas is used in parasols, patio awnings, beach chairs and nautical rigging. In fashion it is used in military-style sports jackets for outdoor activities, as well as bags, sacks, luggage, backpacks and

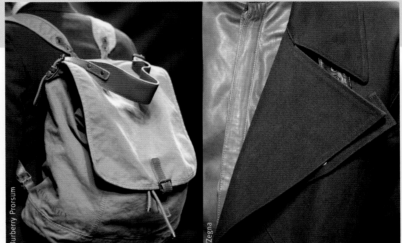

Burberry Prorsum

Zzegna

Versace

Dsquared2

Burberry Prorsum

Burberry Prorsum

briefcases. Sometimes canvas is also used to make hats, shoes and colonial-style belts.

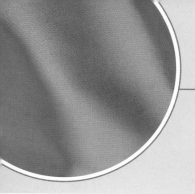

NYLON

Nylon is a resistant synthetic fabric made from 100% high-quality polyamide fiber (6 or 6,6 nylon). It is a plain woven material, tight and shot but extremely light. The nylon in the fabric produces a rigid feel and characteristic reflections. It is a robust, durable material able to resist bad weather, given that it is immune to atmospheric and bacterial agents. Nylon is also produced in combination with natural fibers that strengthen its solidity and consistency, in diverse weights according to its intended use. In blends, a 50% proportion of the two materials must be respected to guarantee the behavior of this fabric. In fashion, nylon is used in umbrellas, K-Way raincoats, rain jackets with hoods, parkas with openings and zipper pockets, and rain hats. Because it is easy to maintain, the material is also suitable for shoulder bags and fanny packs, makeup kits and book bags and backpacks, suitcases, footwear, etc. Among the latest products are designs with divisions and compartments, conceived as transformable objects that, through different closing systems, straps, cords and sliders, go from being simple coverings for the body to multifunctional hybrid garments.

C'n'C

Emporio Armani

Michalsky

Neil Barrett

Gaetano Navarra

YARN-DYED FABRICS

(2)

DYED YARNS

Dyed yarn or dyed thread is the fabric of any fiber or weave made with threads previously dyed different colors. This type of fabric, highly prized in the market due to its quality, requires a longer production time than that of any other piece-dyed fabric, both in the design stage and in the preparation of the materials and practical execution. Dyed yarn also necessitates a study to program the arrangement of the warp on the loom as well as the different weft changes (which slow the machines down) according to the warp pattern instructions and fabric pattern repeat that specify the exact succession and alternation of the colors used to define decorative effects and motifs. Dyed yarns include plain and linear fabrics, pale materials, bicolor fabrics and all fabrics produced in such a way that the complex arrangement of colors produces more elaborate and thus more results than single-dye productions.

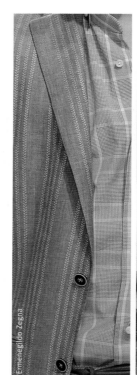

Ermenegildo Zegna

Sportmax

C.P. Company

Laura Biagiotti

Kenzo

Anna Sui

Vivienne Westwood Red Label

Michalsky

Narciso Rodriguez

Kenzo

Stella McCartney

Piece-dyed fabric, as its name suggests, is a single-color fabric made from raw yarn and dyed through successive immersions in an ink bath of the desired color. This dyeing system is chosen according to the commercial demands of the job and is the opposite of thread dyeing, technically more intricate and expensive. Piece-dyed fabric has a dual advantage. On the one hand, it can be quickly transformed into the latest fabric while at the same time its production can begin even after the launching of the sales campaign. In fact, with the help of media resources and dissemination through industry magazines, consumer preferences are more clearly defined in order to contribute to the success of seasonal colors, with which occasionally it is possible to reorganize business priorities. This product versatility is highly prized by "fast fashion" manufacturing companies that need to tailor their offer quickly. On the other hand, given that the use of coarse yarn eliminates the need to store colors that later might not be used, piece dyeing is a good system for enabling textile manufacturers to reduce risk.

Narciso Rodriguez

Shot silk is made using warp and weft threads of different colors, often within a range of accessories. Shot silk displays different colors depending on how we look at it. The effect is due to the light and our viewing angle, as long as silk yarns or continuous sheen artificial fibers are used, not opaque cotton threads. Frequently, the weave is a plain taffeta one that acquires three-dimensionality through the brilliance of the opposing iridescent yarns. Shot silk displays different reflections and shading under different sources of light, whether artificial light or the faint glow of a candle. Different scenic effects can be obtained combining warm and cool dyes that highlight a color that is only insinuated and then suddenly revealed, especially with motion. Shot silk fabric is particularly feminine. In elegant tones, it is very frequently used in lingerie.

Vivienne Westwood

Issey Miyake

Vivienne Westwood

Elena Mirò

Angelo Marani

CHAMBRAY

Chambray is a pure cotton fabric with a cloth weave made up of color warp threads and white weft threads that create a mixed fiber effect or checkerboard effect with small checks. The name comes from the French city of Cambray, where the fabric orginally came from. Chambray is soft and fluid, though it is resistant and used in the construction of easy-to-care-for summer garments such as shirts, camisoles and light dresses with Sangallo lace adornments that add a "Lolita" touch. The fabric possesses a naive, almost child-like charm. It is very light and agreeable, and often comes in pastel tones (aquamarine, faded blues, candy pink, salmon and yellow primrose). Conversely, in dark tones it is similar to work clothes, given that the mixed fiber withstands grime and hides stains. In Italy, dark chambray was popularly known as tela spazzino, or street sweeper fabric, because in the past a similar fabric was used to make the wide camisoles and aprons used for street sweeping and cleaning tasks.

Enrico Coveri

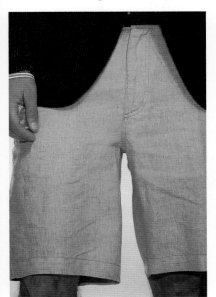

Ermenegildo Zegna

Louis Vuitton

Frankie Morello

VERTICAL STRIPES

A fabric with stripes in colors different from that of the background and arranged vertically. It is made up of sections of warp threads of different colors positioned at intervals while the weft threads are all the same color. Infrequently used in medieval times – they were associated with the devil –, vertical stripes gradually took hold, becoming one of the fabrics used to make uniforms worn by valets, pages, servants and other service personnel. Later, vertical stripes extended to the "harlequin" style of heralds and falconers, the uniforms of the papal guards and the German Landsknecht mercenary soliders. In period paintings we often find exotic figures of African or Turkish origin who for centuries appeared in clothes with horizontal stripes, as if this were the telltale sign of individuals who didn't belong to civilized society. In the 17th century, stripes survived in the livery of coach drivers and the vests of butlers serving the nobility, but also in the wall cladding and tapestries of stately mansions, ultimately figuring as an important element in men's and women's clothing. Dull or bright, of satin, taffeta or precious Peking silk, inserted in sinuous floral elements or flecked with small diagonal grooves, vertical stripes interrupt the monotony of solid surfaces with their dynamic, relentless rhythm.

Vivienne Westwood

Viktor & Rolf

Marc Jacobs

Dries Van Noten

HORIZONTAL STRIPES

Fabrics with horizontal stripes can be of any fiber, including synthetic ones and blends. They are characterized by the horizontal stripes that cross the entire length of the material from seam to seam. Horizontal stripes can come in a variety of colors (a minimum of two), in regular intervals or not, depending on individual tastes and the desired results. When the stripes are vibrantly colored, the fabrics are called *bayaderas*, a name that alludes to the Hindu dancers who wore colorful striped attire made of silk or cotton. To produce a fabric with horizontal stripes requires a warp uniform in color and a weft arranged in alternating colors, combining their repetition sequentially. Wearing clothes with vertical or horizontal stripes was frowned upon in the Middle Ages. Particularly, brightly colored striped garments were viewed as an expression of difference and subversion of the social order, and were reserved for disparaged figures such as traitors, the sick and convicted criminals. Toward the middle of the 13th century, Carmelite monks who wore a dark habit and a striped robe of Oriental origin which they refused to relinquish were disrespectfully called *freres barrés*, ("striped monks"; in old French *barré* also means "bastard"). Later, horizontal stripes came to be a sign of the incarceration of prisoners in jails. Today, this association is obsolete. Horizontal stripes appear in the eye-catching colors of flags and the white and blue of sailors' attire, and are used in beach, leisure and sports wear. Clothing with horizontal stripes require a simple linear pattern and careful study of proportions, given that the horizontal sequence tends to visually expand in that direction, with the resulting broadening of the figure.

Aquilano e Rimondi

Marc by Marc Jacobs

Angiomania

Vivienne Westwood

Paul Smith

DKNY

Matthew Williamson

PIN STRIPES

One of the most common examples of vertical stripes is the pin stripe. Against a dark background (black, gray, blue or another color) pin stripes stand out as very thin white stripes similar to chalk lines. Pin stripe fabric is very common in men's clothing, made with combed woolen yarn or flannel (the label recommends wearing it with a matching shirt and tie). At times, if it is a woolen fabric, the stripes can be intermittent or blurred, obtained through a mild refining process. It is the fabric used in the traditional double-breasted blazer emblematic of executives and businessmen irresistibly drawn to the mystique

Etro

Paul Smith

and aesthetic attractiveness of this garment, including the summer version in yarn-dyed linen, cotton and viscose. Considered very elegant in the twenties and thirties, and popular with gangsters such as Al Capone and Bonnie and Clyde as well as with the gamblers in the stories of Damon Runyon, pin-striped clothes were complemented by two-tone shoes and wide-brimmed hats. In the Chicago of those years jazz bands also were fond of pin stripes, combining them with lustrous satin shirts and brilliantly colored ties. It is no accident that pin stripes have remained a classic, taken up ironically by musicians such as Fred Buscaglione and Bob Dylan, who an article once described as "the prophet in the pin-striped suit". Its consecration as an emblem of power occurred during World War II, when Winston Churchill, the British prime minister with close ties to the English aristocracy, began wearing three-piece pinstriped flannel suits to protocol engagements. The choice of this attire carried a coded political message directed at the German enemy across the world, as evidenced by a photograph from 1940 of Churchill, pistol in hand, with a cigar in his mouth and his signature bowler hat, like a Chicago gangster in action. Today, pin stripes are still fashionable, commonly appearing in women's clothing as well, in the dresses, tailored suits and coats that we find in the collections of Armani, Ferré and Gaultier.

Emporio Armani

Gianfranco Ferré

Daks

Vivienne Westwood

Jean Paul Gaultier

CHECKS

Checked fabric consists of a single weave of different-colored warp and weft threads used to create a pattern of rectangular and square shapes. The squaring can be regular or irregular, and the sizes and colors vary depending on the desired effect. At least two colors are used, often strongly contrasted. The divisions of the spaces and the color contrasts impact the overall effect on the entirety of the surface used, which is carefully considered in relation to the height and size of the person who will wear the garment. Checks are used in clothes, accessories and decoration. The cut and production of check fabric requires close attention in order to find the harmony between the dimensions of the design and the pattern repeat that the fabric reproduces, especially when it includes pleats, cuffs, pockets or insertions. According to the standard rules adopted to carry out the placement of the fabric in the cut, check fa-

bric corresponds to class 5. The wider the pattern, the greater the excess fabric; in addition, it must be taken into account that an irregular check design will require more cloth, given that the pattern must of necessity be arranged in a single direction.

Aquilano e Rimondi

Versus

Roccobarocco

Diane von Fürstenberg

Z Spoke

OVERCHECK

Kenzo

Yarn-dyed fabric of almost any fiber that reproduces an overcheck pattern created by the orthogonal intersection of fine colored stripes, individual or joined at different intervals, also adulterated and in various thicknesses. The pattern recalls the grids of iron-barred windows – hence its name in Italian: *finestrato*. The larger the space between the vertical and horizontal lines and the more forceful the chromatic contrast between the grid and the background, the greater the optical effect of expansion of volume. Overcheck fabric is used in coats, dresses and both sports-style and elegant men and women's vests.

Vivienne Westwood Red Label

Marc by Marc Jacobs

CHECKERBOARD

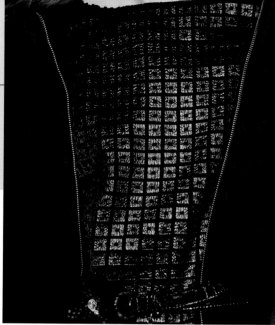

Frankie Morello

Yarn-dyed fabric of any fiber that reproduces a checkerboard pattern, as its name suggests. It is obtained by juxtaposing in both directions groups of dark-colored threads with light-colored threads, which are repeated regularly with taffeta fabric, creating by the superimposition of color areas of diverse intensity. In general, two pure effects – light and dark – are obtained, in addition to a third mixed effect, produced by the intersection of the two colors. In wool, it is the typical check pattern of Canadian lumberjack shirts, suitable for a casual informal look, while the cotton version is characteristic of the camping blanket used for picnics. This type of fabric can also be obtained by contrasting the weave, often with a checkerboard effect highlighted by the use of bright threads, or can be used as the basis of elaborate decorations on complex fabrics for evening gowns. Checkerboard is a very common pattern in the history of fabrics given that its production is particularly compatible with the orthogonal functioning of the loom. The checkerboard pattern is an archetypal symbol of the balance

Roberto Cavalli

between opposing and contrary forces. It appears in the textile products of many ethnic groups, applied in tapestries, rugs and accessories in various geographic zones of the world, and appears in a wide range of very diverse cultures. Its transformations were an object of study in the rationalist design of fabrics created for the industry in the textile workshops of the Bauhaus school.

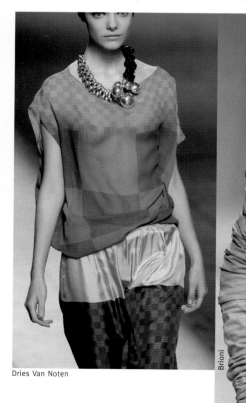

Dries Van Noten

Brioni

Yarn-dyed fabric of any fiber, similar to checkerboard but much smaller. In delicate pastel tones, Vichy fabric is often used in shirts for its light and orderly appearance. The pattern of small squares was common in carded yarns produced in the spa town of Vichy, in the French region of Auvergne, and was used to make children's robes, initially in black and white and white and brown colors. The pattern became fashionable in 1959, when the magazine *Elle* devoted a famous cover to actress Brigette Bardot, who was fond of wearing Vichy cotton balconette bras on the mischievous beaches of Saint Tropez and who for her wedding with actor Jacques Charrier chose a dress, demure and malicious at the same time, with a circular skirt made of a white and pink checkered fabric created by fashion designer Jacques Esterel. From the juxtaposition of a demure, naïve fabric and a pattern of lines that highlighted the shapes of the body emerged the intriguing fascination with the woman-girl notion to which Brigette always remained faithful, appearing in dresses of this kind in many of her movies. Today, Vichy has made a comeback in elegant classic men's shirts as well as in maxi bags and wedge sandals.

Betsey Johnson

Betsey Johnson

Luella

Etro

Dolce & Gabbana

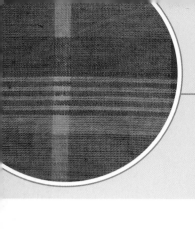

MADRAS

A cool lightweight fabric from the Indian city of the same name. It is a plain-weave cotton material, with characteristic check patterns in bright colors created by interweaving threads of different colors, whether in the warp or in the weft. This type of cloth was originally dyed using natural substances and produced on manual looms with fine fibers similar to gauze. These characteristics of authentic madras cause the color to tend to lose some of its sheen and become lighter over time, creating an effect known as "bleeding madras", highly regarded by those in the know. Today, madras is also made from striped silk and overcheck fabric. It is used in summer clothing for shirts, camisoles, dresses, pants and light unisex jackets, as well as in decoration for coverings and curtains. Creole fruit sellers in Martinique wore the typical checkered kerchiefs as turbans: the *téte-a-madras*. This headdress had many variants, among them one with a small ring at the top on which were placed large baskets of bananas. Another, the *tétea-bouts*, had knotted points above the head. The points had symbolic value in courtship: one point meant, "My heart is free", while two meant, "I'm engaged but available."

Michalsky

Issey Miyake

Vivienne Westwood

Kenzo

C.P. Company

Etro

Vivienne Westwood Red Label

TAFFETA WEAVE DERIVATIVES

3

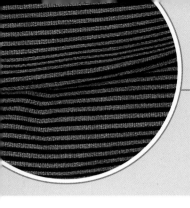

R I B B E D

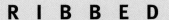

Generic name for fabrics of any fiber and consistency with a three-dimensional surface featuring transversal (warp reps) or longitudinal (weft reps) ribs in relief. The base weave is always a taffeta fabric that doubles the coverage points, producing floating threads in one or the other direction. Transversal (horizontal) ribs are obtained with warp threads that the cover the weft. Longitudinal (vertical) ribs are obtained with weft threads that partly cover the warp. Ribbed fabric is resistant and compact, with very different faces, and highly suitable for shaped yet linear garments.

Hugo Boss

Prada

Hugo Boss

Gucci

Sportmax

Versace

Dirk Bikkembergs

CANETTE

Fabric with larger ribs than those of ribbed fabric and more pronounced than poplin ones, with a plain weave in which the warp is finer than the weft, which is thick and rounded. The fabric produces an effect of striations in relief, formed by a horizontal sequence of ribs repeated over the entire surface of the fabric. Canette also appears in the form of a ribbon, with an internal cotton warp and in different heights, thicknesses and consistencies that make it suitable for outlines, adornments and innumerable decorative effects, even with materials of diverse colors. In tailoring, canette is also used to fasten waistbands in skirts and pants and in the internal perimeter of men's hats.

Giorgio Armani

Trussardi

Calvin Klein

Vivienne Westwood

Herve Leger

FAILLE

Silk fabric of French origin made from wool or viscose. The classic version features very fine horizontal ribs across its entire length, equal and visible on both sides of the surface. A second version exists called French faille, with flat ribs more raised and separated from each other. The flattened effect is obtained by inserting more weft threads per pass and a supplementary warp thread that remains inside and keeps the ribs separated and aligned with the background. Classical faille is soft, compact, lightweight and springy and drapes well. It is often used in haute couture and luxury ready-to-wear garments. Its slightly raised effect was highly valued by designers such as Christian Dior, who used faille liberally in jackets, skirts and dresses with a sober and scenic style.

A. Basile

Bill Blass

Paola Frani

30 Paar Haende

OTTOMAN

Ottoman fabrics feature large flat horizontal stripes with perceptible spaces in between (3 and 10 ribs per cm). They are obtained by alternating a grosgrain weave with a plain weave, with thin dense warp threads interwoven with two types of weft threads: a more robust one that forms the internal filling and another finer one visible on the outside of the fabric. Ottoman fabric can be made of silk, wool, rayon or cotton. The stripes can be of different thicknesses. It is used in coats and elegant garments as a decorative element. The name derives from Osman I, founder of the first Ottoman dynasty, originally from Asia Minor who settled in Anatolia and built a vast empire that included territories in the Balkans, the Middle East and North Africa. The Ottoman sultans lived opulently in the grandiose palace of Topkapi, in Istanbul. This official residence housed textile factories that produced precious fabrics marked with the sultan's seal and reserved for court dignitaries and their families.

Chanel

Aquilano e Rimondi

Versace

Aigner

Aquilano e Rimondi

Dior

Gianfranco Ferrè

33

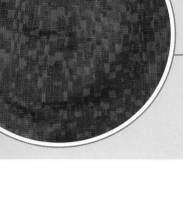

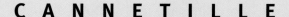

Fabric derived from grosgrain with a flat, checkered appearance resulting from the alternate staggering of the ribs. Cannetille fabrics include a supplementary warp and may have complex, geometric patterns. They are commonly used to embellish ties and in decorative coverings. In the 18th century, cannetille was used to define the innumerable details of *chinoiserie* decoration, which reproduced graceful figurative scenes with gardens, ruins, pagodas and fountains that were alternated with floral motifs, conks, cornucopias and *rocaille* volutes. Today, it is used in interesting projects that experiment with fabrics, such as

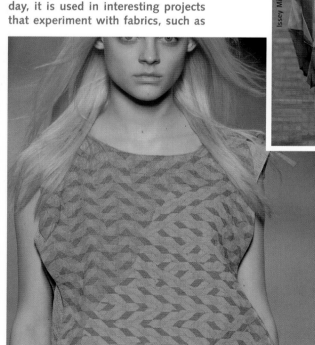

Issey Miyake

Issey Miyake

Issey Miyake

those developed by Japanese designers who like to play with the impact of light and imperceptible three-dimensional effects thanks to the sensible and studied alternation of the ribs. When color is added to this, the result can be entire pieces, including large ones, with a strong visual impact, as seen in some of the collections of Issaye Miyake.

Issey Miyake

Issey Miyake

GROS DE TOURS

Ann Demeulemeester

Gianfranco Ferré

Etro

Dior

Gianfranco Ferré

Dior

Old name for classic grosgrain, gros de Tours is a ribbed fabric with two wefts with no reverse side. It is obtained with one warp interlaced with two alternate wefts in a plain weave. It has a compact, rigid surface with transverse and parallel ribs in the direction of the weft that are formed by floating warp threads, twisted and very fine, that envelop the weft completely and cover it. It can be made of silk, cotton, polyester or other synthetic fibers. There are many kinds of grosgrain, distinguished by the number of wefts inserted. The simplest variety is medium grosgrain, which alternates sequences of one or two wefts. Sometimes gros de Tours appears in the form of ribbons or passementerie. In these cases, the weft, formed by a ribbed thread, is evident only in profile along the border of the selvage, and the ribbon is called grosgrain. It is also used in accessories such as bags, shoes and belts as well as in decoration. In the 18th century, this fabric was a French specialty, initially made with a single ink in Tours, a city that later specialized in different qualities of the material, among them Dama del Tours and Royal Tours, in satin and in versions with seven colors or in gold. In later centuries, gros de Naples appeared, featuring very prominent ribs formed by a two- or three-ply weft.

PANAMA

Gucci

Chanel

Lacoste

Plain-weave fabric in which weft and warp threads are crisscrossed in pairs. The fabric is obtained with pairs of two- or three-ply weft and warp threads of plain cloth. The resulting effect is a grid, as in basket weave. If the expansion is exaggerated, the fabric loses consistency due to the length of the loose weft and warp threads. Originally used in hemp and jute sacks for holding coffee, today it is made with coarse cotton, hemp or linen yarns. Panama fabric has a very resistant structure, and is used in men and women's clothing and in decoration. Some panama fabrics have a rustic but elegant effect, enriched by the lustrous/opaque dichotomy of the yarns. The name extended to the hats made in the equatorial regions of Central America with fine white-palm fibers that have a subtle surface interwoven in a very simple, tight and regular way.

AIDA CLOTH

Kenzo

Gucci

John Galliano

Kenzo

Aida cloth has an embroidery canvas structure, a term that indicates a fabric with a long but robust and resistant weft of canvas yarn originally used to make cloths. It consists of an interwoven taffeta weave according to a natte pattern variant: 4 warp threads and 4 weft threads grouped together to reproduce a checkered pattern, similar to a repeated series of small San Andres crosses. It is a fabric used as a base for embroidery and above all in craftwork and the hobbies sector. The regularly arranged threads leave clearly visible interstices that serve as references for threading the needle in cross-stitch and half-stitch work. In thick wool embroidery, the base is completely covered in soft, voluminous thread to form multi-color shapes and compositions that mimic the style of tapestries. For this reason Aida cloth is also called Arras cloth, a town in the region of Passo di Calais famous for the production of wool and fabrics with designs, known originally as *pann di razzo* (tapestry cloth). For cross-stitch embroidery in clothing and brides' trousseaus, this small grid was superimposed onto a less regular fabric to facilitate embroidering and was subsequently removed when the work was finished. It had the same function as worsted, a fine-weft fabric on which embroidery was made. To produce Aida cloth, twisted 100% cotton threads of uniform thickness were used, as were wool, linen blend and jute, with Lurex or iridescent threads to create specific effects. It is sold in various colors and many varieties. The name of the fabric tends to be accompanied by a number that indicates the size of the checks and is adapted to the system of linear measure of the country where the fabric is manufactured. In the metric decimal system it is indicated by the number of checks per 10 cm, while in the Anglo-Saxon system the count, or the number of checks per inch, is mentioned.

4

DIAGONAL WEAVE FABRICS

WOOL GABARDINE

Louis Vuitton

Louis Vuitton

Sonia Rykiel

Vera Wang

A word of Spanish origin formed by combining *gabán* (overcoat) and *tabardina* (short coat similar to a tabard), wool gabardine is a resistant fabric with a diagonal weave in which the reverse side takes precedence over the outside, characterized by oblique, tightly woven, regular fabric. The warp threads are twice as dense as the weft, and are very fine and twisted. The diagonal, dramatically inclined (45 degrees and 63 degrees), is not very prominent, rising to the left in the case of highly twisted thread. On the inside it has a flatter appearance reinforced by the cut and ironing. The structure of this fabric makes it extremely practical and easy to maintain. It can made of wool, cotton or mixed fabric, and depending on the material used and the weight of the fabric, it adapts well to summer or winter, though gabardine is a midseason fabric par excellence. In the combed-wool version, it has a rough feel with a

Dsquared2

weight of 250-350 g/m². The diagonal character in relief can also have slight napping. While not very soft to the touch, it lends itself to drape and, needless to say, tailoring. It is used in the manufacture of jackets, coats, dresses, skirts and clean-cut suits. The so-called Eisenhower jacket is made with gabardine fabric, a garment with a diagonal structure that reaches just below the waist with four pockets, a collar and placket, inspired by the battle jacket worn by the legendary general during the war.

COTTON GABARDINE

Cotton gabardine, with a weight of 250-400 g/m², is used for military-style pants and sporty hats in traditional khaki color – a term derived from the Hindustan word "khaki", which means "sand-colored". It is believed that Indian regiments used it for the first time during the siege of Delhi, in 1857. With a specific finishing treatment and in the colors creamy beige, nut, brown and black, it is used in men's raincoats such as the one Humphrey Bogart wore in *Casablanca*. In 1902, English entrepreneur Thomas Burberry had the idea of registering gabardine as a commercial brand. In the 1970s, shirts with military insignia, safari jackets, anoraks and cargo pants made of gabardine became protest symbols adopted by youth culture, taking them to an extreme in their style of dress, an instance of the paradoxical "terrorist chic" about which Michael Selzer theorized.

Gucci

Junn J

Aquascutum

Céline

DRILL

Tremendously versatile fabric of carded cotton, particularly resistant to chafing and tearing and originally used in work clothes. It has a 2/1 twill weave, rods to the left, similar to denim, though piece-dyed. It comes in various weights and colors, sometimes piece over-dyed, and used in casual clothing in the production of jackets and pants for summer, especially Bermuda shorts in classic navy blue or neutral colors such as Havana brown or pinkish beige. Traditionally, this fabric was used in the mid-19th century for British and French military uniforms. Drill is used to make straight-leg, flexible, comfortable pants, with a slightly slim fit, pleated waist and a smooth or wrinkled finish known as "chino". This garment, normally worn by Chinese and Filipino peasants (Chinese shirt), became very popular in the United States, moving from military uniforms to civilian clothing when veterans of the Spanish-American War who had fought in the Phillipines came home. In the United States chinos were worn during the Second World War to compensate for the scarcity of khaki fabric, in the version without central pleats and smooth in the back. In the 50s and 60s, it was combined with a blazer with golden buttons or the classic Harris tweed jacket, becoming the currency among university students as a less casual alternative to jeans.

Dsquared2

Moschino Cheap & Chic

Paul Smith

Michalsky

Undercover

43

DENIM

Sturdy, rigid, compact cotton fabric with 2/1, 2/2, 2/3 twill weave and diagonal lines running from right to left. It is woven with Z-twist yarns, dyed indigo in the warp and ecru in the weft. The blue color of the fabric is due to the fact that the warp threads take precedence on the outside. Denim is commonly referred to as "blue jeans", though the name comes from the expression "de Nimes", the French city where resistant economical fabrics, dyed indigo, were manufactured and then sold in the United States as fabric for boats and covers for carriages. Denim is very similar to the blue canvas, always dyed indigo, called Genova canvas (hence the term "blue jeans") used in popular attire and some work uniforms. The distinctiveness of denim lies in its gradual fading caused by chafing due to a vat-dyeing technique that is very solid but targets the external layer of the thread without reaching the inside. The different blue tones of denim are obtained with various dye passes gradually stratified in the fabric. With use, denim acquires a washed-out and worn look at the highest frictions points (knees, pockets and buttons). Levi Strauss, who popularized denim overalls – a one-piece garment with a U-shaped crotch and straps and reinforced with copper rivets – among American gold-seekers, invented jeans. Machinists and members of the armed forces subsequently began wearing this garment. Overalls also formed part of country and rodeo attire, which contributed

ZZegna

to reinforcing the popular myth of American identity. In the 1950s, denim embodied the "rebel-without-a-cause" generation gap phenomenon and spread throughout the world as a symbol of transgression and freedom. In the 1970s, the market extended to women and children, with the appearance of tight-fitting jeans worn like a second skin, with a strong fashion component due to the finish and additional treatment of the fabric. Today, the warp thread is dyed all colors and is marketed as colored denim or black denim. There is

Jean Paul Gaultier

Dolce & Gabbana

Dolce & Gabbana

Diesel Black Gold

Iceberg

printed, embroidered, studded, painted, faded, over-dyed, stone-washed, frayed and broken denim used to make not only informal unisex pants, jackets and shirts, but also dresses, skirts, designer clothes, bags, shoes and decorative accessories of diverse colors to satisfy all tastes.

Frankie Morello

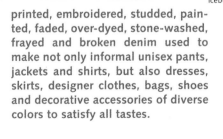

Dolce & Gabbana

Strong, rigid, compact fabric rough to the touch and woven with combed cotton threads. It can consist of a blend of linen and cotton or cotton and polyester. It is also called "twill cavalry" due to the weave provided by a Levantine interweave of 2/1 or 3/1 twill, with a slightly inclined ribbed effect and arranged in pairs. It emerged as a medium-weight fabric suitable for sportive clothes, specifically *riding jackets* and other garments for horseback ri-

Paul Smith

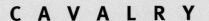

Armani Privè

ding and other outdoor activities. It is a very resistant yet elastic fabric and thus does not wrinkle easily. A more pronounced diagonal variety is called "tricotine" because it mimics the diagonal appearance of knit work. Due to these characteristics cavalry twill is the fabric of choice for making the pants of the classic *odd jacket*, softened by a composition made up of 97% cotton and 3% spandex, that are

Aquascutum

combined with a sports style jacket of British inspiration, in tweed, Shetland or tartan, an outfit that is unfailingly elegant. Odd jackets can be light blue, egg, sandy beige, khaki, light or dark brown, forest green or navy blue, with the aim of creating a more refined chromatic harmony by varying the color of accessories. With its compact regular surface, cavalry twill recalls the sober, strict look of the uniforms worn by chauffeurs and bellboys, and adapts very well to garments subjected to intense wear and tear such as military uniforms. Occasionally, this type of fabric has been disparaged as a boring expression of an impersonal and anonymous taste, although, in reality, given its availability in different weights, it lends itself to many stylistic interpretations. The more robust and lightweight variety, between 400 and 500 g/m³, is frequently used in leisure wear, infusing these garments with the charm of austere English elegance, such as British warm, an updated version of a winter coat with a military cut that today is often worn in civilian life. Designers such as Marc Jacobs have chosen cavalry twill for men and women's suits and jackets, subjecting them to a soft-brushed or rinse-wash treatment that personalizes the surface.

Etro

Bill Blass

WHIPCORD

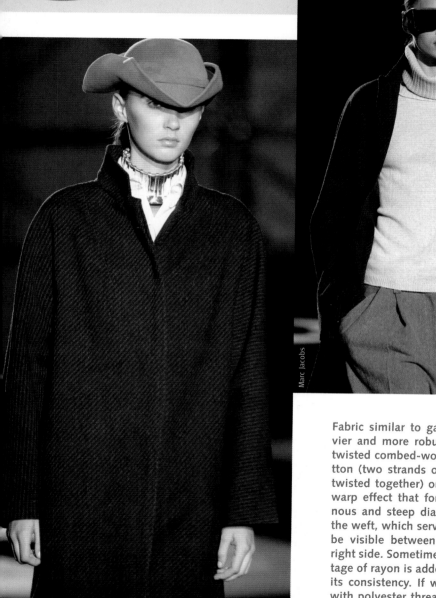

Marc Jacobs

Marc Jacobs

Fabric similar to gabardine yet heavier and more robust. It is made of twisted combed-wool or mouliné cotton (two strands of different colors twisted together) or speckled with a warp effect that forms very voluminous and steep diagonal ribs, while the weft, which serves as filling, may be visible between the ribs on the right side. Sometimes a small percentage of rayon is added, which softens its consistency. If whipcord is made with polyester thread, the volume of the ribs is intensified. Whipcord is di-

fferent from covercoat in that, though it has the same effect, it is more trimmed. Its structure is very compact, fulled, woven with twill, especially resistant and slightly rough, and at times impenetrable to sewing with a needle. Whipcord is an anti-wrinkle fabric that offers a certain amount of thermal resistance and withstands repeated washes well. For all these reasons, it is a durable material, suited to the production of working clothes and uniforms. The term "whipcord" is a compound noun consisting of "whip" and "cord", and literally means "cord for whipping" or lash, a highly twisted or woven cord that horsemen sometimes use to whip their horses. The etymology is from the equestrian world and refers to the rigidness of the rib, of the twisted thread, and the resistant nature of the interwoven material. Viking whipcord braiding is a special fabric technique used to create small cords to close garments or embellish small jewelry. Whipcording is also called interlocking because the fabric is made up of four braided strands that form a stronger cord; generally, the strands are tied to bobbins that act as weights. It can also be made with a single-dye or in bands or diagonals in two colors. The technique, a variation of the Japanese *kumihimo* method, uses two interwoven pieces arranged directly in front of each other; one end of the work is fixed to a support parallel to the floor, the balls of material on the right are launched simultaneously, and the ac-

Miss Sixty

Y3

tion is then repeated with the balls on the left. The preferred colors for whipcord are fall tones, dark gray and moss green, in wool between 16 and 18 ounces for pants and jackets; for working clothes, cotton of 9 to 12 ounces is used. It is used mostly in outdoor clothing such as parkas and light coats. Whipcord is used to make the weekender jacket produced by Filson, an American company specializing, since 1897, in the manufacture of quality outdoor garments sold throughout the world (they are even shipped by mail to Greenland). This design, featuring numerous pockets for carrying whatever one needs, is the typical product intended for men who work outside, such as hunters, fishermen, engineers, and explorers, sailors and miners. Yet, due to its technical features, the garment also lends itself easily as an article of clothing suitable for urban leisure time.

COVERCOAT

Combed or carded fabric, made with highly twisted speckled yarns (three combined strands of different colors), with a diagonal weave characterized by ribs in prominent relief. It is a sturdy and resistant fabric, compact yet slightly elastic, and therefore maintains its shape well. It is typical of English country clothes, suitable for outerwear, especially riding jackets, with a close-fitting line, characterized by two lateral openings (or a central one in the back) and pockets with placket, and is used above all for horse-riding. Cover coat fabric is preferably used in dark blend colors, particularly green and brown tones in different weights, for making pants, jackets and light coats. Medium-weight cover coat is one of the nearly indispensable classics in the male wardrobe, cut like a long

Etro

Antonio Berardi

Burberry Prorsum

solidly made coat down to the knee, with simple hidden buttons, velvet collar and four lines of parallel seams at the height of the cuffs and hems. Occasionally, it is similar in appearance to gabardines, with a more comfortable volume, wide pleats in the back and tapered in the waist, usually made of pure virgin wool and also in a reversible version combined with waterproof gabardine cotton, such that it can be worn on both sides. In the heavier version, around 400-500 g/m², some cover coats have broad shoulders and a slightly flared cut, suitable for winter

even in place of a coat, with padded lining and a fur collar. Known brands such as Loro Piana, Zegna, Trussardi, Hugo Boss, Clavin Klein and Burberry offer unisex versions.

DIAGONAL WEAVE DERIVATIVES

5

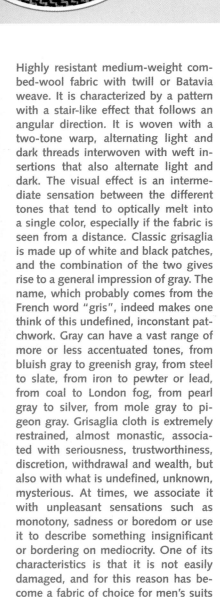

GRISAGLIA

Highly resistant medium-weight combed-wool fabric with twill or Batavia weave. It is characterized by a pattern with a stair-like effect that follows an angular direction. It is woven with a two-tone warp, alternating light and dark threads interwoven with weft insertions that also alternate light and dark. The visual effect is an intermediate sensation between the different tones that tend to optically melt into a single color, especially if the fabric is seen from a distance. Classic grisaglia is made up of white and black patches, and the combination of the two gives rise to a general impression of gray. The name, which probably comes from the French word "gris", indeed makes one think of this undefined, inconstant patchwork. Gray can have a vast range of more or less accentuated tones, from bluish gray to greenish gray, from steel to slate, from iron to pewter or lead, from coal to London fog, from pearl gray to silver, from mole gray to pigeon gray. Grisaglia cloth is extremely restrained, almost monastic, associated with seriousness, trustworthiness, discretion, withdrawal and wealth, but also with what is undefined, unknown, mysterious. At times, we associate it with unpleasant sensations such as monotony, sadness or boredom or use it to describe something insignificant or bordering on mediocrity. One of its characteristics is that it is not easily damaged, and for this reason has become a fabric of choice for men's suits and pants. The peak of grey attire for men was at the end of the 18th century

B. Pieters

when in England it became necessary to draw a clear distinction between the clothing of the two sexes. Light tones and painstakingly worked fabrics, particularly affected and ostentatious, gave way to a monotone uniform consisting of a three-piece gray suit, derby hat and cane, more suited to the personality and social role of the bourgeoisie. Current fashion retains vague reminiscences of this past, and the grey suit is strongly recommended or taken as a given in formal situations. Its weight fluctuates between 230 and 430 grams per square meter.

Alberta Ferretti

Federico Sangalli

Costume National

Alberta Ferretti

The word "twill" comes from the word "two" and generally is used to indicate a diagonal weave. It is a textile usually made from silk or similar fibers, though also from cotton or wool, with a 2/2 twill weave, characterized by a barely perceptible 45 degree diagonal. Occasionally a raw silk warp and a more pronounced weft are used, causing the diagonal to emerge. With a special matte-finish treatment twill becomes surá, a fabric frequently used in ties, kerchiefs and foulards. Twill is suitable for blouses and accessories and as a base on which colored graphic motifs are printed that acquire movement against a not completely solid background. A thick twill, consisting of eight yarns, is the support base for Hermes ties, while rubber twill, obtained by immersing the fabric in a rubber-based hardening bath, was the preferred fabric of Ferragamo collections, which proposed ties with small animal motifs printed all over the cloth. In printed cotton with a finish similar to gauze on the reverse side twill is used in men's shirts and children's pajamas.

Marni

Dries Van Noten

Anna Sui

Emilio Pucci

SOLARO

A yarn-dyed gabardine fabric, with a Batavia weave and average weight of 300 g/m², produced with contrasting colored threads that give it an unmistakable, changing and iridescent surface. It is also known as sunshot and *solaire* in French, and is military in origin. Solaro® is a registered English trademark; it can be dyed the classic beige color (herring-bone pattern) on the outside and light pink on the reverse side. It is a classic example of how the language of fashion continuously borrows meanings that go beyond the purely aesthetic element of form and materials. Gianni Agnelli, who wore it as a crossover suit on summer holidays spent in the United States, made Solaro fashionable. Ever since, the complete "Solaro" suit has been an almost indispensable classic in the wardrobes of men who prefer a sober elegant style. Unwritten rules veto wearing a vest with a "Solaro" and prohibit combining it with garments of other weaves or whimsical attire.

Chanel

Paul & Joe

Very soft woolen fabric with diagonal, Batavia or herringbone weave, woven with yarn from Shetland Island. It has a mesh surface in a single color or with Scottish motifs, with a long, flat pile that hides the details of the fabric. Originally used for men's clothes, it is often available in elegant pastel tones that define an impeccable ultra-feminine Chanel-type cut with passementerie and gilded buttons. The serious but at the same time creative charm of Shetland, typical of the refined gentleman of the past, was magisterially embodied by actor Cary Grant in a famous scene from the movie *To Catch a Thief.* On the beach in Nice, sitting in a white convertible next to Grace Kelly, the actor allows himself to indulge in a bit of male vanity in the form of a blue Shetland jacket.

Y3

Sportmax

BCBG

Aquascutum

HERRINGBONE

Diane Von Furstenberg

Herringbone is a classic pattern in men's jackets. The arrangement of the spikes is called "broken twill", a construction typical of buildings in Roman times (*opus spicatum*, literally "spiked work"). The herringbone pattern is achieved by the interlacing of weft tacking stitch. This intertwining recalls the structure of ears of wheat or fish bones. It is almost always made in two colors with contrasting tones to obtain a more pronounced effect. There are different varieties of the fabric, such as spezzata herringbone, in which the diagonal-line pattern alternates but is interrupted before the lines unite or cross halfway. The size of the pattern repeat determines the type of use. Larger patterns are reserved for jackets and coats, which have a strong visual impact. Herringbone fabric is available in different colors: gray, green, brown and blue in light, medium or dark shades. In 1940, Herringbone twill, cut out of green herringbone fabric, became the uniform of choice of German forces during World World Two due its extreme comfort. Grey herringbone personifies the contemporary elegance of a garment somewhere between daily attire and leisure time and forms part of the basic selection of the American company Brooks Brothers, which recommended combining it with a white Oxford-cloth shirt with a button collar and a black knit or striped silk tie. There is also varied herringbone, a version that includes multi-color threads in the fabric.

Donna Karan

Dolce & Gabbana

Alberto Biani

Gucci

Antonio Marras

Pollini

Dolce & Gabbana

CHEVIOT

Slightly wavy, flexible, medium-weight woolen fabric that gets its name from a breed of sheep from the Cheviot Mountains, which separate Scotland from England. The fleece of Cheviot sheep is highly prized for being not only long and lustrous but stout and firm as well. Cheviot wool can be carded or combed, is used in medium-fine yarns with a single or double twist and is generally woven with a crossed twill weave, created through the repetitions of a weave with two twills pointing in different directions forming two intersecting lines on the fabric that are repeated

Céline

according to the pattern repeat. Sometimes cheviot is woven in a manner that forms a diagonal design in the shape of fish scales, frequently accentuated by the use of contrasting warp and weft threads. Cheviot is typical of English sportswear and has its French equivalent in *cheviotte*. Normally it used to make heavy clothing, both men and women's garments, with weights varying between 350-400 and 600 g/m², including coats, pants and skirts. Tailors have given this somewhat rough fabric the humorous nickname "bulletproof" in allusion to its notable resistance.

Giorgio Armani

Roberto Cavalli

ZIGZAG

A single or two-tone fabric with two diagonal weaves of the same kind arranged in opposite directions (S and Z) at regular intervals that combine with each other. Intersecting at a predetermined distance, the zigzag stitch forms a wavy pattern with points that alternately point up and down. The points can be single or double, for which a herringbone 4 weave is used. It is made with thick cotton, linen or hemp with twist in the warp and a simple weft weave, also known as sackcloth, a highly resistant yarn- or piece-dyed textile ideal for tablecloths and fabrics for sacks or deck chairs. In Italian it is called *traliccio* (three threads) because it is woven with three threads.

There is also a composite version used to make mattress covers, with a weave or pattern obtained with various combinations such as a "fish-scale" pattern. This fish-scale zigzag motif goes very well with threads of diverse colors as well as with various types of materials (for example, wool and silk) arranged in the weft and warp in a way that produces a contrasting clear-opaque, soft-hard effect. The wool version is particularly prized in women's clothing for classic suits and dresses, while the cotton or mixed fiber version is preferred for shirt making.

Etro

Les Copains

Marc Jacobs

Combed, carded or cool wool fabric. It has a twill or Batavia weave with a characteristic design of two-tone checks and a possible optional third color. The most classic glen plaid fabric is black and white with or without a subtle red or sky-blue stripe. Crow's foot stitch is visible inside the well-defined checks. The use of this pattern is very old and has its origin in the English upper classes that moved to Scotland. Unable to use the designs of local clans, these English aristocrats adopted this type of check design as a distinctive emblem, though they called it *glenurqhart*. Sometimes the fabric is also called Prince of Wales check, a reference to Edward VIII, Prince of Wales, who abdicated the English throne to marry the electrifying Wally Simpson, a member of the middle class. Transformed into cult attire, the informal suit worn by Edward VIII became an indispensable element in the wardrobe of anyone who wanted to identify himself with English sobriety. Glen plaid is made with Saxony, a type of wool that takes its name from the region of Saxon where it is from, and its classic supreme elegance is in keeping with an austere, tasteful cut. It is ideal for both formal and lighthearted occasions, combined with a blue shirt and silk tie with jacquard patterns or with solid shirts with a button-down collar and a regimental tie.

Paul Smith

Dior

Yves Saint Laurent

Angelo Marani

Gianfranco Ferré

Daks

Dolce & Gabbana

BARLEYCORN

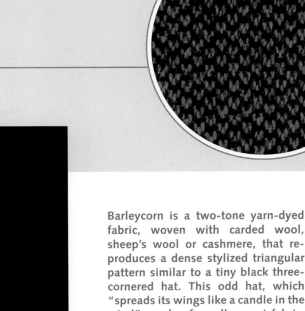

Barleycorn is a two-tone yarn-dyed fabric, woven with carded wool, sheep's wool or cashmere, that reproduces a dense stylized triangular pattern similar to a tiny black three-cornered hat. This odd hat, which "spreads its wings like a candle in the wind", made of woolly, recut fabric, lined internally with silk and always adorned with a silk ribbon, was worn by prelates and monsignors in the 16th and 17th centuries. Barleycorn fabric is obtained by contrasting warp and weft threads, which are interlaced in a Batavia base weave. It is a typical example of sober yet sporty men's tailoring cloth, especially its sheep's wool and cashmere version, which weighs around 350-400 g/m². That said, it is also used for elegant suits and jackets, where the use of translucent synthetic fibers, often tone-on-tone, contribute to creating an impression of false unity. Its name in Italian is *capello di prete* (priest's hat). *Il cappello del prete* is the title of a detective novel, written in 1888 by Emilio De Marchi and considered one of the first works of the genre, whose plot revolves around the twists and turns of a hat. The novel was made into a movie in 1943 by Ferdinando Maria Poggioli and adapted for television in 1970 in a version directed by Sandro Bolchi.

ZZegna

HOUNDSTOOTH

Fabric of French origin, yarn-dyed two or more colors, formed by simple twist threads with a Batavia weave (2:2 twill), and obtained with alternating bands of four light and four dark threads that form a design of small checks. Houndstooth check (*pied de poule* in French) is produced by the intersection of vertical and horizontal stripes formed by black and white diagonal bands that always repeat in the same way on the entirety of the surface. It is woven mainly with wool.

There are many varieties, which are distinguished by their design or size. The smaller version of houndstooth check is a classic fabric in men's tailoring, woven with combed or carded wool or light wool, although it also appears relatively frequently in cotton and synthetic fabrics. Its two-tone version features such designs as the classic glen plaid check.

Chloé

Aquascutum   Chanel

Ashish

Slightly elongated pattern that vaguely recalls a star. Its larger version, pied de coq, is sometimes made with irregular woolen yarns that give it a shantung effect and make it more elegant, suited to today's tailored cut. One of the latest collections, personally endorsed by fashion designer Alexander McQueen, included a giant pied de coq pattern among preferred recurring motifs.

Vivienne Westwood Red Label

Alexander McQueen

Roccobarocco

Roccobarocco

Cynthia Steffe

Marithé & François Girbaud

Roccobarocco

T A R T A N

The word comes from the old French term *tiritaine*, which means "rough and wooly". It is also called Scotch plaid due to the fact that it is a yarn-dyed fabric woven with wool from Scotland, where it was created to distinguish, through the combination of traditional colors, the lineages around which the Celtic communities were grouped into clans. Tartan fabric is used to make the classic Scottish kilt worn by men as official attire in ceremonies. There are more than seventy-five traditional tartan patterns, but only a few are widespread. The design consists of brightly colored checks that repeat at regular intervals in the warp and weft, with a diagonal weave to create a symmetrical pattern. In every tartan design we can observe a spacious single-color background demarcated on four sides by successions of polychromatic stripes. In the fabric composition each color appears to be pure but is actually mixed 50% with another dye. Tartan colors are determined according to the rules of heraldic tradition (in the past these were limited to red, blue, pale blue, bottle green, black and white). Today, there are many varieties of motifs with unusual colors, such as the ones fashion designer Vivienne Westwood used in the late 1990s. Tartan provides a pleasant contrasting effect if used as a liner in coats and raincoats. Examples of this are the trench coats worn by English officials and the famous gabardine that actor Humphrey Bogart was fond of. It is a multi-faceted fabric, used in clothing or in decoration to cover walls, armchairs and ottomans. It has always been a fashion favorite because it reflects classical elegance while at the same time being completely up-to-date.

Vivienne Westwood Red Label

Dolce & Gabbana

Dolce & Gabbana

Dolce & Gabbana

Yohji Yamamoto

Dsquared2

Dolce & Gabbana

Dsquared2

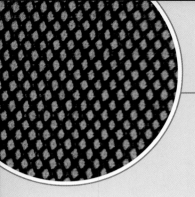

Combed wool fabric, typical of semi-formal men's tailoring. It comes in various weights and is obtained by alternating two light and two dark warp and weft threads with a hint of 1A-2B-1A color, using a diamond weave. The resulting design creates a small jagged diamond with a dot in the center that vaguely recalls the eye of a partridge. It has the appearance of a dense light pointillism spread evenly against a dark background. Today, it is made with almost all types of fibers and is very common in women's clothing (pants suits and sober, elegant outerwear preferred by a public that, without abandoning the imagination, respects classical tradition). For garments with a more youthful air such as sport-style jackets and redingotes, it comes in a variety of lively colors that accentuate the light-dark color contrast or the carded effect that highlights the wooly pile.

Lanvin

Byblos

Bill Blass

SATIN WEAVE FABRICS

6

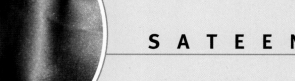

SATEEN

Fabric with a smooth, uniform and soft appearance. It is woven with a satin weave in which the warp yarns are floated over weft yarns and the stitches of the weft weave are separated and arranged in a non-consecutive, though regular, order called "progressive number" that leaves them hidden. Sateen has two opposing sides: a smooth, glossy front side and a dull back. Like all sheeny fabrics, it has variable tones depending on the incidence of light on its surface, thus conferring on the person who wears it a radiant and luxurious look. It is a highly prized fabric, produced in the past exclusively in China under the North Song Dynasty (960-1127), although its golden age of use was during the Ming and Quing era, especially as a foundation for the silk embroidery on the attire of dignitaries of the imperial court. The word "sateen" comes from "Zaitun", the name the Arabs gave to the city of Zhangzhou, where sateen was made. Yarn-dyed sateen is extremely versatile, grants volume to drape and contributes more body to flounces. Piece-dyed sateen accentuates the soft feel and drop in designs with more fluid lines. It is used in a single color as well as in printed and embroidered patterns. The preferred material is silk, the surface of which is embellished by the floating yarns. It also appears in artificial fibers such as rayon or mixed with synthetic fibers like polyester, though the quality is notably inferior. The most common versions of sateen have a regular weave pattern, woven in 5 threads (Chinese

Oscar de la Renta

Cacharel

Dolce & Gabbana

satin) or 8 (duchesse satin), while the irregular version of the fabric uses a weave pattern of 4 (Turkish sateen) or 6 (regina satin). There is also sateen with wider patterns, such as 7-thread satin (meraviglioso satin), and 9- 12- 16- and 24-thread sateen, though these are not used for very often because the floating threads tend to tangle and break. The fabric was very much in vogue in the 1930s, during the "white telephone" period, for it brightened the pale features of such platinum-blonde Hollywood stars as Jean Harlow, accentuating her curves and falling in a way that discreetly caressed the body. The diva wore sateen garments with sliding lines, the backs well defined by the adhering fabric, and a diagonal cut with fluttering godet sleeves. For the afternoon, white or ivory sateen, of lustrous silk, tightfitting to the knee, has subtle straps that cross in the back to define a plunging eye-catching neckline. Another memorable image, even more voluptuous and sensual, is the corset dress that the explosive Gilda wore in the eponymous movie of 1946, a role played magnificently by Rita Hayworth. Nowadays, sateen, normally combined with embroidery, is the preferred fabric for such lingerie as panties, baby dolls and culottes, as the fabric adheres smoothly without compressing, although there are also stretch and bi-stretch versions that ensure attachment. For men, sateen is frequently used in the classic tuxedo collar, though is also found in psychedelic versions in shirts with refined prints.

Etro

DUCHESSE

Burberry Prorsum

Stéphane Rolland

Valentin Yudashkin

Chanel

Jean Paul Gaultier

100% silk fabric of medium-high weight. Robust and compact, slightly rigid to the touch with a smooth surface, Duchesse is very lustrous on the outside and usually woven with 8-Harness satin weave. Some varieties use very fine wild silk threads, high-quality cotton for the weft, viscose rayon threads or chemical fibers that can also be woven in 7-, 10- or 12-Harness Satin. Duchesse has a high warp thread count (up to 230/cm), sometimes of organdy silk that completely covers the surface. It has a sparkling appearance and can be a single color or striped. When made from natural silk, it is used in elegant haute-couture garments with a trapezoidal cut and volumetric structure, or for bridal gowns with a wraparound body and voluminous train. It also used in women's accessories that match dresses, such as capes, stoles, ties, bags, shoes and jeweled belts, while the chemical-fiber version is commonly used in linings. Duchesse is the traditional fabric of classic ballet slippers, fragile and delicate in appearance, with laces at the calf and a structure reinforced with wood in the toe. In decoration, it is used in accessories and in coverings for furniture.

SATINETTE

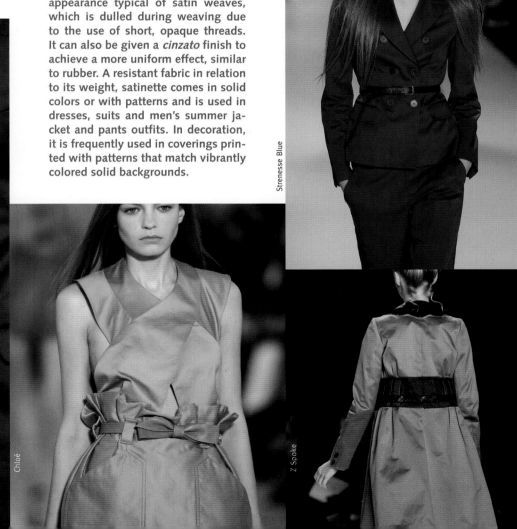

Medium-weight cotton fabric with a 5- Harness satin weave and a very smooth lustrous surface and dull back. On average, it has a maximum thread count of 60 threads and 40 wefts/cm. The use of very fine threads makes it extremely light. These characteristics justify its name. For convenience in weaving, the outside of the fabric is considered the dull side. The textile used in the warp determines the fabric sheen. If made with pure cotton, it must be subjected to calendaring during the finishing stage so that it acquires the lustrous appearance typical of satin weaves, which is dulled during weaving due to the use of short, opaque threads. It can also be given a *cinzato* finish to achieve a more uniform effect, similar to rubber. A resistant fabric in relation to its weight, satinette comes in solid colors or with patterns and is used in dresses, suits and men's summer jacket and pants outfits. In decoration, it is frequently used in coverings printed with patterns that match vibrantly colored solid backgrounds.

Strenesse Blue

Chloé

Z Spoke

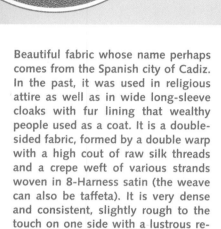

CADY SILK

Beautiful fabric whose name perhaps comes from the Spanish city of Cadiz. In the past, it was used in religious attire as well as in wide long-sleeve cloaks with fur lining that wealthy people used as a coat. It is a double-sided fabric, formed by a double warp with a high cout of raw silk threads and a crepe weft of various strands woven in 8-Harness satin (the weave can also be taffeta). It is very dense and consistent, slightly rough to the touch on one side with a lustrous regular finish on the other. Cady silk has

Givenchy

excellent drape. There are also versions in wool, cotton and viscose. In the 1930s, Cady crepe was introduced into fashion, suitable to the taste in vogue at the time for fluid garments that drape well with little support and adorned with bows whose ends fell harmoniously in soft stoles. In her bias-cut garments, French designer Madeleine Vionnet used a fabric blend named Rosalba (49% natural, 51% artificial silk), one of the first artificial fabrics worthy of comparison to silk. Today, Cady silk comes in different

Bill Blass

Balenciaga

Gucci

Elie Saab

Krizia

Lorenzo Riva

weights and, piece-dyed, in a wide range of tones. Black is preferred for tube dresses and princess dresses that are tightfitting but with undulating lines. It is frequently used in saturated colors for draped evening gowns, with an oval neckline and a special cut, in ivory tones and pure white for traditional bridal gowns.

SFUMATO

During weaving, beautiful chromatic effects can be created on a textile surface with abstract faded blurs or defined patterns achieved through shading. *Sfumato* (or shading) satin is obtained by the regular addition of supplementary stitches, which gradually transform a warp effect into a weft effect through coordinated repetitions. The different color tones in the weft and warp alternate quantitatively and define the color degradation in a sequence of horizontal, vertical and mixed stripes. Playing with different combinations of weave patterns, adding stitches from any other satin weave (e.g., 8-Harness Satin) or

Zero+María Cornejo

Céline

Kenzo

Salvatore Ferragamo

taffeta, produces a fabric with a more complex design, one whose appearance recalls the pointillism technique used in the painting of Seurat. Sfumato fabrics are not made exclusively of satin, but can be fashioned out of a number of herringbone materials.

LIGHTWEIGHT FABRICS

7

CALICO

Hussein Chalavan

de from coarse cotton, very neutral or raw, with a medium thread count and a parchment effect, available in different weights depending on its use. In its heavier versions it can be calendared or sized and is used primarily in decoration and theatrical scenery. Normally, the fabric dyes well and is printed with detailed patterns in bright hues. It is used for curtains, aprons and decorative accessories. Provencal-style women's dresses popularized by the company

Souleiado used a raw calico background printed with stamps carved from wood and molds chiseled in copper plates to reproduce the famous Indiennes. Designs with printed edges along a selvage or arranged horizontally on the fabric require careful study of the arrangement of the design and precise calculation of the consumption of cloth.

Lightweight fabric generically referred to as calico, from the Indian port city of Calicut, where it was made by traditional weavers called càliyans and, with the help of mordant, was adorned with patterns painted and xylographed by hand. The catalog of patterns required the fabric to be cut in large rectangles with long floral points on the edges and a large branch with flowers, leaves and birds in the middle. In Europe, the East India Company imported these fabrics that were used as coverlets. Raw calico was also imported. It is inferior cotton, less fine than muslin, and called "grandma's dishrag". It sometimes has an imperfect structure and is used in pillow cases and bed sheets. In France, calico with two-tone floral designs and animated scenes, which imitated decorations on porcelain, and printed with etched copper plates were called Toiles de Jouy. Today, this term is used to identify a plain-weave fabric ma-

Yohji Yamamoto

Ralph Lauren

Jo No Fui

Peter Som

Hermès

PERCALE

Fabric probably of Persian origin whose name perhaps derives from the word *pargale*, which means "piece of cloth", or from the town of Pargali. It is classified as a very fine fabric, similar to madapolam, a cotton fabric from the Indian city of Madapollam. It is woven with very fine cotton threads mercerized separately or mixed with combed cotton, or also with linen or polyester threads. Percale has a high warp count (from 80 to 120 per cm). It is even finer than muslin, high density, closely woven, and very smooth to the touch. It can be white or dyed pastel colors, starched and calendared. In the past, it was the fabric par excellence for white clothes, used mainly for bed covers, handkerchiefs, undergarments and nightshirts. In its printed version it was also used in men's shirts, summer clothes and shirts for children.

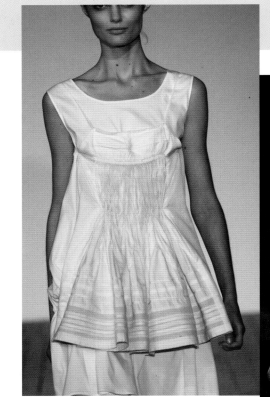

Ter et Bantine

Anglomania

Anglomania

Salvatore Ferragamo

PELLE D'UOVO MUSLIN

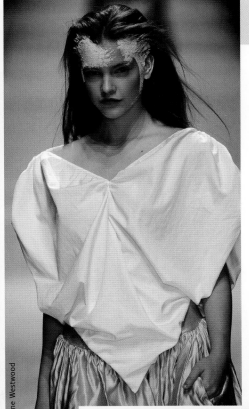

Vivienne Westwood

The Italian term *pelle d'uvo* refers to a very fine, lightweight fabric that weighs around 90 g/m². It is woven with taffeta using extremely fine yarns combed and twisted to create a very smooth surface. The structure of this fabric also comes from madapolam, a lightweight cloth similar to muslin, made in pure white or colors, with the same warp and weft reduction, produced in a factory owned by the East India Company in the Southern Indian town of Madapollam. The fabric is made from cotton or linen, at times semi-transparent to the point that it is compared, due to its extreme fineness, to the protective internal membrane of an egg. This substance is formed by a fine transparent but not in the least bit fragile colorless double layer that adheres to the shell except at the point where it separates to form an air chamber. The fabric is occasionally subjected to calendaring and is commonly used in fine garments and as a background for embroidery. In home textiles it is normally used for Nordic goose-feather duvet covers, as its high thread count prevents the stuffing from coming out.

Marios Schwab

Blacky Dress

Versace

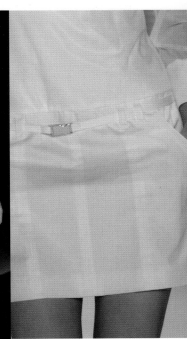

Blacky Dress

POPLIN

Fendi

Etro

Alexander Berardi

Poplin is a tightly woven fabric cool and dry to the touch. It is woven with cotton or silk threads or artificial fibers, usually a blend. It has very small crosswise ribs, barely visible, obtained with a reps weave, a variation of a plain weave with predominance in the warp. It is made with mercerized threads, handled like gauze and twisted in the warp to a higher degree and more subtly than those arranged in the weft. The result of this combination is a silky, smooth appearance. The warp thread count is greater, normally double, that of the weft, with around one hundred threads per square inch. Poplin has a noble origin. In the past it was a very fie woolen fabric used exclusively by the pope, as its name in French (*popeline*) indicates. It is a resistant fabric, though very fine and light, with a weight of 110 to 115 g/m², used in white and pastel tones in shirt making. The most highly regarded kind is Sea Island poplin, a fabric with an even higher thread count (around 140 per square inch) than classic poplin, which increases the effect of silky consistency. It lends itself to small striped and checked patterns. Poplin is also made in intense vivacious colors, with a medium weight, to follow seasonal trends. It is suitable for many garments, including pants, vests and summer jackets. One of the most highly prized 100% poplin finishes is paper touch poplin, which provides a dry, crinkly effect. It can be waterproofed for raincoats and spring jackets.

Isabel Marant

Frankie Morello

BATISTE

Batiste is a lightweight, sheer, transparent fabric that takes its name from its inventor, Baptiste Cambray, a weaver born in the village of Cantaing-sur-Escaut in the district of Cambrai, today part of the French region of Cambresis and at the beginning of the 13th century part of the German empire. Baptiste Cambray came up with a weaving process that allowed for the production of very fine linen fabrics. Since then, batiste, also called Cambray cloth, has been made on a large scale according to traditional methods and exported with increasing success. It was very common in trousseaus, used to make high-quality intimate garments such as petticoats, nightgowns, women's blouses, camisoles for newborns and handkerchiefs. Other sources attribute the name to the use of a strongly fulled weave (*buttuto*, in Italian). Batiste is resistant and lustrous, made up of pure linen warp and weft threads of the same name, and combed and mercerized. To be an authentic batiste cloth, the fabric must have, in both directions, a thread count of at least 36 threads per centimeter. With successive mechanizations, numerous versions were produced, such as mako batiste, made from pure cotton with long mercerized fibers, and, later, batiste cristalline, mixed with a small percentage of polyester or viscose that provides it with more luster. Other varieties are batiste opalina, made from soft cotton with a milky appearance, or batiste glace, made from translucent, rigid and transparent cotton. It is a very light fabric that weighs between 50 and 70 g/m² and is used to make lingerie, shirts and summer dresses.

Issa

Gianfranco Ferré

Julien Macdonald

John Galliano

Gaetano Navarra

MUSLIN

Muslin is a fine and subtle plain-weave fabric woven with highly twisted long-fiber cotton warp and weft threads. The name comes from the Iraqi city of Mossul, although its origin is documented in the city of Dacca, in Bangladesh. Other sources attribute the name to its surface, which has small bubbles that make it similar to a mousse. It was introduced in Europe in the 17th century. Used in white, raw, dyed and printed variations, due to its practical qualities it became a true fashion phenomenon. In the 18th century, in the city of Tarare, a town in the French region of Rodano-Alpes, there was a dyeing, starch finishing and embroidery district specializing in the manufacturing of muslins that diversified production using silk, cotton or blended fibers. Muslin that was soft to the touch, with an ethereal semitransparent appearance, was produced in San Gallo and Zurigo, originally solely from cotton. Printed and embroidered muslin gained favor among women in the 19th century, not to mention the bucolic transgression of the "queen's shirt"(*chemise a la reine*) – a summer garment of simple, loose lines made of two-layer muslin fastened tightly at the waist by a long ribbon and made fashionable by Marie Antoinette – and the delicate tunics with a neo-classical air worn by Josephine Bonaparte and, later, stoles, collars, cuffs, flounces and gathers of the fronts of negligees and Romantic-style petticoats. In the early 20th century, cotton muslin was used in lingerie, while wool muslin was used for printed dresses and shawls of the Belle Epoque. Nowadays, it is made in many different varieties, such as carded cotton, cotton and polyester blend, woven with combed Merina wool yarn with a variable weight of 50 to 90 g/m². To be called muslin, the weft threads of the fabric must be finer than the warp threads, with a thread count of around 180 threads per 6.54 cm. It can be made in printed patterns and also embroidered. Silk muslin, similar to chiffon on account of its lightness, though more transparent due to its more open structure, has a drier feel. Muslin can be lustrous or matted. All types of muslin are used in children's clothing, blouses and dresses (collars and cuffs) and in accessories such as scarves, shawls, foulards and handkerchiefs. Sheer flounces of stratified muslin in total white or total black versions characterized the volumes in a collection named "Burnt", created by young fashion designer Robert Wunper.

Isaac Mizrahi

Valentino

Hugo Boss

Gianfranco Ferré

FOULARD

Dolce & Gabbana

Alviero Martini

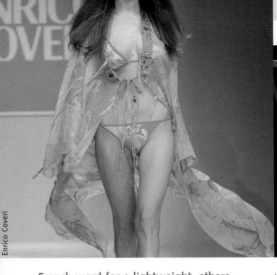

Enrico Coveri

JC de Castelbajac

Dolce & Gabbana

French word for a lightweight, ethereal silk, cotton or synthetic-fiber fabric, with twill weave finished so that the cloth acquires a soft feel and especially lustrous appearance. Foulard is usually printed according to a consolidated sketch with one or more motifs in the center framed by adornments, simple or paired, of various kinds. It is used for dresses, blouses, evening gowns, kimonos, handkerchiefs, pareos and shawls. The name *foulard* also designates a headscarf of silk checks, the famous Hermes accessory, which can be knotted in different ways on the body as a top or pareo, on the head, at the wrist, around the waist… The famous image of Grace Kelly, an icon of refined fashion who later became the princess of Monaco, wearing a foulard folded into a triangle and knotted under her chin is a look imitated by women all over the world. All Hollywood divas worthy of the name have experimented with a more spectacular variation, one in which a foulard is wrapped around the neck two times, covering it completely, and then tied in the front. This style, combined with large sunglasses, was adopted during the *dolce vita* period. The foulard "a la Cleopatra", arranged so that it covers the forehead and hair and is ultimately knotted at the nape of the neck, became fashionable in imitation of the Egyptian claft, after the impressive screen performance of Elizabeth Taylor in the role of Cleopatra. In subsequent years, foulards were knotted loosely at the neck and also around the straps of ladies' handbags as a touch of distinction. Young people in the sixties used a small unisex foulard folded flat and knotted tightly around the neck, with short ends that dropped to the sides. It was worn with an open shirt, imitating the characteristic image of Tex Willer or legendary figures such as Elvis Presley.

ANGEL SKIN

Francesco Scognamiglio

Lightweight, soft and fluid fabric with a satiny granular surface invented in the 1930s from albene, an acetate matte thread that, thanks to new knowledge about polymers, was converted into matte through a pigment introduced in the colloidal mass before extrusion. This opaqueness differentiated angel skin from other satin-weave fabrics, which used lustrous threads such as rayon or viscose in imitation of natural silk. Normally, angel skin uses 12-Harness Satin that allows for good drape. In those years, the same fabric was used to make pajamas and beach wear that later became the first wide pants for women, soft, fluid and loose at the bottom. The term "peau de soie"(silk skin) refers to a cloth produced in the 20th century in Padua known in England as Paduasoy. Occasionally it has a two-side surface obtained by modifying 5-Harness Satin or 8-Harness Satin, such that the floating warp threads appear on both sides of the fabric. A third variation is "swan skin", a 5-Harness Satin with crepe threads. This material is very light and soft, drapes well and is so fluffy it is compared with the chalk-white plumage of the elegant avian with the long fine neck. It is used in refined lingerie and elegant evening gowns.

Antonio Berardi

Isabel Marant

La Perla

Jean Paul Gaultier

BYSSUS CLOTH

Byssus cloth is a rare, very expensive fabric, practically impossible to find, also known as sea silk. It is made only in certain remote places on the island of Sant'Antioco, in Sardinia, from the filaments of the pinna nobilis, a bivalve mollusk with an elongated shell (a species considered in danger of extinction) that lives in the waters of the Mediterranean Sea. These animals, which secrete a silky, lustrous saliva that they use to anchor themselves to rocks on the sea floor, have been recognized since antiquity as a precious resource for producing high-quality natural silk, spun and woven to produce clothing for very important figures. Fisherman discovered the excellent hemostatic qualities of sea silk. The term "byssus" extended, by similarity, to all impalpable lightweight semitransparent plain-weave fabrics made from very fine linen, silk or dense cotton used as background for embroidery.

Mark Fast

Salvatore Ferragamo

30 Paar Haende

Byblos

PARACHUTE

C.P. Company

Lightweight, graceful and almost imperceptible fabric produced mainly with heavily milled silk cloth. In 1514 Leonardo da Vinci had an intuition: "If a man had wings made of gummed linen ten fathoms sideways and another twelve fathoms high, he could jump from any height and not get hurt." The first to try a silk parachute was Jean Pierre Blanchard, who died during a jump in 1809. The prototype was improved by building a structure with an apical hole in the cupola, which had a surface area of 48 m² and was made up of 24 segments sewn together in such a way that they could withstand the pull during opening. Due to its resistance and capacity for retaining air, during the Second World War parachute fabric was put to military and technical use in parachutes for pilots. Its conversion for practical purposes in the production of luxury items, which hadn't found an adequate outlet at the time, left its mark on the name of this

type of fabric. On July 1, 1945, Albertina Magliani Gianpellegrini realized her dream of having a white wedding in a very special dress, one made from the silk parachute that Scotchman David Kirkpatrick, a parachutist in Cusna, gave her husband as a gift when he was a partisan. Today, parachute cloth is used in fashion to provide volume without a support structure and frequently is combined with a coulisse finish that gives it resistance and breadth. It is also used to make long skirts, pants, blouses and shoes. In the 1970s, parachute silk was replaced by nylon, which is less porous, and new fabrics emerged as the fruit of research in the United States, one of which was F/111, which requires little sizing and has a programmable degree of porosity.

Strenesse Blue

Custo Barcelona

C.P. Company

Paul Smith

ORGANZA SILK

Valentino

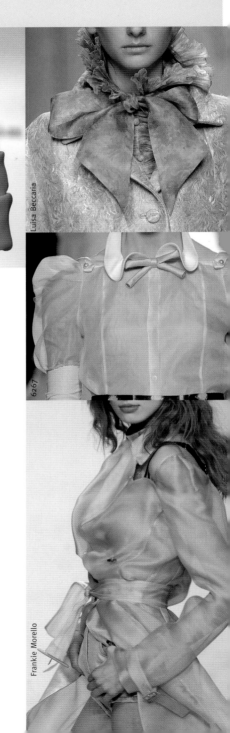

Mila Schön

Luisa Beccaria

6267

Frankie Morello

Its name comes from Urghenz (Turkistan), though in Europe it is also called organdy. It is a lightweight fabric of around 40 g/m², dense though transparent, preferably constructed with a plain weave and woven with special organza silk warp and weft threads or only warp threads. Organza is a highly resistant flexible thread made from the highest quality treated silk fibers, with a pronounced Z-twist (500-600 twists per meter). There are different types of organza, including organza grenadine, medium organza, strafilato (extra yarn) organza or common organza. Organza has a luxurious appearance and is dry to the touch, a feel strengthened in the finish through sizing. It is used in elegant blouses with oblique flounces, in waves and stratifications on very elaborate evening gowns, and is particularly suitable for bridal wear and embroidered veils. It appears frequently in ceremonial headdresses. A famous Givenchy perfume takes its name from the fabric, thus equating the sheer consistency and almost intangible quality of the material with a fragrance intended for the sophisticated woman.

COTTON ORGANZA

Extremely fine, veiled and sheer fabric, similar to muslin yet more rigid and durable. It is obtained with a plain weave through pronounced twisting of exclusively cotton fibers. In the past, this material was used, almost always in white, for lining the inside of dresses or for doubling a particularly fine fabric and granting it more stability. Like other types of organza, it can be printed or embroidered. It is often used in pastel tones for women's shirts, romantic dresses with flounces, or children's wear with pleats.

Bora Aksu

Roberto Cavalli

Jean Paul Gaultier

Polyester organza is softer and less treated than cotton or silk organza and can also be made from mixed fibers such as rayon-acetate. The finish, which does not increase stiffness, disappears after the first wash. It is characterized by a more accessible price than other elegant fibers. Nowadays, it is produced in several versions, among them wrinkled, solid and iridescent. Polyester organza is used to make garments intended for mass production that require a lightweight structure without sacrificing ease of maintenance. It is suitable for dresses, skirts, shirts, foulards, shawls and women's ties. It is also used, in the form of a ribbon, for hairdressing decorations and on gift boxes. In decoration, it is used to make economical curtains that can be enhanced with intricately worked adornments or embroidery in numerous colors. The contrast between the highly elaborate work and the ethereal consistency of the fabric creates a sensation of movement and ensures penetration of light.

Viktor & Rolf

Dior

Blugirl

Thakoon

CHIFFON

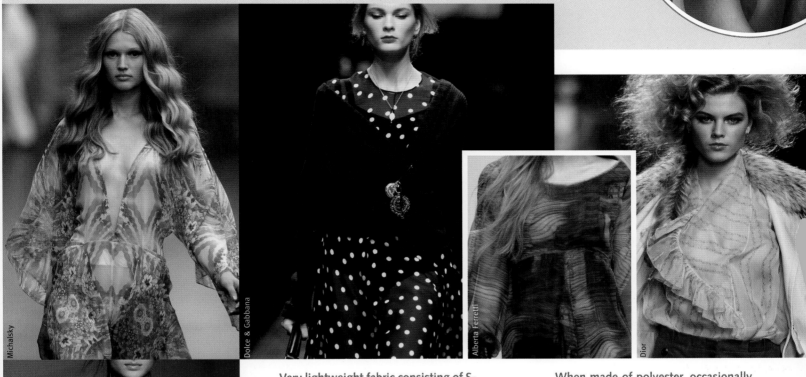

Michalsky

Dolce & Gabbana

Alberta Ferretti

Dior

Emanuel Ungaro

Very lightweight fabric consisting of S- and Z-twist yarns with a plain weave. It is used in light dresses, shawls and stoles. Its grainy surface has a slight horizontal crimp and a fine, veiled appearance. Chiffon weighs between 40 and 50 g/m². Its feel, particularly soft, enhances luxurious seductive garments that drape well. The name derives from the French word *chiffe*, which translates literally as "rag". It is a sheer material, though fragile and delicate, and requires careful maintenance to prevent the fabric threads from running. Silk chiffon is very elegant, though wrinkles easily, and is used primarily in evening gowns with flounces, superimposed layers and sheer trains, as well as in shirts, shawls and highly prized undergarments.

When made of polyester, occasionally in elastic versions, it receives a chemical treatment that makes it softer and, therefore, more economical and affordable for making t-shirts, foulards and belts. Cotton chiffon or chiffon made from other fibers not as attractive as silk can also be found in stores. The spectacular cocktail dress with a tight-fitting bustier and asymmetrical drape – created by Greek designer Christina Stambolian – that Lady Diana wore in 1994 to a party and that subsequently came to be known as the "revenge dress" was made of pleated black chiffon.

VOILE

Plain-weave fabric consisting of coarse, very fine quality threads. It can be woven with cotton, treated silk or wool, or combined with viscose or polyester, which makes it softer and more fluid. It has the same number of high-twist warp and weft threads. Bleached first and then dyed a wide range of colors, voile is sheer and lightweight. It weighs around 40 g/m², but can be

Antonio Berardi

Dior

reduced to 26/-28 g/m². Due to its transparency, accentuated by the reduced volume of the fibers that make it up, voile is used in fashion for revealing and concealing purposes. Silk voile, sized pleated and printed, is also used for stoles and foulards. It offers good drape and embossing results, and is used as inserts and shirt fronts in blouses and, above all, in headdresses, bridal wear and evening gowns. Cotton voile can also be mercerized and calendared and is suitable for shirts, summer pants and dresses with veils. The name comes from *velum*, a Latin word that designated a particularly thin fabric that veiled the head and sometimes the face of women or that enveloped precious objects such as chalices during religious services.

Alberta Ferretti

Dior

Blugirl

La Perla

Jean Paul Gaultier

GAZAR

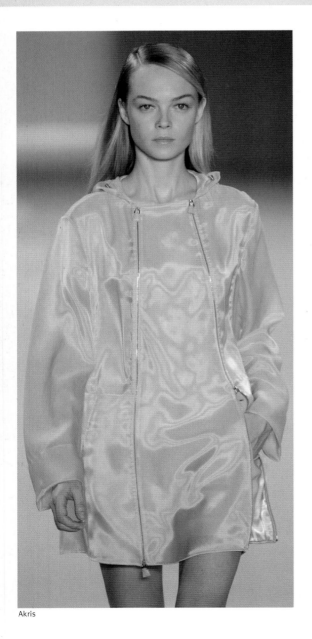

Akris

Marni

Lanvin

A stiff fabric of pure silk, similar to double or triple organza but stronger and less transparent. It has small horizontal striations and is crinkly to the touch. While gazar has a compact structure, it is light and ethereal and highly regarded in haute couture. Silk gazar dresses are the unmistakable cornerstone of the style of such dressmaking masters as Lanvin, Fausto Sarli and Ferre. It is used mainly for volumetric flounces, pleats and drape in the construction of sculptural dresses, and also occasionally appears in petticoats. Silk gazar can made in printed patterns or receive a lamina-ted finish that updates its classical look and provides garments extra stiffness. White and ivory silk gazar was used to make the bridal gown of Kate Middleton, the consort of Prince William of England, designed by Sarah Burton for Alexander McQueen. The gown, linear yet sophisticated, consisted of a corset cinched at the waist with hand-embroidered Cluny and Chantilly lace, a long voluminous skirt and a nearly three-meter train.

Marni

Lanvin

SHEER GAUZE

Sheer gauze with waved yarn is the gauze par excellence. Initially, it was made in England; later, the bobbinet machine invented by John Heathcoat in 1806 was patented and used to produce mechanical tulle. The weave contains some straight and tenser warp threads, held in place by others that are more twisted and longer called leno yarns, which are inserted in the mesh and reciprocally interlaced adopting a slanted position. The weft, introduced normally, remains parallel but is rearranged or spaced out to form an open weave. To make a specific English leno-gauze weave, a special assembly of the loom is necessary. At times, in the absence of the traditional selvage, sheer gauze is used to make the nearly invisible lateral finish of many fabrics. The "sheer gauze" selvage continues to visibly twist between the two warp threads, usually of polyester, that enclose a

Gaetano Navarra

weft thread at each turn. Gauze fabric produces a sheer yet stable weave, with a particularly durable and solid structure that allows light and air to pass through. Depending on what it will be used for, it can be of synthetic fiber (nylon) or natural materials. This material can be used to make sturdy reinforcement supports for curtains, mosquito nets or petticoats and crinoline for bridal gowns. It can also be used as the base and filling for hats. Crinoline, a petticoat made of stiff and sized fabric, held in place by a support frame that increased the volume of the skirts, was invented by the Frenchman Oudinot and became a highly popular women's accessory in the 19th century. The name "crinoline" designated both the structure of the petticoat, supported by a metal hoop, and the fabric of which it was made, initially consisting of stiff natural horsehairs.

Marni

Valentino

Céline

Anglomania

Armani Privé

GAUZE

Lightweight, transparent fabric with a thin plain weave, possibly from the city of Gaza in Palestine. Gauze fabric (huck lace) has some tenser warp yarns along with others that are more twisted and looser and that interlace following a sinuous course. This creates a very open textile structure, one with empty spaces but at the same time stable. It can be made from cotton, silk or other materials. It can be somewhat stiff and is used mainly in a single color, with several layers superimposed or printed to create the effect of more movement. Due to their similarity, the term has been extended to all similar plain-weave fabrics with a low thread count. Among them are openwork fabrics with different designs, woven with frequent floating warp and weft threads, with an attractively frivolous appearance, though they are very delicate as the threads get caught up easily. Reinforced with edges made from thicker cloth, gauze is used in curtains, mosquito nets, tablecloths, towels and decorative accessories, as well as in shoes, skirts and blouses. Another variety is "fake gauze", a material with a linear but loosely woven structure used to make bandages.

Alberta Ferretti

Blumarine

Sharon Wauchob

Luisa Beccaria

Dries Van Noten

8

FABRICS WITH BLUR EFFECTS

MELANGE FABRIC

A fabric of any fiber spun with mixed yarn, created by the combination of several components or bands of the same component. It is made in adulterated, blurry, almost dirty colors with chiaroscuro effects. It can be *camaieu*, pale and diffuse, with faded tone-by-tone color progressions that imitate the effect of *cammei* (from the Old French *camahue*, or "chiaroscuro"). It also can consist of fabric blends in blurrier and more contrasting colors. Different color yarns are blended before spinning, that is, in fiber. The blend produces good results in wool, especially carded wool, and can be sheer and compact or consist of a long pile with a generally low count, whether in cloth or knitted fabric. It can be made up of fiber blends of many blurred and contrasting shades. Among the mixed fibers the most typical are variegated fabric (three-layer novelty yarn); heathe-

red (stained with many colors but without tonal contrast or made up of many equal elements of different colors that form a peculiar blur); and *moulinè*, from the verb *mouliner*, or "to twist the yarn" (a yarn consisting of two threads of different colors, joined and twisted, the alternation of which produces on the whole a sheer and delicate heather with a characteristic lustrous effect). Shetland is a fabric woven with a blend. The concept of blending includes the combination or concurrence of materials with different characteristics, such as wool and silk, which are joined to achieve, for instance, super-Mogador, a yarn used by Ermenegildo Zegna for weaving winter ties.

Bottega Veneta

Dior

Enrico Coveri

Gucci

Alexander Wang

END-ON-END

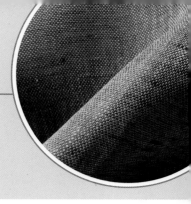

Yarn-dyed fabric with a slightly irregular and heathered surface, with a two-tone optical effect regardless of the weave, which can be plain or twill as well as a derivative such as Batavia twill. It is characterized by the particular arrangement of the threads, which form opposing chiaroscuro coloring. Often woven with wool, linen and cotton yarns, it is also called "salt and pepper". End-on-end produces a miniscule vertical pin-stripe effect (visible on the outside and the inside) created by threads joined in alternating sequence, with a note of 1A -1B color in the warp and uniform color in the weft. If the end-on-end effect is also repeated in the weft, alternating 2A-2B in both directions, a tiny grid is obtained. However, if the colors of nearby filling and warp yarns are not very different, the result is a false solid color. The term *fil a fil* is a French expression that literally means the "end-on-end" or "thread-to-thread" weaving arrangement of the fabric. This type of fabric is particularly suitable for woolen products and tailoring and is used to make jackets, pants and men and women's suits. In cotton, it is used very frequently in shirt making.

Marc Jacobs   Marc Jacobs

Gaetano Navarra   Marc Jacobs   Emporio Armani   Kristina Ti

CHINE

Devi Kroell

Cynthia Steffe

Temperley London

Drosophila

Dries Van Noten

A fabric with figurative or geometric designs with intentionally undulating, blurry, washed-out and almost confusing outlines. The word comes from the French verb *chiner*, or "to heather" (to dye the threads in a fabric different colors). It has its origin in a technique popular in France in the first half of the 18th century for making *Chinè à la branche*, fabrics produced in Europe that imitated the decorative effects of certain oriental products made by a similar process known as *ikat* (tied). It is done by protecting parts of the yarn (sometimes in skeins) that, divided into small bundles, are reserved for well-tied areas to prevent the penetration of color during immersion in coloring agent baths. The loose parts are dyed, while the reserved areas remain white and can be colored in succession by a system of inverting the bindings. This results in spaced dyeing. A fabric in which the reserved dye is applied to warp threads is known as simple *ikat*, while in double ikat, the reserves are done in order and in the weft. Crossing of threads with different dyes and arrangement according to the desired sequence produces designs with geometric heathered outlines such as checks, diagonals and chevrons. The preferred fabric for chine and ikat are taffeta and satin. The ikat technique was practiced by ancient Hindu communities and pre-Colombian peoples in Peru and later spread to many countries. Nowadays, multicolor silk ikat fabrics from Uzbekistan, Malaysia and Indonesia are highly regarded, as are traditionally crafted cotton ikat products from the Ivory Coast. Japanese kasuri are ikats with alternating printed patterns. The chine a las chaine effect is achieved at times by a more complex process, one involving additional stages: a first refined silk warp thread is woven in taffeta with a false weft with a low thread count (between 3 and 6 per cm) for the sole purpose of keeping the threads together. The resulting fabric is printed using a system of blocks or plates. Later, the first weft is removed and the warp printed in reserve is used for the final weaving, this time with a denser weft, between 30 and 50 insertions per cm. Thus, small transferences are created among the threads that produce variations in the outlines of the designs. To speed the process up and reduce costs, the warp is printed on directly through a system of paper or plastic film transfer that provides different colors, resulting in a heathered pattern. Chine effects are particularly good in silk, and currently they are most frequently used in decorative fabrics and ties. They are also often used to enhance jacquard fabrics. In its cheaper cotton version, chine is used in the construction of shirts, pants and ethnic-style clothing.

WOOL CREPE

Medium-weight worsted fabric and taffeta fabric produced by alternating regular twist yarns with crepe yarns, which are highly twisted unstable fibers that uncurl when free of tension after exiting the loom. The result is the wool crepe's characteristic rough appearance, full of pockmarks. Sometimes a crepe weave is used, a fabric without a reverse side or a neutral material that offers good balance with light and heavy effects, suitable for adding movement to the irregular pattern of crepe yarns. The name is derived from the Latin word *crispus* (curly). Despite its dry grainy feel, wool crepe hangs well and lends itself easily to drape. It is piece dyed. The twist of crepe yarn, obtained through humidification, oscillates between 2,000 and 4,000 twists per meter. The fabric was the preferred material for producing mourning attire, dyed white for children and black for adults, as its particularly dull appearance and almost rough feel underscored the attitude of renouncing social life and luxury. In the mid-17th century, it was very common in Bologna, and later was exported to France. Around the middle of the 19th century, crepe played a key role in the industrialization of the art of weaving, given that the yarn, reinforced by increased torque, was able to better withstand friction with the mechanical parts of high-speed weaving machines. Its structure allowed for a series of variants, called *crepella* (lightweight, soft crepe) and *crespon* (heavier and more rigid with light ribbing produced by yarns twisted in a

single direction, obtained through differences in the direction of the twist, the number of twists per meter, the composition of the fiber, the thickness of the yarn and the arrangement in the warp and weft. This singular quality made crepe a favorite fabric among French fashion designers, who made a warhorse of it, infusing a classic of masculine and feminine elegance with good taste, fantasy, creativity and skill of execution.

Lanvin   Etro   Barbara Bui

Narciso Rodriguez

Martin Margiela   Dolce & Gabbana   Sportmax

CREPE DE CHINE

A light, resistant, plain-woven fabric originally from China produced consisting of a simple all-silk warp with no twist and a 100% raw-silk weft made up of two or three layers and highly twisted threads. The wefts are introduced into the fabric alternating the direction of the twist "two-and-two", with two picks of filling to the left and two picks of filling to the right, such that the inclination of the first ones compensates for or neutralizes that of the second. With successive purging and dyeing stages, crepe fabric twists on itself, causing the material to shrink between 10 and 15% in the direction of the height. Crepe de chine owes its name to the fact that it was imported from the Far East to France, where it was so highly prized that at the beginning of the 19th century, an attempt was made to produce it industrially. There are many varieties, the most common being a medium-gloss fabric produced with raw silk that is subsequently pasted to obtain a curled effect and a glossy fabric in which treated-silk or polyester wefts are used always alternating crimped threads and normal ones in both directions. Occasionally elastic crepe threads are used in the warp or weft. Crepe de chine has a compact, glossy appearance that highlights draped designs; its silky nature requires skillful sewing, though the material doesn't fray easily. Its economic version, mixed with polyester, isn't as lustrous but provides optimum results. Piece dyed or printed, cre-

S. Rykiel

pe de Chine is used very frequently in women's fashion. In the seventies and eighties the fabric symbolized the aspirations of the middle class to be different as well as sobriety and good taste. In those years, the crepe de Chine camisole or blouse was a classic among refined women, who could choose from a wide range of glossy dyes. Crepe de Chine shoes, foulards and ties printed with a limitless variety of patterns were responsible for making the fortunes of many generations of businessmen in the city of Como and the territory of Lario, which specialized in printed silk.

Antonio Berardi

Mariella Burani

BCBG   Lutz   Unrath & Strano

SATIN CREPE

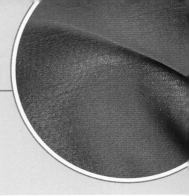

Hermès

A soft, silky, medium-light weight crepe fabric, glossy on one side and dull on the other. It has a 5-Harness Satin weave (other crepes are plain woven) formed by untwisted warp threads predominant on the glossy side of the fabric and crimped silk weft threads with an alternating twist that are foremost on the dull side. The filling yarn count is nearly half that of the warp. Occasionally we find shot and even printed versions. They are varieties of satin crepe with a satin weave: charmeuse or crepe-back satin, a fabric with two faces (satin/silk crepe) characterized by a consistent but fluid feel, and crepe de meteor, called this because of the extreme sheen of its surface, smooth on one side and rough on the other, like georgette.

Dior

John Galliano

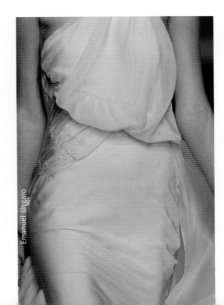

Emanuel Ungaro

Haider Ackermann

VALENTINO
TISSUS

CREPE GEORGETTE

Giambattista Valli

Light, transparent fabric whose name comes from French fashion designer Georgette de la Plante. Similar to chiffon but duller and grainier, it is considered a plain crepe (crimped in the warp and weft) and is difficult to produce compared with other crepes (ones crimped only in the weft). Georgette is made exclusively with highly twisted worsted silk yarns and opposing twists (2I/2D). The weft count is less than the warp, and the crepe effect/face is visible on both sides. Despite being plain woven, its surface is undulating and mobile, it has very large shrinkage (almost ¼ of the initial length and width) and is very dry to the touch. To increase the crimped effect, the fabric can be made with a crepe weave. It is also made in low-cost versions of viscose or mixed with rayon or cotton. One variety is Roman crepe, a georgette with a Panama weave created by alternating S- and Z-twist weft yarns (2/S-1/Z-2/S). The fabric molds the figure well, is light and enveloping, offers good support despite being relatively thin, and is made in solid colors and prints. Its average weight is around 50 g/m².

Jonathan Saunders

Luisa Beccaria

Yves Saint Laurent

Dior

Blumarine

CREPE MOROCAIN

A fabric made according to the same principles as Crepe-de-Chine (weft more twisted than warp), though heavier and more consistent, formed by finer Z-twist silk yarns and a denser crepe-fabric weft (from 6 to 12 strands) that can be of wild silk or cotton. This structure gives it a strong horizontal rib effect, similar to Canton crepe, which has a protuberant pleated surface. There are silk versions, more highly esteemed, and other more economical ones made from continuous filament fibers such as rayon. Its weight ranges from 80 to 100 g/m². Crepe morocain is suitable for very elegant coats and eveningwear as well as for garments that require a resistant structure like that of this closely woven fabric. In lighter versions it is also used as lining for luxury garments and furs.

Brioni

Issey Miyake

Gucci

Derek Lam

Antonio Marras

Sable fabric is grainy and semi-opaque in appearance though soft to the touch, imitating a smooth surface covered with grains of sand. It is characterized by its particular base weave, obtained by joining portions from other weaves (plain, Batavia twill and Levantine, heavy and light) but with the same number of threads. Alternation of the weft yarns is combined to create a rough but balanced fabric, without an outside or an inside. The structure of sable is varied, with a very large pattern repeat on an arrangement of an enlarged thread weave, multiple of the base weave. There are combinations of 66 or 120 threads times 40 or 60 wefts. Sable requires rational use of yarns (contrasting colors in the warp and weft) and careful study of weaving effects. It is a classic example of the concurrence of composition novelty and technological research in the creation of new textiles. At times, sable uses highly twisted crepe-spun material, which makes it a more swollen and three-dimensional fabric called sable crepe. It can be made of wool, silk, silk blend or synthetic fibers. It is used above all in women's clothes and ties.

Armani Privè

Jil Sander

Bill Blass

111

PIQUE-KNIT

Piqué knit has an effect similar to that of sable. Its name comes from a novelty pattern derived from twill. It is created by a combination of small geometric patterns set against each other with light-heavy effect, twirled or juxtaposed with 90 degree rotations on one side or at an angle. It is characterized by its irregular surface, dull and grainy, similar to granite, the result of the play of the weave. It can be made of combed wool with different colors in the warp and weft. It weighs around 350-450 g/m² and is used in such garments as jackets and suits. Pique made of silk or artificial fibers is much lighter and is frequently used as a background for printing patterns on ties. Its lightest version is called *grain de poudre* (grain of powder), while *barathea*, of wool-cotton or wool-mohair, is used to make tuxedos. Certain types of pique with irregular, crimped or *boucle* yarns, of wool, cotton or viscose, are also used in decoration.

Louis Vuitton

Peter Pilotto

Marios Schwab

SEERSUCKER

Seersucker is a cotton fabric from India whose name originates from "shir o shakar", which according to its Hindi, Urdu and Persian roots can be translated as "milk and sugar". The English term is a compound word made up of *seer* (Indian weight of measurement) and *sucker* (vent). Seersucker has a very decorative look, with horizontal or, more frequently, vertical lines in the form of stripes or checks. In the past, it was hand spun with cotton and silk threads that, properly alternated, produced stripes grouped together in areas with different characteristics of stretch and shrinkage. In general, it is obtained by arranging warp threads with different twists in the loom, alternating groups of tense threads with looser ones such that the fabric acquires a natural effect of roughness. These features keep the fabric away from the skin, facilitating the passage of air; for this reason seersucker is suitable for summer garments such as shirts, shorts and jackets the don't require ironing. Seersucker permits dressing with impeccable elegance even in very warm climates. Its elasticity, which tends to weaken over time, is independent of the technique used to obtain this quality: through weaving, through thermal compression or through chemical finishing processes. In the United States, seersucker fabric was popular among workers. Later, it was discovered by the upper classes and became part of the wardrobes of Southern gentlemen, in the form of the classic white-and-blue blazer known as the Oxford-striped seersucker jacket.

Cacharel

Moschino Cheap & Chic

Etro

Paul & Joe

Gabriele Colangelo

CRAQUELÉ

Chanel

Albino

Isabel Marant

Historic yarn-dyed or piece-dyed fabric with a crimped fragmented three-dimensional appearance. This feature is the result of the arrangement of warp and weft yarns on the loom with different tensions. When the finished fabric is removed from the loom, the tensest threads, normally situated in the weft and occasionally in the warp, cause the curling. Craquelé can be made with a variety of materials, such as silk, cotton or synthetic fibers. Sometimes it includes crepe yarns, which curl in the piece-dyeing stage, or bathed-silk threads, which recover their elasticity when they dry. Both systems contribute to producing a more wavy effect. Originally, the crimping was achieved using craft techniques on a plain-weave base, passing the silk filling yarn manually. In the early 20th century craquelé began to be manufactured on semi-automatic looms. It is used in ladies' clothing and fashion garments. Prada has unveiled a lacquered version.

Bottega Veneta

Céline

FABRICS WITH RELIEF

9

IRIDESCENT FABRIC

Gianfranco Ferré

Iridescent fabric alternates opalescent yarns with plain and regular ones, forming a heterogeneous surface. This effect is due to elongated enlargements of the yarn in highlights that encompass in its own twist the thickest parts of the fiber. Different thicknesses are obtained by stretching the yarn. Depending on the type of fabric desired, simple, enhanced or flammé yarns can be used, producing more irregular fabrics. Similar to tiny tongues of fire, iridescent elements are arranged in the fabric as miniscule brushstrokes whose strong visual impact grants personality to the fabric. Iridescent yarns can be of the same tone or of contrasting colors. Some fabrics have iridescent parts only in the direction of the warp while others have enlargements both in the warp and weft. Iridescent fabric is very effective in shirt making and is also used in ladies' suits and dresses. In decoration accessories, they appear against very light backgrounds in curtains of different consistency and transparency made from linen, cotton and synthetic fibers.

Aquilano e Rimondi

Marc by Marc Jacobs

Lorenzo Riva

Gianfranco Ferré

A plain-woven fabric with an irregular appearance, originally made with wild Chinese silk produced by silk worms from the oaks in the province of Chan Tong and woven on manual looms. The yarn is two-stranded (produced simultaneously by two worms enclosed in the same cocoon) and irregular, always yarn -dyed and either dry or soft to the touch. Similar types are produced in the region of Ho-Nan (Ho-nan fabric, with an irregular feel and spun on a manual loom) and in the region of Lianing (Antung fabric, spun on a mechanical loom). In India it is known as *tussah*, a silk fiber spun and woven by hand and used to make *tussor* fabric. Shantung silk is also produced in Japan, Indonesia and Thailand. Nowadays, it is a fabric often characterized by a lustrous surface with spaced striations due to irregular spinning (*malfilé*), used solely in the weft or in both directions. The irregularities and knots are not defects but constitute the characteristic feature of this fabric, which doesn't ruin, is resistant to use and slightly elastic. Solid dyeing highlights its structure, which can also be made of cotton mixed with silk, viscose or synthetic fibers. It is found for the most part in elegant blouses, tailored suits and dresses and summer overcoats, in addition to men's ties with a limitless range of tones that reflect light with the slightest movement. Shantung is also frequently used in decoration, although it's delicate, forming halos and stains on contact with water.

Michael Kors

C'n'C

Balenciaga

Balenciaga

BOURRETTE

An irregular, dull, slightly grainy, silk fabric, plain woven or woven using pure bourrette yarn or mixed with other fibers. This yarn is composed of surplus combed yarn and short silk fibers (less than 4 cm) that are reused to reduce its high price. It is of irregular thickness, due to the tiny knots and enlargements created by small agglomerations of material generated during spinning. It can have a very rustic or refined appearance and be dyed solid colors or with mixed effect due to the presence of residue from previous productions. It requires careful manufacturing because it is vulnerable to chafing. From the end of the 19th century to the first two decades of the 20th century, entire neighborhoods in Lyon and Basel were devoted to this type of work, for which primarily a female workforce was used to spin chapé silk. Bourrette yarn was also used to make especially light knit garments, characterized by the rustic yet elegant spirit intrinsic to dull silk.

Dries Van Noten

Haider Ackermann

Chanel

Alexander McQueen

BOUCLÉ

A fabric with a springy surface with small curled irregular loops obtained from novelty yarn of the same name. Bouclé, from the French *boucle* (ring, loop), is a binary twisted yarn with two different yarn tensions, such that one forms a series of curls arranged at regular intervals. It is used in woolen and knit fabrics. During weaving, bouclé yarn, for which a carded type is preferably used, forms a more or less granular, compact and soft three-dimensional surface dotted with tiny loops and curled knots. It is suitable for making jackets, trouser suits and medium-weight or winter coats especially fluffy, soft to the touch and very feminine. Yarn dyed, bouclé can be made in solid or novelty colors, especially with linear and geometric patterns. Cardigans and sweaters can have a crimped appearance when the loops are very small.

Aquascutum

Max Mara

Kenzo

Etro

Enrico Coveri

BOUTONNÉ

This is a three-dimensional surface dotted with knots, small agglomerations of short fibers, hair and nubs formed during spinning and incorporated into the yarn, which tends to be a carded yarn with a lot of volume. The nubs are created with special spindles that act in such a way that when two yarns are twisted together they have a tendency to turn on their axis in an inverse direction to the twist. Novelty boutonné yarns are formed with a core yarn and a knot or effect yarn. The thread yarn can be simple, enhanced or alternating knots. The procedure is the following: one yarn advances with steady speed while the other moves alternatively at the same velocity as the first and much slower, though maintaining the same length of yarn. When it slows down, the second yarn wraps around the first, ultimately forming small knots at different distances. Then the yarn starts running again, with many small, hairy bumps spread across the body of the yarn (the nubs). Generally, these knots create an effect of little balls of contrasting colors. Boutonné can include dye shadows and count effects and length of pattern repeat between the component yarns, in keeping with seasonal fashions. The knots are arranged irregularly on the background. The boutonné technique used to make novelty yarns is applied to men's and women's garments, in cotton and linen, and extends to orthogonal fabric such as Donegal tweed or tweed knickerbocker and knit fabrics.

Carolina Herrera

C. P. Company

Jil Sander

Donna Karan

Veronique Leroy

TWEED

Paul Smith

Albino

Fabric with a rough, thick and somewhat bristly appearance, made with a diagonal weave or derivatives using carded wool of muted natural colors and with a characteristic chiaroscuro design obtained with mixed yarns, bouclé or boutonné of various colors. The color of the warp is different than the weft, and generally has a count of 12 threads per centimeter. In the past grey and black yarns were used, and the classic pattern was herringbone. Today, tweed appears in the classic colors of the English countryside, from moss green to burnt brown, as well as in checked, overchecked and classic Scottish tartan versions. It is consistent, solid and somewhat coarse to the touch, though with the addition of synthetic fibers it acquires more softness. It has high thermal stability and is 100% hydroscopic. Given that over time tweed tends to fray in areas most vulnerable to chafing (e.g., at the elbows), the sleeves of jackets are often reinforced with suede patches. According to English tradition, to preserve its elegant and at the same time gritty attractiveness, a tweed jacket should never be pressed. Over time, tweed has come to be associated with traditional and eccentric male figures such as Sherlock Holmes and Phileas Fogg, the main character in the novel *Around the World in 80 Days*. The name comes from the Tweed River, in England, which runs through the manufacturing area on the border between Scotland and England. According to other sources, the name is a distortion of the term twill, a very common fabric in local textile towns in the 19th century. There are various types of tweed, differentiated by the area of origin. These include classic varieties with interesting micro- and macro-tweed effects and re-interpretations updated by fashion designers made from mohair wool or a silk blend with Lurex buttons.

Albino

HARRIS TWEED

Called *clò mòr* in Gallic, Harris Tweed is a variety of tweed whose rough masculine appearance, with flattened white hairs on a Batavia twill weave, distinguishes it from other tweeds. It owed its widespread popularity to the Countess of Dunmore, who encouraged its production among weavers in Harris, a southern region on Lewis Island, in the Hebrides archipelago, to the north of Scotland. The fabric quickly spread to the islands of Uist and Barra. Genuine Harris Tweed is made with the pure virgin wool of the famous Blackface ram. The carded and spun wool was dyed by hand with vegetal substances extracted from local blueberries, saffron, peat and lichen. The fabric was woven exclusively on manual looms. The Harris Tweed trademark was registered in 1909, using as an emblem a world map with a cross above it taken directly from the coat-of-arms of the Count and Countess of Dunmore. Today, Harris Tweed is no longer a craft fabric, though it has preserved its identity despite an industrial output of three million meters per year.

Jil Sander

Marras

Sportmax

DONEGAL TWEED

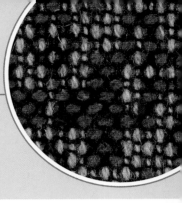

Donegal tweed (or Irish tweed) is a soft tweed fabric from Donegal, a county founded by the Vikings and named *Dun nan Gall*. At one time it was produced mainly in Ardara, the former tweed capital. Nowadays, it is woven with irregular yarns such as multicolored boutonné and produced with combed or carded wool as well as cotton. Donegal tweed contains a chromatic blend formed by colored specks, like flowers in an Irish field, that interrupt the uniform surface. This fabric, occasionally of plain weave instead of twill, is very wintry, suitable for coats, jackets and trouser suits. Some versions are made with thicker homespun threads with locks of woolen hair in relief or the more modern laminated threads, forming an attractive contrast between rustic, dull wool and the beauty of the metallic sheen. Donegal boutonné tweed was used to make the Norfolk jacket, worn in the latter half of the 1880s in the refined atmosphere of English sports clubs. It is a four-button garment with small lapels, two flap pockets and strap-like pleats that extend down the back. The Norfolk eventually became a classic jacket used exclusively in sports.

Jil Sander

Chapurin

Sportmax

Carolina Herrera

CHANEL

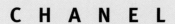

Chanel is a yarned-dyed fabric with an irregular three-dimensional surface formed by differently colored novelty yarns (experimental twists due to their nature and construction techniques such as slub, boutonné, loop and bouclé) that alternate in the fabric in the directions of the warp and weft. The weave can be a simple plain weave. The fabric is springy, soft and delicate, above all because it contains pastel tones similar to caramel that combine with each other to form small barely visible checks. This fabric, basically an English tweed, was chosen by fashion designer Coco Chanel in 1954 for her signature suit, a design whose charm combines masculine and feminine qualities and

Antonio Marras

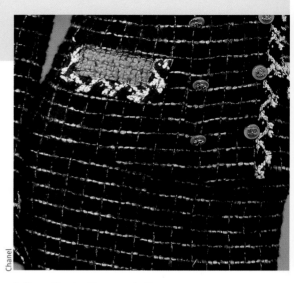

Chanel

fully reflects the revolutionary concept of fashion proposed by the international queen of chic. The classic Chanel has a close-fitting waist, with a slightly flared skirt and collarless cardigan-style jacket open in front. An apparently simple and linear design, it grants extreme importance to details such as the four pockets, grosgrain or novelty passementerie edges and golden buttons. The outfit is completed with a silk blouse that matches the lining of the jacket, the typical chain stitch sewn on the inside, a long string of pearls and the indispensable camellia. The day President Kennedy was assassinated in Dallas, Jacqueline Kennedy was wearing a pink wool Coco Chanel jacket. Today, the Chanel suit evokes the nostalgia of a remote polished elegance, and Chanel is considered an essential fabric, one even woven with gold- and silver-laminated threads. Designer Karl Lagerfeld, at the helm at since Chanel 1983, took pleasure in offering numerous versions in which he adapted form

Chanel

Chanel

Chanel

Chanel

and fabric to the whims of women seeking novelty without renouncing a sober and classical style. The SS 2009 collection includes Chanel fabric dotted with soft silicone, a high-tech material that formed a grid in relief and contributed a very modern air in tune with our times.

Chanel

Chanel

KNICKERBOCKER

A homespun fabric from the United States similar to Donegal and woven with coarse thread. It has a nappy surface made up of small knots and buttons that contrast with the background. The name comes from the pseudonym Dietrich Knickerbocker, adopted in 1809 by American author Washington Irving for his novel *History of New York*. This fabric was used to make the knicker or knickerbocker suit, with zouave pants tied below the knee with a ribbon or a button like those worn by the Dutch immigrants who founded New Amsterdam, the future New York. It is a somewhat rustic, carded fabric, used for sport-style men's jackets. At the end of the 19th century, the knotted material of the pants became part of traditional golf attire. In the 1920s it was the favorite of the Duke of Windsor for jacket and pants combinations that he wore even in the city.

Chanel

Gaetano Navarra

Gaetano Navarra

10

FABRICS WITH WEAVE EFFECT

CRETONNE

Derived cotton fabric formed by resistant threads, often mercerized, with a weave featuring light effects in relief, intricately worked or striped. It is a very dense and robust medium-weight material (around 150 g/m²). Large floral patterns are printed on the outside, while the inside is subjected to chemical treatment. It is used in decoration, especially for upholstering mass-produced affordable armchairs and sofas. Light cretonne is used in towels, bedcovers, curtains and wall coverings, while in fashion it is used to make blouses and shirts with a bucolic flavor, gardening aprons, children's beachwear and ladies' summer dresses. Its origin and name are from the French village of Creton, in Normandy. In the southern part of this French region, in Pays d'Auge, Vimoutiers was a village very active in the 19th century textile industry where Paul Creton, considered the inventor of the product in 1640, lived. Originally, cretonne was a strong plain-weave fabric woven with hemp fiber in the warp and greige linen in the weft. A law in 1738 required that the fabric be made exclusively with pure linen. In the 19th century cretonne was used to upholster sofas in the homes of the bourgeoisie. In the collective imagination, cretonne evokes a somewhat outmoded style of the 40s and 50s, recalling the faded sofas of old aunts and grandmothers, or certain accessories with washed-out colors such as bags or beach bags or ones for storing needlework. Occasionally, a young designer with northern European tastes will salvage cretonne for clothes or accessories that evoke its original, poetic flavor.

Vivienne Westwood

Vivienne Westwood

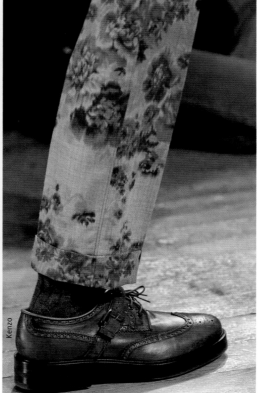

Kenzo

Missoni

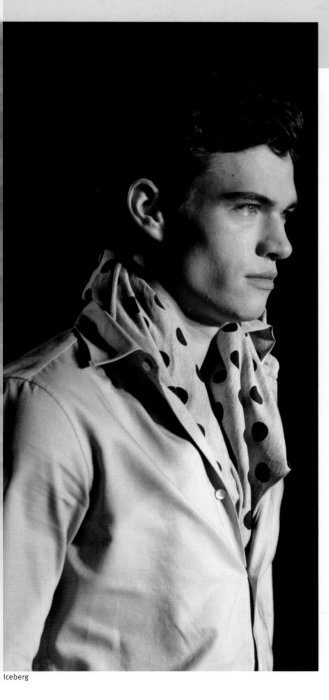

Iceberg

A pure cotton or polyester blend with a panama weave from the eponymous English city. Technically, Oxford cloth is obtained by clinching weft and warp threads of the same thickness or with fine threads folded in the warp and simple and thicker in the weft, which is springier. It is characterized by having colored warp threads and white weft threads, which accentuates the "basket" effect with tiny grids made of little white dots on a colored or finely striped surface. The term "pinpoint" refers to a more refined fabric resulting from the evolution of Oxford cloth. It is a type of long-fiber twisted cotton fabric that, while maintaining a grainy feel and colored warp threads, has a very dense weft that makes it similar to poplin, consisting of a numerous pinpoints. Another variety is Royal Oxford, with colored and colorless threads, though more subtle, that give rise to a softer fabric with an almost silken appearance. Oxford cloth is soft and lustrous, cool to the touch and medium weight, around 125-135 g/m². It is suitable for the construction of button-down-collar men's shirts, the points of which are fastened down by buttons. This type of shirt was the favorite of polo players in the second half of the 20th century, as the buttons prevented the points of the collar from flapping during heated competition that simultaneously required maintaining a certain degree of composure. Brooks Clothing Company, a United States company founded in 1818, specialized in the manufacture of this type of shirt, for which it used different varieties of Oxford cloth. Later, it changed its name to Brooks Brothers and, preserving the classic cut, introduced a wide array of colors, some of which were very eye-catching. The Oxford-cloth shirt is still an international point of reference for masculine elegance.

Dolce & Gabbana

PIQUE

Its name comes from the French verb *piquer*, meaning, "to sew". It is a cotton fabric with several layers and a notable relief effect. It can be simple, composed of two warps, one with a taffeta weft background and the other a tenser pique weft, which forms the weave. The tenser weave points define the outline of the fabric design. English pique weave, which produces a horizontal relief effect, is distinct from simple pique due to a second series of softer supplementary weft threads that alternate with the first ones and remain on the inside forming an enveloping layer. Pique fabrics often have napping on the inside. A third kind of

Vivienne Westwood

pique is wavy pique, called this because it alternates areas of covered weft with exposed ones, creating reliefs and depressions. The result is a soft and fresh composite fabric. Fabrics with this structure vary notably in weight depending on the consistency and composition of the threads. In its heavier versions, pique fabric is suitable for bedclothes, especially bedspreads and duvets. The term pique alludes to a ribbed fabric with a pattern of longitudinal stripes, little dots, diamonds or checks added through a supplementary warp and weft. Pique with very thin stripes is referred to as "pinstripe". It is a very light, summery fabric used to

Ermenegildo Zegna

Mariella Burani

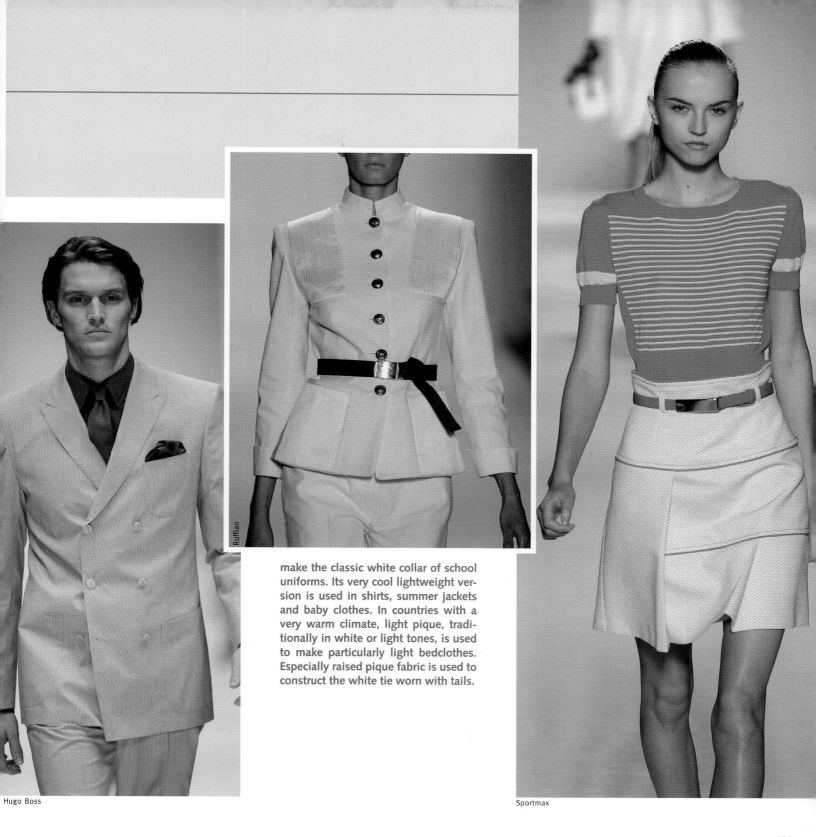

Ruffian

make the classic white collar of school uniforms. Its very cool lightweight version is used in shirts, summer jackets and baby clothes. In countries with a very warm climate, light pique, traditionally in white or light tones, is used to make particularly light bedclothes. Especially raised pique fabric is used to construct the white tie worn with tails.

Hugo Boss

Sportmax

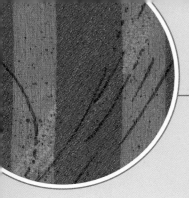

PEKIN

Initially a silk fabric painted in gouache probably of Chinese origin, it appeared in France in the 18th century and was one of the favorite materials of the Marquise de Pompadour. The term derives from Pei-ping, the ancient name of the city of Peking. It is characterized by its two warps distinguished by color or thread count, which produce vertical stripes juxtaposed and alternated in a longitudinal direction. This creates a fabric with stripes differentiated by the contrast of different weaves arranged at intervals. Pekin can have two or more simples weaves, for example, plain and twill, alternating a lustrous satin stripe and a dull gros de Tours or ribbed one or a single 5-Harness Satin weave with two fabric faces, one light and one heavy. There are damascened, crimped and Scotch pekin or pekin with small floral patterns. The pekin effect is defined by the name of the weave. In simple versions it is made in different weights for shirts, dresses and jackets. In composite versions it used mostly in decoration, although it is also highly valued by English and French designers for updating or recreating period styles.

Thakoon

Jean Paul Gaultier

Dior

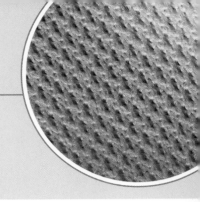

cause of this characteristic depth, the structure of honeycomb is also called guafre fabric. There are many varieties, suitable both for clothing and decoration. The embossed surface is particularly apt for retaining moisture and facilitates water absorption. For this reason, it is often used, with cotton and linen fibers, for napkins, towels, bathrobes and cleaning cloths. It also insulates against the heat, given that it incorporates air. Wool honeycomb, for instance, is used to make bedspreads. The honeycomb effect is also achieved with smocking embroidery that crimps the fabric, producing small rectangles or diamonds. Often an elastic thread is sewn on the inside to make honeycomb springier and more versatile. It is a classic fabric in elegant dresses for adolescent girls, usually with an embroidered bodice.

Carven

Louis Vuitton

Combed fabric similar to pique. Honeycomb has a characteristic structure that reproduces a three-dimensional screen made up of cavities and niches that alternate and cross diagonally to form small quadrangular or hexagonal cells similar to those of a honeycomb. The surface is identical on the outside and the inside. The fabric is woven with floating threads in the warp and weft, which are reduced or grow toward the interior of each cell according to the desired design. The floating threads are arranged under each other in such a way that longer ones are slightly raised and form a kind of crest. The resulting effect is similar to a honeycomb. Be-

Ermanno Scervino

Hussein Chalayan

SLIGHT RELIEF

Michael Kors

Michael Kors

Gianfranco Ferré

This group consists of all fabrics with small patterns in relief obtained by a series of opposing weaves with a pattern repeat greater than 28 threads. The most original effects are achieved using yarns of different materials and colors, which create contrasting or very faint motifs (e.g., coal gray with gray and black checks). These fabrics can be of any weight and produce a multitude of decorative effects. Depending on the type of yarn, the weight and the design, they are used in clothing or decoration. Cotton varieties are used mainly in shirt making, with highly valued effects of false uniformity. Wool versions are used in garments with a linear structure such as tube dresses, sleeveless dresses, skirts and vests. These are sewn to make a garment that goes with everything: the sport-style jacket which, thanks to its tonal and graphic qualities, harmonizes with practically all elements of the wardrobe and allows for creating always fresh outfits that can be personalized through the proper use of accessories.

Marni   Peter Pilotto   Peter Pilotto

COMPOSITE FABRICS

11

A fabric of opposing weaves that form small, bright and lustrous patterns against a dull background as a result of weaving. It is a relatively easy fabric to make, with only one warp and one weft, woven exclusively in cotton, with a structure similar to that of poplin and often with a taffeta base. The motifs consist of dots or small geometric or floral motifs obtained with brief floating warp and weft threads with which small weave effects are created. Varying the colors of the warp and weft threads produces variations of intermediate dyeing in the background and strongly contrasted dyeing in the pattern. Its name in Italian, *brillanti-na*, alludes to the lustrous appearance of the fabric, enhanced by the use of silk or synthetic yarns. Its structure lends itself to a series of novelty combinations freely interpreted by textile designers, who adapt them to the requirements of the latest trends. Percaline is a classic fabric, preferably made of cotton, used in elegant and sports-style men's shirts. White shirts with fine, sophisticated, almost silver reflections, worn with a black tuxedo, are made out of percaline. Other varieties, of synthetic fibers, are used in ties, linings with attractive added effects and light relief against the background, and ladies' clothing, especially blouses, in which percaline creates soft visual movements. Herringbone percaline, woven with a cotton warp and combed-wool or angora weft, is a lustrous fabric used in men's suits and warm winter linings.

Antonio Marras

Alberto Biani

Antonio Marras

Frankie Morello

Byblos

DAMASK

A fabric with no reverse side, once made in the Orient, mostly of silk. The technique, of Chinese origin, extended to Persia and Damascus (Syria), a city that specialized in its manufacture and sale. Its most basic version consists of only one warp and one weft, with threads of any natural fiber (cotton) or artificial fiber (rayon) with a 5- or 8-Harness Satin weave, made with heavy effect (warp side) on the surface of the fabric. It is a totally monochromatic, flat and smooth fabric, with motifs the same color as the background. These patterns are obtained with slight effect (the reverse side of the weave itself), emphasizing the weft, which contrasts with the background due to the difference in sheen. From this combination many varieties are made, some of which are the fruit of different interpretations, periods and geographic places. Damask de Tours, for example, is produced by combining two fibers, satin and gros de Tours; damask de Lyon (background and motif alternate satin and herringbone weave) and summer damask (taffeta background and satin motif) always obtained by opposing bright and dark effects due to the use of different weaves. Oriental damask uses a heavy 5-Harness Satin background and features motifs defined by floating weft threads in order, with small edges made of simple taffeta. Damask is one of the most used fabrics in history, particularly by cultures with advanced knowledge of textile art. Damask was used in Catholic liturgical garments such as dalmatics and tunics, as well as in decorative coverings, canopies and furniture. In late sixteenth-century men and women's clothing damask was enriched with heraldic-like symbolic motifs such as diamonds, crowns, amphorae and fleur-de-lis, though in subsequent centuries the patterns were sometimes completed with broken wefts or brocades. Today, different types of damask are used in diverse areas. The raw materials used play a significant role, as does the count of the threads, which are selected in combinations most suited to the fabric's intended use.

Michael Kors

Angelo Marani

John Galliano

Etro

Giambattista Valli

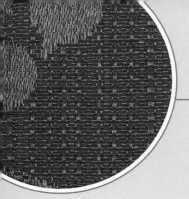

DAMASCATO

A fabric derived from classic damask, woven with quality colored threads in the warp and weft (for example, silk and cotton or cotton and linen). Damascato fabrics include all monochrome or polychrome fabrics with a chiaroscuro design with contrasting brightness and darkness, the result of the opposition of the fabric and weave effects of shaded satin. In Flanders, highly regarded monochrome damascato and intricately worked fabrics were made using Flanders linen, a lustrous material with a very fine thread count, smooth and dry to the touch, obtained through a complex and meticulous production process, all of which made it a luxury product prized throughout Europe. Flanders cloths, with damascato decorations woven with stylized geometric or floral motifs, tended to have a tight thread count, resulting in a fine, delicate fabric that was also compact and resistant. Because of these features, damascato has been used in table linens and decoration as a classy alternative to solid-color cloths. Today, the original linen has been replaced by mercerized cotton, synthetic fibers or different novelty materials, of pastel or bright colors, while industrial production on jacquard looms has lowered the cost and made the fabric accessible and suited to the demands of fashion.

Vivienne Westwood Red Label

Aquascutum

Derercuny

Antonio Marras

Lorenzo Riva

JACQUARD

Jacquard is a composite fabric with complex motifs that includes various subclasses of fabric such as damask, Gobelin, lance, fil coupe, etc. Its name comes from Joseph-Marie Jacquard (Lyon 1752 – Oulins 1834), a machinist in the French textile industry and inventor of a device that substituted the traditional loom – a series of cords or heddles operated by hand that raised the warp threads, threaded in meshes that determined the weaving – with a more modern system of punched cards. The laced cards passed sequentially through needles that acted as readers when crossing the perforations. A mechanism of connected hooks raised the threads, allowing

Louis Vuitton

Aquascutum

the passage of the weft. This system permitted memorizing the complete production cycle of the composite fabric (including the selvage) according to a code of fillings and empty spaces obtained from reading the punched card of the design, carried out in accordance with the desired weave and the evolution of the anticipated threads. Jacquard's invention, the basic principles of which have remained unchanged, in addition to speeding up operation, allowed for arranging a vast array of designs and adornments that could be filed and easily reproduced on the spot, thus contributing in a significant way to the rapid spread in popularity of composite fabrics in clothing and decoration. Fabrics woven on Jacquard looms are noteworthy for the beauty of the design and fibers used, usually of high quality. They are characterized by the presence of different weaves formed simultaneously, since, technically speaking, each thread can follow its individual progress vis-à-vis the others. Jacquard fabric, which today is produced on electronic machines controlled by a computer, experiments with the different interwoven threads,

Devi Kroell

combining them, emphasizing a bright color over a dark one, making them appear and disappear through complicated warp or weft effects, alternating the sizes, number and arrangement of motifs, multiplying composition color and alternating shadings. It is used for making clothes and in decoration and can be printed on. In the high-end tie sector, catering to a demanding public, jacquard fabrics contain elegant weaving effects and innumerable small Jacquard motifs in relief.

Iceberg

Albino

Antonio Berardi

LANCÉ

Multi-colored composite fabric that imitates the effect of traditional brocades, beautiful silk materials with discontinuous decorative effects on the outside created by the introduction of partial weft brocades of silk or laminated threads. The brocade weft, inserted with the help of small needles, only enters in the area of the design, with continuous movement back and forth without cutting, which allows for keeping the plain background of the fabric lighter. Lance also permits the use of supplementary weft threads partially visible on the outside of the fabric, launched from selvage to selvage throughout the length of the fabric. These weft threads, whose colors are defined by numbers, delineate the design with a great deal of finesse and

Enrico Coveri

shape the outlines and reliefs, being woven on the outside of the fabric, while they remain floating on the inside when not required for the pattern. Sometimes these floating threads are cut after weaving or are joined to the satin background with a very wide weave repeat. Lance is used frequently for ties and elegant ladies' wear, as it allows for a wide variety of textures and rich graphic definition of details. Its use extends to textiles for decoration, though due to their extreme delicateness, all lance fabrics must be lined. "Lavalliere", a type of bow tie knotted in the shape of a butterfly with stripes that descended flatly on the chest and that was very much in vogue in the 19th century among artists and intellectuals of the Third Republic in France, was made out of silk lance with small decorative motifs.

Marc by Marc Jacobs

Badgley Mischka

Vivienne Westwood

Paul Smith

and subtle dyes. The origin of the name messicana perhaps is related to the traditionally crafted pre-Colombian fabrics made exclusively by women on waist looms, which rested on the stomach at one end and were tied to a post or column at the other. This type of loom can be used to make very long but, needless to say, thin fabrics. Nowadays, messicana is mostly used in period décor. Occasionally, designers such as V. Westwood and C. Lacroix choose this material to evoke an affected look or provide a romantic kitschy air. Messicana fabric is also used in markedly ethnic styles that place the geometric work typical of South American craftwork in relief, obtained with supplementary partial wefts that alternate and form stripes with the background.

A typical fabric used for decoration with a plain and partially composite background and longitudinal stripes, popular in the France of Louis XV and Madame de Pompadour. It has stripes with polychrome patterns, especially floral, leaf or garland motifs on a plain taffeta background, alternating with simple weave stripes of 8-Harness Satin. It has several warps: one for the plain fabric base and one or other supplementary ones partially arranged that form wavy longitudinal patterns. The chain of effect forms on the outside more or less long stripes that cover the base fabric and remain on the inside when they do not appear on the outside. Often these fabrics contain a combination of fine

Bottega Veneta

Ter et Bantine

Gucci

FIL COUPÉ

Louis Vuitton

3.1 Phillip Lim

Angelo Marani

A lightweight composite fabric, of silk or synthetic fiber, often with a chiffon base. The name comes from the French term that alludes to the visual element of the fabric. At the same time, it indicates the manufacturing process used, according to the cutting technique (*fil coupé*) of the floating threads. Coupe is characterized by geometric or stylized motifs that form a flat and shiny pattern in relief almost always outlined in satin weave and achieved by introducing floating threads in some areas that are cut after weaving. The threads are cut at variable distances, producing a three-dimensional effect of dense stripes on the outside of the fabric that grants the design fuzzy, irregular, almost undefined outlines. The fabric is woven on a jacquard loom and allows for the use of supplementary warp and weft threads, of colors and materials substantially different than those of the background, which tend to be finer and have more highly twisted threads to form a frizzy but transparent structure from which hang threads slightly

Gattinoni

Dior

Angelo Marani

shading the base. The supplementary threads arranged in the direction of the warp or, more often, the weft, are *launched*, crossing the entire fabric from selvage to selvage and remaining loose even when they don't form part of the surface fabric of the motifs, according to the technique also used in lance. Fil coupe is a fabric with a forceful decorative impact, due to the contrast between the transparent, fragile and delicate appearance and striped patterns, three-dimensional and beautiful, that seems almost embroidered. It is suitable for shirts and elegant women's wear and can be made in printed patterns. It is also very frequently used in curtains.

Antonio Marras

GOBELIN

Balmain

A somewhat thick composite fabric with a theatrical, eye-catching appearance, characterized by thin horizontal stripes and large complex motifs similar to those seen on tapestry. Some particularly prized Gobelin fabrics are made with a single pattern repeat that occupies the entire height of the fabric. The traditional motifs are, above all, highly detailed flowers and natural landscapes, meticulous mythological scenes and stylistic elements with a retro air once used in upholstery. It is woven on a jacquard loom with different warp beams and several shuttles for the weft threads. Gobelin requires four warps: one ecru-colored backing warp; one black or neutral-colored weave warp with more tension in it; and two vividly colored twisted warps and three wefts: two carded wefts (ecru for the background and black for the work) and a black or neutral-colored twisted-thread weave. Each warp produces two color tones depending on whether it is interwoven with a light or dark weft. Mixed effects are obtained by alternating the course of the threads. While the warp is solely cotton or, less commonly, wool, the weft threads can be wool, silk or linen, sometimes even laminated. Its heavy consistency, due to the use of very fine warp threads and thicker, stouter weft threads, results in a surface very resistant to use. Modern Gobelin is made from cotton, with a thread count of 12-14 cm of warp threads and 9 cm of weft threads. It is used mostly in subdued tones as a covering for couches, sofas, ottomans and siding. Modern design, with the intention of adapting Gobelin to contemporary decoration, has introduced new themes in the patterns, including abstract ones. It is used in jackets, pants, footwear, bags and suitcases, as well as in details such as collars, revers collars, waistbands, pockets, etc. The name comes from Manufacture des Gobelins, a family of scarlet dye specialists that founded a tapestry factory in a windmill in Faubourg Saint Marcel. During the reign of Louis XIV, at the behest of Minister Jean-Baptiste Colbert, the Gobelins workshop buildings became the headquarters of Manufacture Royale des Meubles de la Couronne, which produced decorative luxury objects for the nobility under the direction of painter Charles Le Brun. The factory had low-warp looms for weaving small pieces and high-warp looms for large pieces, which were operated in a flourishing production of high-quality tapestries. Today, the factory is located at 42 Avenue Des Gobelins, in the 13th arrondissement of Paris, where the company has its headquarters, a museum and some workshops that continue producing tapestries for the decoration of public buildings.

Marios Schwab

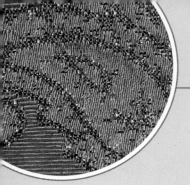

B R O C A D E

Derercuny

Paul & Joe

A beautiful composite fabric, probably of Oriental origin, produced by joining brocaded supplementary wefts with gold or silver thread, polychrome silk, crimped and curled, or in chenille yarns, also called "effect wefts", which only appear in certain areas of the fabric to underscore details or define particular effects. Its name comes from the Latin word *broccus*, an allusion to brocades, adornments woven in relief with threads rolled up in small shuttles called *spolini*. *Spolinato*, a synonym for brocade fabric, derives from this technique. The fabric background, normally plain satin, ribbed or twill fabric, can have a warp and weft of silk, cotton, wool or almost any other fiber. The weaving is carried on a jacquard loom for composite fabrics (damask, lampas, velvet, etc.) with launched fine-count wefts and contrasting dyes on the reverse side of the upper cloth. The hand-woven brocaded wefts are continuous, limited to the small sizes of the motifs, without cutting the threads along the length of the outlines of the design. The return of the weft is always visible on the back. Brocades require special skills on the part of the weaver, especially in the changing of colors and in the added wefts, enjambments and superimpositions of which should be avoided. To resolve these snags, a technique called "point rentre" was invented in the 18th century. Another matter is *brocatello*, a fabric with two warps and two wefts, with a firm background consisting of a hemp or linen weft on which satin motifs with a launched silk weft are introdu-

ced, forming relief. This fabric belongs to the family of old lampas fabrics, used for the most part in décor fabrics, both in the past and the present day. Brocade wefts were produced to obtain lightweight cloths with elaborate and complex motifs that showed parts enriched with valuable materials visible only on the front, given their high cost, notably increasing the luster and sumptuousness of the garment and the social prestige of the person who could afford to wear it. Today, brocade has been substituted almost completely by electronic jacquard weaving, though it survives as an ornamental fabric that suggests an image of splendor in luxury decorations.

DOUBLE-KNIT FABRICS

12

T W O - F A C E

Jil Sander

Bottega Veneta

Max Mara

Fabric characterized by the absence of a back and with a distinct appearance on both sides. It is called "double weave" because it can be used equally on both sides. It is woven in different ways: by alternating colors, by opposing weaves or by opposing and alternating both. Fabrics have a double-weave warp and weft with three types of threads with a double warp and a single weft, or more wefts of different colors and consistencies that cross a single warp but each of which passes only one side. This group of fabrics includes lampas and derived materials used for decoration. It lends itself well to making fabrics for ties with very fine count silk threads with two different face sides that can be turned at the wearer's whim or according to daily circumstances. It is also used for men's shirts, in fabrics with two warps that have a version on one side for external use and another for accessory or complementary purposes. The latter tends to be visible in cuffed sleeves and open collars. In these cases, the loom is arranged to produce two types of fabric simultaneously, a simple one, which constitutes the interior area, and a double fabric, which represents the worked effect. However, more frequently, the fabric is made up of four types of thread that form a single, more consistent double fabric, in which the front and back are interchangeable and have an identical design with alternating and opposing colors. The two layers are closely linked with various weaving techniques that can have the same weaves or a different but compatible one. Another method uses five or more sets of threads for defining two distinct completely independent surfaces, joined by a fifth common element that serves to unite the warp or weft, and neither of the two surfaces can be considered the front of the cloth. The two layers can be separated removing the joining thread. One of the most typical examples of double weave is the two-color wool fabric used in the seventies by fashion designer Mila Schon. Whole dress, coat and suit collections with flatfell seam interior or exterior finishes were produced that allowed for complete reversibility of garments. This type of contrasting fashion characterized certain elements of refined elegance in Italian fashion that had an internatio-

146

nal impact. Reversible material is still used, combining classical tradition and modernity, at times heightening the differentiation of the two face sides of the fabric through the use of different finishes.

Mila Schön

Moschino Cheap & Chic

Giles

Cavendish

Chanel

MATELASSÉ

A quilted fabric, heavy but soft, with a knit-cloth effect in which several weft and warp threads join to form two layers of bonded material. The term derives from the Italian *matelassé*, which means "stuffed" or "packed". There are many types of matelassé, which are obtained by the aesthetic and harmonious combination of materials, colors, thread thicknesses and weaves. Matelassé can have a plain background, with a linear weave like taffeta, twill or satin, with the interwoven pattern made during the production process. A series of warp threads remains tense, while the other stays loose; in this way, outlines and filler are formed on the surface, which appears to be quilted. (Supplementary wefts that add internal thickness to the two layers strengthen this effect). Another option is for the fabric to have a background featuring the effects of floating filler yarns, percaline and damask, always with three-dimensional relief created beforehand by the different tensions given to the warp and weft rather than by the filler. A jacquard loom is needed to make matelassé. It is suitable for bodices, jackets, coats and eveningwear. It mostly used in coverings for furniture and bed linen, given that its composite nature allows for conceiving and producing different coordinates for adapting it to all kinds of decorative accessories according to the latest fashion trends.

Gabriele Colangelo

Laura Biagiotti

148

Aramand Basi

DKNY

Isabel Marant

Corrado De Biase

CLOQUÉ

A type of double cloth with two different face sides due to the type of threads and weaving, made according to the English piqué system. It consists of one warp and one base weft, usually of fine cotton threads with a medium twist interwoven at internals with an underlying pique chain made with a second, far tenser weft of curly sunken thread forming patterns successively in relief. This system of threads traps a thick weft in its interior that acts as padding and contributes to creating a wavy, patterned layer. After weaving, a wet finish is applied to the fabric that causes the curly threads to dra-matically contract. At this point, these threads compress the lower part of the fabric and pull at the stitching of the second warp, visible on the upper face. This causes the decorative motifs of the upper layer to expand and assume a convex appearance. The same effect is achieved substituting the curly threads for woolen ones, which retract due to the high temperature and humidity, while the threads and cotton weft maintain their original sizes.

Armani Privè

Burberry Prorsum

Giambattista Valli

Jean Paul Gaultier

Jean Paul Gaultier

"BACKED" FABRIC

A layered fabric obtained by superimposing several surfaces (for example, an openwork fabric and a mesh fabric) that can have a different mercerization, joined by sizing and heat and invisible weaving stitches. It is a false double face, conceived for use on both sides with reversible functions that serve both the front and back of the garment indiscriminately. When the fabric has a sheet of polyurethane foam attached through different techniques (fusion, adhesion, woven or put together on site) it is said that it is subjected to a laminating process. These fine coverings can be adhesives for use as thermal adhesives on large surfaces. Their thickness ranges from 2 to 4 mm. They are inexpensive but are sticky and not very elastic to the touch, which causes resistance to the cut of the designs during production and moves with difficulty in sewing machines. In addition, the foam layer changes over time, degrading and flattening out with use and tending to pull at the external fabric. The coupling of two fabrics allows for interesting combinations that lend themselves to a wide spectrum of interpretations and experiments.

Mouflon wool folded with organic fur transforms the surface of a protective fabric, while a wool fabric base coupled to a chiffon weave gives the fabric a delicate feel. Recently, Ermano Scervino experimented with denim folded with macramé, applied with special tools similar to abrasive discs, creating the kind of surprising effects characteristic of nearly all his collections.

Yves Saint Laurent

Missoni

Balenciaga

Bottega Veneta

Y3

TUFTED FABRIC

A fabric made by sewing with special needles threads of different weights and thicknesses horizontally or vertically, one next to the other, with the aim of obtaining a uniform and compact surface. The meeting points are made with a chain-stitch mesh or knitted fabric effect and allow for the addition of a vast range of items for use in garments and for technical, industrial, geotextile, etc. purposes. Its lightness and variety of colors make it suitable for midseason clothes such as raincoats, recently re-launched by North American fashion designers, in classic or vibrant colors and often with a matching skirt or dress worn underneath. It is also suited to the new notion of the "deconstructed" blazer, also made in night versions, with needlework throughout the fabric and lamé remnants. Recently, a special type of shirt called a "two-in-one" appeared on the market. It is made with two striped fabrics, one with a natural fiber base, joined by invisible stitches, allowing the busy wearer to change in a minute without having to go home. In 1995, the company Federico Aspesi di Gallarate, a leader in the production of machine embroidery, perfected the use of a new needle machine that operates on finished fabrics and that is used in the jeans sector, making it possible to give denim more consistency, particularly suitable to cold winter climates, and whose new appearance has proven especially popular in the United States and Far East, with increases in sales in those parts of the world. Some needlework fabrics with dense horizontal stitching, carried out with special machinery, are made from non-woven fabrics joining layers of natural or, especially, synthetic fibers, or interlacing more layers of threads to significantly increase resistance in this direction. Fabrics of this kind are used for interlinings or as filler in decoration, and are produced with inexpensive materials.

Armani Privè

C'n'C

Burberry Prorsum

Louis Vuitton

Ann Demeulemeester

Bottega Veneta

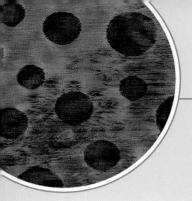

T U B U L A R

Three-dimensional tubular section fabric, double or triple, with a warm, springy, soft appearance. It is made on two planes that intersect at regular intervals. It can include more warps and wefts, alternated to achieve the respective surfaces. The weave ranges from plain tubular taffeta, solid-dye or two-color, to a weave with mixed effects consisting of color or with alternating colored dyes that can give rise to stripes, checks or pretty patterns, always small or medium repeat to change the tubular nature of the fabric, which must be fixed between the two component layers and contain a certain amount of air. There are tubular fabrics made from other materials such as twill, satin, Batavia, etc., as well as ones that have an interior layer of filling (with a thicker yet lighter weft and of carded thread), added at regular intervals to give volume to the fabric and make it warmer and more comfortable to the touch. This type of fabric is used in wraparound jackets, asymmetrical coats with a characteristic ovoid shape, with semi-circular or wide collars, used very frequently by contemporary Japanese designers.

Carolina Herrera

Armani Privè

13

VELVET AND SIMILAR FABRICS

COTTON VELVET

Jean Paul Gaultier

Marco De Vincenzo

The warmest of the cotton fabrics due to the fact that its pile, no more than 3 cm long, is an insulator. In Italian, it is called *velluto* (in French, *velours*), derived from the Latin *vellus* (hair), which refers to its characteristic hair cover of varying lengths and types. It is smooth and lustrous with uniform and straight tufts secured to the background, almost always a plain or silk weave. The tufts are distributed across the entire surface in a single direction, and consequently the fabric requires a meticulous production process. The tufts, fixed in the form of a V, are easier to iron and need less meticulous care than those fixed in a W, which have a double weave. The anchoring can be reinforced applying synthetic resin on the reverse side of the fabric. Cotton velvet, an all-purpose fabric made in many weights, has a classical image, yet, because of its versatility, lends itself to diverse fashion uses. Velveton is the name for a smooth weft velvet that uses one warp and two kinds of weft and is characterized by tufts of hair that form floating threads in the supplementary weft that are then cut in mechanical finishing operations. The first cotton velvet with a classic weft was produced industrially in English factories in Manchester. Common velvet is made using the double piece system, in which two fabrics are produced simultaneously, one against the other, each one consisting of a warp and weft but joined to a common third warp, which forms the pile of both. The distance at which the two fabrics are arranged regulates the length of the pile. The tufts of hair are cut in the center with an extremely sharp knife, which slices forward and backward. When removed from the blade, the double fabric is divided in two and rolled up in two different bobbins. Two-piece velvet is made in widths of 40, 90 and 150 cm. Cotton velvet is piece dyed, and a variety of functional and aesthetic finishes can be applied to it: brushing in both directions leaves the pile uniform and dense; the application of synthetic resins makes the hair more elastic, such that it recovers its original position when flattened. The cut regulates the pile at the desired height. Velvet can be treated to give it more feel or a weathered, aged, mottled, printed, rubbed, lustrous, matted, etc. appearance. It is a fabric suitable for any use, particularly in men and women's clothing, granting them considerable elegance. The typical slippers worn with the traditional suit from the Italian region of Friuli, worn during World War I by alpine troops on account of their being light and noiseless, are made of velvet. Today's version is the comfortable slippers worn by such famous fashionistas as Elkann and Madonna.

Jean Paul Gaultier

Etro

WOOL VELVET

Gucci

Giorgio Armani

A compact fabric with a soft pile used primarily in decoration due to its solidity and ductility. It is used in coverings for armchairs, sofas and theatrical backdrops. Wool is the least flammable of the natural fibers and, therefore, is used in velvet theater seats or in fabrics used in large backdrops or in curtains. Wool velvet, mixed with linen, is also used in carpets and floor coverings. The coverings in luxury trains that offered maximum comfort during long journeys were made of velvet. In Utrecht, Holland, a special type of mohair wool velvet with a linen background was manufactured. The Pilgrim's hat was a hat worn in the 17th century by the Puritans, who despised wigs and headdress with showy adornments. Sometimes longhair wool velvet was produced for making clothes, especially voluminous yet soft outerwear such as capes, overcoats and jackets. Velvet made from special wool such as cashmere or alpaca in ultra-chic designs is very highly prized.

Donna Karan

Giorgio Armani

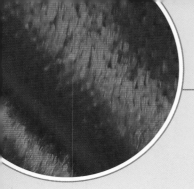

SILK VELVET

A fabric with a very soft and shiny surface. During the Renaissance, there were masters (*veludieri*) who specialized in its production. In Venice, the *veludieri*, whose patron saint was Saint Mark, formed their own guild, separate from the other silk professions, and in 1420 they obtained branched divisions according to the kind of work they did. "Cut velvet" became popular in fashion in the first decades of the 16th century, as can be seen in the portraits of such illustrious figures as Leonor Gonzaga, Duchess of Urbino, in a painting by Titian (1536-38). The Swiss Guard, painted by Rafael (1511-14), wore multi-color cut velvet attire. The black velvet made in Genoa was particularly treasured because of the quality of the silk and the perfection of the dyeing. Today, silk velvet continues to be an expensive fabric chosen for its silky feel, particularly sumptuous, and for its particular light effects, which can vary from intense to faint, from shiny to delicate. Due to its features, it used in contemporary fashion in evening dresses and wedding gowns as well as in capes for formal occasions.

Ports 1961

Stéphane Rolland

Aquilano e Rimondi

Hermès

Aquilano e Rimondi

VISCOSE VELVET

The soft pile of velvet acquires fresh sheen with the use of viscose, which gives weft velvet an elegant touch, traditionally with a sportier look. Fashion designer Enrico Coveri said that velvet has the advantage of making the design of clothes less structured and softer. Plain viscose velvet is very practical and flatters the face, which is why it is used in hats, and also looks very good in eveningwear.

It is a versatile fabric that can be trimmed or calendared employing techniques that make it special and original. Designers such as Agatha Ruiz de la Prada make coats, tailored suits, dresses and playful tops that have fun with the vibrancy of the color, with eye-catching and stimulating tones.

Angelo Marani

Angelo Marani

Agatha Ruiz de la Prada

Agatha Ruiz de la Prada

A generic term used to designate types of velvet whose patterns, defined by pile in relief, can vary both in appearance and form. In the past, a special loom was needed for this; today, a jacquard loom is used. When the patterns are complex, the details are defined using "curled velvet" (with whole rings), "*allucciolato* velvet"

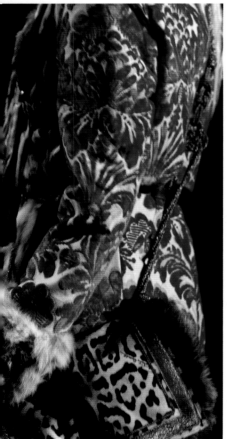

Roberto Cavalli

(with gold-thread rings) or "against-the-cut velvet" (with hairs of different lengths) such that the decoration mimics a bas-relief. Due to the alternation of different colors and yarns, "goldsmith velvet" (with curled parts and cut parts), which capitalizes on the different refractions of light on the textile support, came to be spoken of. The combination of various techniques in a single fabric increased its value even more. Patterned velvet was only used in details such as sleeves, bodices and collars in clothes in the 16th century. Many portraits of English nobility painted by Holbein evidence this trend. All the effects of patterned velvet – which essentially is velour – are used in fashion and decoration and are chosen according to structure, sizes of the pattern repeat and fabric weight. One technique employed in this type of velvet involves the use of special iron objects placed in the direction of the weft and in which the warp hair is inserted to form loops that are later cut and made into tufts. Patterned velvet is also used to make bags, shoes and boots that often appear in the collections of Fendi, Dolce & Gabbana, Cavalli and Gucci.

Gucci

Bottega Veneta

Angelo Marani

Jean Paul Gaultier

Central Saint Martins

Louis Vuitton

RIBBED VELVET

A plain or twill weave cotton fabric with fairly tightly packed ribbing in relief on the front of the material that underscores the background and almost seems sculpted. It is also called cord velvet. The ribs, parallel to the selvages, are made up of tufts of hair woven with supplementary floating weft threads cut at the ends with special multi-leaf cutters. The tufts alternate with hairless areas, forming a succession of stripes instead of covering the entire fabric surface. The ribs can be of different thickness, large or very fine according to the number of repetitions of the sequences of the more or less tightly packed tufts of hairs. There are various kinds: flat, convex or with double ribbing, and the tufts can have a different length. Some have 350 and 500 stripes with well-defined ribs; others have 1000 and 2000 stripes, suited to the lighter weight of winter shirts. The ribbing offers thermal protection and is found in men's suit and pants

Max Mara

sets that are combined with garments made of fabrics woolier to the touch. While in keeping with tradition, ribbed velvet benefits from research into new weaves, use of special yarn-dyed fibers and the combination of the thread with different materials and finishes, making it a fabric always in fashion and very much in demand.

Carolina Herrera

Eley Kishimoto

Betty Jackson

Gucci

Ermenegildo Zegna

VELVETEEN

Louis Vuitton

Strong, resistant fabric with convex ribs that have a tendency to wear out from chafing. The first velveteen was produced at the end of the 18th century under the name bombe velvet and grew in popularity in later centuries. It was the ideal fabric base of the country attire of English gentlemen, used in the construction of vests, jackets and hunting coats. Velveteen coats were a symbol of non-conformity, often worn by artists and intellectuals. Today, velveteen is used in menswear and women's clothing, in active and leisure wear, as well as in adornments, borders, inserts, collars and pockets.

Max Mara

Issey Miyake

Number Nine

Dolce & Gabbana

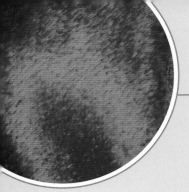

Alberta Ferretti

Stéphane Rolland

Marc Jacobs

Derek Lam

Emilio Pucci

Relatively light fabric (around 180 g/m²), very lustrous, with varied and fragmented light effects. It is a velour fabric with an almost always cotton background twisted in two strands and a silk warp pile (occasionally organdy) much longer than that of common velvet. The hair is flattened, pressed and stretched in succession, and given a mechanical press finish with cylinders. The result is a compact, silky and reflective surface that acquires shifting reflections due to the effect of light. Because of its sheen, the fabric is also called mirror velvet. In addition to silk, the hair can be made of wool, viscose or synthetic fibers such as polyester. Panne velvet is different from plush velvet, an acrylic fabric that imitates fur and has longer, more directed pile. Occasionally, it is similar to embossed velvet, since during pressing with metallic cylinders it receives a fine embossing at certain points to increase the decorative effect. It is also similar to froissè velvet, which is puckered and wrinkled. The basic concept of this variety is the break from visual uniformity of the shiny surface, something that makes it especially suitable for ruffling and iridescent effects typical of elegant garments and eve-ning dresses. Very luminous, fine to the touch, with smooth and fluid drape, it lends itself to pieces by prominent designers such as the long velvet silk panne skirts by Gucci and Rolland, the eccentric detours charged with vitality by John Galliano, and the soft Bohemian atmospheres of Derek Lam.

Ann Demeulemeester   Laura Biagiotti

Custo Barcelona

Etro

The soft, compact textile base of velvet lends itself very well to printed patterns. The length of the hair must be reduced to allow the colors to adhere well to the support. The most common technique is rotary printing with cylinders (in the past copper cylinders but today steel), which allow for a well-defined pattern. The cylinders have small orifices close to the areas where the color needs to adhere and pass successively over the fabric, spread out on special printing tables, depositing the color contained in the cylinders. A cylinder is used for each color of the pattern to be printed. The transfer printing system is applied to velvet with specific effects obtained through heat-compressed sheets applied to the fabric pile. Printing allows for more personalization of velvet and better adaptation of the material to the demands of each individual designer. Mariano Fortuny, who lived in Venice at the beginning of the 20th century, experimented with velvet printing techniques applying stenciled gold and silver. This method gave his fabrics a weathered and aged look, yet at the same time beautiful and luminous, a dichotomy that gave rise to a unique immediately identifiable style. The glossy velvet background, in colors inspired by the city of canals, was enriched by the application of traditional metallic pigments whose formulas the artist kept secret because, though he'd patented some of the procedures in Paris, he was very reluctant to reveal their composition. Among contemporary designers, a big

Dolce & Gabbana

Anna Sui

Antonio Marras

Mariella Burani

admirer of printed velvet is undoubtedly Etro, who often directs its collections at current-day dandies.

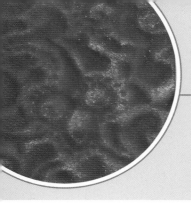

DEVORE VELVET

Special velvet from which some areas of pile are chemically eliminated (*devoured*) in a way that makes the background visible. The term comes from the French verb *devorer*. Alternating fillings and empty spaces allows for highlighting details of the motif one wishes to reproduce. Devore velvet can consist of one or more colors, sometimes superimposed with printing processes. Technically it is obtained by spraying a special corrosive paste on a mixed fabric base with cellulose, protein or chemical fibers. The effect of the chemical agent and the high air temperature eliminate the cellulose, while silk, wool and polyester remain unchanged. Strikingly beautiful effects are obtained on velvet with viscose hair, which disintegrates at some points and transmits particularly warm light where it remains. Devore velvet is used in elegant garments and fluid designs in which movement underscores the technical features of the textile surface thanks to the play of light.

Donna Karan

Emilio Pucci

Anna Sui

John Galliano

Emilio Pucci

CHENILLE

Issey Miyake

Veronique Leroy

Hussein Chalayan

Ann Demeulemeester

Burberry Prorsum

A fabric with a velvety appearance and a surface with a long pile, obtained with weft thread. The name of the fabric, invented in France around 1600, derives from the French word *chenille*, which means caterpillar, an animal characterized by its abundant little legs, all voluminous and soft. Chenille yarn is wrapped in hair, obtained by cutting in thin strips a fabric with a structure of warp threads grouped at regular intervals and with floating weft threads cut with a blade. The resulting strips are twisted to provide the yarn with resistance and are then re-used in weaving as the weft. Other methods use a yarn made up of two fibers of different materials, cotton and silk or synthetic fiber: one is fine and resistant; the other is thicker and soft. These are twisted together and later cut. There are many novelty varieties that often are used in passementerie. The chenillette, also called cure-pipe, enwraps a metallic thread. The textile surface of chenille can be silk, cotton, wool, rayon, acrylic, viscose or polyester fiber. Chenille is woven on a loom, with a plain or jacquard weave and with a flattened pile effect, in the shape of a sponge. In other instances it is knitted, which is evident in the pile. The fabric can be of various weights, according to its intended use. In casual fashion it is used (in its elastic version as well) in beachwear, dance attire, one-pieces, meshes and active wear in general. In decoration it is used in curtains, period coverings, doors and bed covers. It can be pieced dyed, printed or tooled. Chenille appeared en masse in the thirties as a fabric adaptable to trends and evolutions in fashion, and was extremely popular in the sixties, especially in printed patterns with brightly colored graphic images and designs. Since then, its seductive attraction has underscored the sinuous movements of many Goth- and Romantic-style models on international catwalks, featuring all the colors of the rainbow and the magical and mysterious tones of aquamarine and violet. Ermenegildo Zegna has used chenille in attractive silk ties for men. In 1990, the Chenille International Manufacturers Association (CIMA) was formed.

TERRY CLOTH

A fabric with a spongy, three-dimensional appearance, with a sequence of loops of more or less tightly packed threads spread across its surface, formed by a loose-tension supplementary warp called a warp-knitted terry. The first warp end (background) is interwoven with the weft with a medium grosgrain weave and forms the base of the fabric. The use of low-tension cotton threads gives the fabric the capacity to absorb a lot of water. The layer of loops can be arranged only on one side in plain terry cloth and on both sides in double-looped terry cloth, for which three different warps are needed, part on one side and part on the other on the alternate terrycloth, thus determining its degree of absorption. Terry cloth is made on special looms that use devices such as a hinged type connecting rod, a comb with a mobile casement box or regulation system. In other languages it is called "sponge" (Italian: spugna, French: eponge), after the soft, elastic skeleton of Porifera (sponges), marine creatures that absorb water. Terrycloth can be cut and brushed to look like chenille cloth and velvet, striped or patterned with longer pile or, more frequently, printed with vividly colored motifs. Velvet terry cloth has a surface with loops on one side and a cut and smooth surface on the other. The fabric is fulled to make it more compact. It is used to make robes and towels as well as beach and cruise wear. In the fifties terry cloth sailor's outfits were common, worn by fashion conscious women. For garments and complementary accessories fashion

Wunderkind

journalists proposed two alternatives: a beach outfit with a Chanel-style cape or half cape, with contrasting trim, or a knee-length dress coat in solid colors or with motifs to match the beach towel, or a longer design consisting of a robe with a hood, striped or with a floral motif, and a belt. Terry cloth can also be produced with the weft mesh technique, introducing a supplementary thread into the regular outside/inside work that forms loops on the surface. Today, patterned terry cloth stockings, with special absorbing power, are used for sports and leisure activities, and its spongy surface is reproduced by certain embroidery machines capable of sewing areas of knit terry cloth on different support fabrics. For the bourgeois man, Versace propo-

Chanel

Herve Leger

sed in the nineties an updated version of the house robe – a symbol of a culture practically vanished today – with a very chic soft terry cloth garment with shiny satin lining, very distinct surfaces that produced a strong effect of contrast.

14

JERSEY

Fabric originally from the island of Jersey, in the Channel Islands, also known as full and short stitch, flat stitch or satin stitch. It is the simplest type of weft knit, obtained with a single series of needles in a single-needle or circular knitting machine. It has a uniform surface of fine stitches achieved with a single thread that runs horizontally to the piece and, finding the needles, feeds the formation of thread connections that constitute the stitch. Jersey has two different sides, flat on the front and piled on the back with a slight mesh effect. The fabric can be woven with yarns of any kind, usually combed. A bi-stretch fabric, jersey has soft filling. It adapts well to body shapes and can be plain or decorated. It is a good material for draped garments, with nice plastic effects, but must be handled carefully when sewing because it tends to stretch along the edges, particularly its elastic versions. It is suitable for internal and external meshes, dresses, etc. The history of jersey fabric intersects with the audacious and adventurous career of Coco Chanel, indisputable queen of French chic who, starting in 1916, popularized the use of this material, which until then had been considered inadequate for tailored garments and used only to make sports clothing and underwear. In her shop on Rue Cambon, only hats were sold, due to a contract that bound her to non-competition agreements with other clothing businesses in the vicinity. To skirt this contractual provision, and also to create an innovative style, Chanel introduced machine-made fabrics, using jersey material acquired at a low price from textile industrialist Jean Rodier for the production of simple gray and dark-blue dresses adorned with long gold chains and pearl necklaces or costume jewelry with imitation gems. These innovations were extremely popular with Chanel's customers, leading the designer to start producing jersey designs that made her creations famous all over the world.

Frankie Morello

Bottega Veneta

WOOL KNIT

Hermès

Betty Jackson

Aigner

Bottega Veneta

In common language, knit is a plain-mesh fabric, like jersey, very light and used in the construction of dresses and unisex sports wear. For a long time, the original jersey fabric was produced with wool fibers, to which cotton and silk were added later. Jersey wool was woven on modest looms on the island of Jersey, in the Channel Islands archipelago, in the English Channel, and was used in the 19th century in heavy-stitch garments, worn initially by English fisherman. It was, nonetheless, a local craft product that sold at a very low price even abroad, Great Britain having waived levying the industrial activity of the islanders, who enjoyed a degree of political autonomy as compensation for the sacrifices they had made during the German occupation in World War II. Its natural softness and stretch make jersey wool a versatile fabric. Today, wool knit is produced in numerous weights with threads of various counts, almost always combed, giving it a light appearance, with a refined and compact finish. The carded thread version is slightly hairier and less compact. Refining and finishing operations became very important, contributing to personalizing the base product, also mixed with other fibers in cutting-edge textiles. Example of this are devore wool knit, which highlights the heathered motifs of camouflage, the lichen effect, the stitch that gives it a worn look through special abrasive washes, and also kid mohair knit, with unrolled and broken pile, and satin and plush knit.

COTTON KNIT

Emma Cook

Calvin Klein

Marithé & François Girbaud

Jeremy Scott

Central Saint Martins

Fabric commonly used in classic white or colored t-shirts, a basic universal garment. Cotton knit has the same softness and resistance to wrinkling as wool, though with more stretch. The technology involved in its production is the same as that used to make wool. In women's and sports wear, cotton jersey with elastane (spandex) fibres is used more often (spandex threads have more stretch and combine practicality and freedom of movement with an impeccable aesthetic quality). The use of biological cotton with certification of authenticity, without using pesticides in the cultivation of the fiber, today adds value to the simplicity of the prototype of the classic t-shirt, created in the United States, worn by many male sex symbols. In the world of cinema this garment has been worn by such famous actors as Paul Newman, in *Cool Hand Luke*, Marlon Brando, in *A Streetcar Named Desire*, and James Dean, in *A Rebel Without a Cause*, making the roles they played more familiar and closer to the public. A designer who exalted for all time the simple t-shirt in its classic navy-blue version is Giorgio Armani, who guaranteed its success when including it in his own wardrobe as a stylistic element of perennial modernity, worn even on not so informal occasions.

SILK KNIT

A very fine, ethereal, decidedly practical fabric that can be woven with sleek yarn or highly twisted yarn, acquiring a unique crepe effect. Because of its silky fluidity it is very suitable for elegant dresses. A brilliant interpreter of silk cotton in printed patterns, with complex op and pop designs and bright, upbeat colors, was without a doubt the Florentine marquise Emilio Pucci. At the of the 1950s he sensed

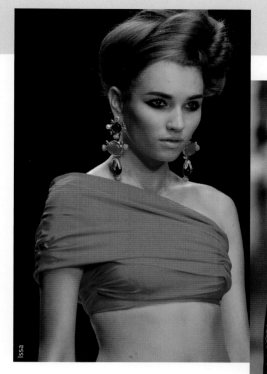

Issa

Bottega Veneta

the enormous potential of this fabric, lightweight and highly resistant to wrinkling, associating it with dresses with simple lines and a basic cut that favored the female figure. Among the designs from that period are the classic shirtdress with a thin belt around the waist and novelty buttons, long fluid tunics that fell all the way to the floor, and shorter blouses combined with wide pants like "palazzo pajamas", successfully launched by Russian fashion designer Irene Galitzine. Roberta di Camerino also introduced in those years exciting silk knit dresses that caressed the body and concealed it behind surprising printed trompe-l'œils that simulated slight pleats in relief and billowy graphic draped elements. These designs

Byblos

Angelo Marani

fused elegance and practicality, as required by the new image of women in keeping with modern times. In more recent versions, we find finishes in which the knit surface is enhanced by crystalline, pearly, translucent or frosted glints. The sculptural dresses with bold metallic flashes created by Frida Giannini for Gucci are distinguished by the softness of their lacquered viscose knit drapery.

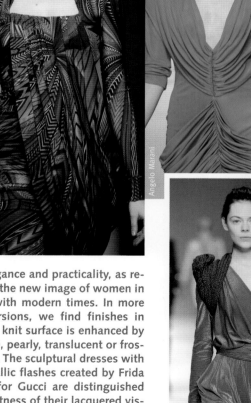

Max Mara

LISLE

Givenchy

Emanuel Ungaro

Emanuel Ungaro

Filoscozia® is a trademark known for the high quality of its products, knitted with threads very soft to the touch that until the middle of the 19th century were imported from England, a country that specialized in the production of cotton threads. Lisle is a knit fabric woven with combed yarns from two twisted yarns, burnt to eliminate excess fluff and mercerized to enhance resistance. It is made with high-quality long fibers from Egypt. The thread count, given by the length recorded in the weight, no less than Ne 50/2, varies greatly according to the intended use of the garments, which range from men's fine socks to undergarments to yarn-dyed men's and women's t-shirts. It is bright and springy fabric, one that is shrink-resistant and keeps its shape, especially if subjected to succes-

Lacoste

sive Sanforized treatment, which significantly stabilizes the dimensions. Lisle feels good against the skin and is very light, as it facilitates the absorption and dispersion of body sweat; it is also easy to maintain. A fine material, it dyes well. It can be made in sharp, bright and lasting colors, highly prized by those in the know. In the fifties polo shirts were made with lisle cotton, long-sleeve men's garments with typical horizontal stripes of alternating colors, characterized by their insouciant informal elegance. The three-button open co-

llar made them very suitable for informal occasions and sports. In 2002, a new brand was created for Filoscozia® Alta Qualita fabric, with an orthogonal structure, which certifies and guarantees a material produced entirely in Italy following controlled transformation cycles.

A variety of jersey though more compact and resistant, it is a fabric with a knit weft structure with ribs crossed in various stripes. It is a mesh material very suitable for cutting, as it is extensible, though not very elastic. It has the same appearance on both sides. It is made with double-knit circular sewing machines with two series of needles arranged at 90 degrees and that operate in opposing positions,

Veronique Leroy

Veronique Leroy

Chapurin

Chapurin

Chapurin

producing a herringbone stitch. Interlock fabric is flexible and particularly breathable, which facilitates the expulsion of moisture toward the exterior layer and always keeps the body dry. Easy to care for, it is always ready for use, as it dries quickly and doesn't need to be ironed after washing. It is springy to the touch and drapes well. It can made of cotton and also of 100% polyester and weighs around 180-200 g/m². Biological cotton dyed with natural coloring agent is ideal for leisure wear like short-sleeve t-shirts, tops and little dresses as well as for sportswear, work clothes and undergarments. Interlock has lent itself to imaginative creations by independent-minded fashion designers, ones not afraid to subvert classical rules.

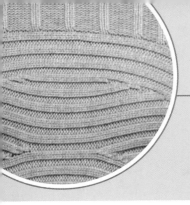

Gianfranco Ferré

Issey Miyake

Issey Miyake

Alexander Wang

A knit fabric with vertical ribs in relief created by alternating stitches on the front and back sides arranged in stripes. It is especially elastic horizontally. There are different versions of the fabric with ribs of varying widths used to make combinations, undershirts, pantyhose and other garments. The structure of ribbed knit fabric can be wool, even woven with expensive cotton yarns, and cover the entire surface, granting it cling, grip and consistency, especially when mixed with elastic yarn. It is called *canale* in Italian in homage to a similar material woven by hand and used mainly to adorn the collars, cuffs and edges of sweaters and other woven garments. Rib knit is used for making large circular collars, springy anoraks, bed

socks and hats for the snow. Vanise rib knit has a motif of various colors from side to side, often in contrasting tones. This technique uses a production method in various layers distributed evenly among all the needles, leaving one color visible on the front of the fabric and the other visible on the back. To alternate the dyed ribs, the thread is inverted in some of the needles. Ribbed fabric needs to be handled carefully as it tends to give with the passage of time and successive washes. White rib knit is used to make the "spaghetti strap" shirt, also known in popular culture as the "bricklayer's t-shirt", an emblematic garment of male members of the urban working class for whom exposing their underwear and showing off their biceps and chest hair are distinctive signs of unbounded manhood. Italian actor Alberto Sordi wore the famous tank top undershirt many times in his much-feted performances when he

wanted to put himself in the skin of the common man. The Italian political leader Umberto Bossi wears this shirt occasionally when attending meetings in Pontida with members of the Lega Nord party, for whom this shirt has become practically a symbol of identity. The somewhat aggressive connotations of this undershirt worn as an outer garment are confirmed by the name "wife beater", a reference to the fact that in police photographs this type of shirt seems to be the preferred garment of men arrested for violence against women. There is no shortage of more aesthetically attractive images, such as that of the muscular rapper Eminem in concert or a very young Marlon Brando in the unforgettable movie *On the Waterfront*.

Gianfranco Ferré

Tubular knit has a fullness that allows for perfect adaptation of the finished garment, even if the article requires a more or less complex pattern. The fabric is made on circular looms, machines based on the use of needles arranged throughout the interior of a perimeter and prepared to work in succession, each turn starting before the preceding one is complete. Through the differentiated regulation of this perimeter the machines allow for the production of seamless tubes of different lengths, each corresponding to a determined size. The terms "body size" and "seamless" are applied to garments without lateral stitching, made from tubular knit fabric, without cutting the sides of the material, yet shaping it at the juncture of the sleeves and that of the collar. In 1998 designer Phillipe Starck created StarkNaked, a revolutionary and versatile 80-denier garment, a seamless tube-shaped design that is long and thin with a very compact structure. Because it is 8% Lycra, this unique article of seamless clothing adheres to the body like a stocking, weighs 200 grams and can be worn inside out, lending itself perfectly to the most disparate fashion styles. The idea was later perfected in StarkNakedHot, with three small distinct tubes added in the form of sleeves, collar and bra and that can be applied to the main tube that forms the dress or skirt through adjustable clasps or straps. The different functions of tubular mesh are the focus a project entitled A-POC (abbreviation for A Piece of

Stella McCartney

Guy Laroche

Argentovivo

Cloth) developed by Issey Miyake. It consists of a roll of tubular knit fabric (stuffed for winter versions) that can be cut to obtain as many seamless pieces as necessary to achieve the desired look.

177

PIQUE KNIT

A knit fabric with relief effects and alternating hollow spaces (pique style) similar to little cells with limited elasticity that form geometric patterns. It is obtained with a plain-knit structure, similar to jersey, the surface of which is plastically altered by the influence of a particular type of weave that uses special stitches that retain some parts while leaving others springier. Fabric woven with low relief, also called "Lacoste", is obtained by alternating strips of normal stitch with others consisting of simple loops. Double pique is a knit structure acquired with loops of free threads. Made of 100% cotton and weighing between 210 and 250 g/m², honeycomb knit is a very light fabric with excellent ventilation and considered easy to maintain. It is used to make t-shirts and the unmistakable Lacoste polo knits in solid colors featuring the widely known symbol of the brand on the chest. Its characteristic good breathability makes honeycomb knit the preferred fabric for sportswear, especially for tennis. In fact, Rene

Lacoste was a seasoned tennis player who, in the twenties, came up with the idea of bringing together in a single design the practical nature of the t-shirt and the elegance of the shirt, with the addition of the crocodile logo, a nickname Lacoste had earned for being an especially tenacious competitor who never released his prey once he had it in his clutches. While honeycomb knit continues to be a classic unisex fabric, it isn't immune to the fascination with seasonal trends, such as when the material is subjected to a special wash that gives it a vintage look. Nowadays, its use extends to all leisure occasions, for which it is practically essential. Even polyester honeycomb, made on raschel looms, has a certain degree of breathability. Silk honeycomb is the signature fabric of handmade knit ties by Ascot, the German manufacturer and international leader in the production of this article of clothing, another classic in men's fashion.

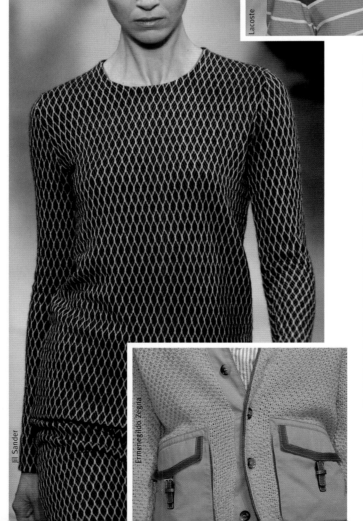

Lacoste

Dolce & Gabbana

Jil Sander

Ermenegildo Zegna

INLAID KNIT

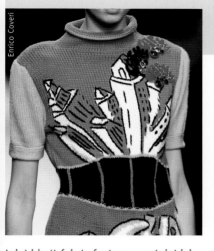

Enrico Coveri

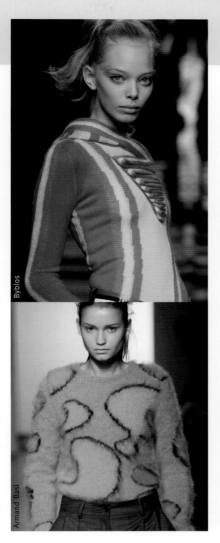

Byblos

Armand Basi

Inlaid knit fabric features an *inlaid* decorative motif, that is, one inserted in the background structure and consisting of a design with large flat sections of colors defined through changing the thread. In a single stitched fringe, a thread of one color is fed up to a certain point, a second one is added to it, then a third, etc., according to a precise design. This type of decoration is recognized for the extremely polished and smooth appearance on both sides of the fabric, while allowing for improvisations through maintaining the relative lightness of the stitch. It has the practical advantage of not having unpleasant broken threads on the reverse side that could tangle. Due to this feature, inlaid knit is highly regarded despite its higher cost compared with faster techniques. In the 1930s designer Elsa Schiaparelli used this type of fabric ironically in surrealistic code inspired by the artistic movements to which her painter friends belonged. Designer Sonia Rykiel also uses blocks of vivid colors for inlaying trompe loeil motifs in springy merino, mohair and cashmere sweaters, while Jean Char-

les de Castelbajac, another master of ludic irony in lively colors, plays with the pictorially attractive side of large figurative motifs, recognizable even from afar.

JC de Castelbajac

JACQUARD KNIT

Intricately worked knit fabric with complex designs obtained by using a selection mechanism to change needles and colors of all kinds, in a way similar to the electronic looms used to weave composite fabrics. The technology of jacquard knit machines allows for a wide variety of motifs in specific areas or covering the entire surface, which reproduce geometric, figurative or abstract motifs, also defined with a large number of colors. It is used both in elegant garments and sportswear. When the threads don't pass through the front of the fabric they remain

DKNY

Etro

Givenchy

floating on the reverse side, with a limited length, returning to the front when the design requires it. This encourages the use of combinations of small motifs of frequently alternating colors to avoid the inconvenience of poorly woven fibers remaining on the back, which easily become entangled and create unattractive tight threads. The patterned Missoni sweaters are famous for their unusual combinations of Impressionist-like colors.

The double-knit jacquard technique is used to make two-tone designs with a positive-negative effect. Other devices allow for creating surfaces with retained stitches that create embossed effects in relief, such as matelassé fabrics. In the SS 2012 collection of designer Gabriele Colangelo, jacquard knit work, woven later with additions of nylon, is reinvented in pictorial code in dresses that reproduce the paintings of Gerhard Richter.

Missoni

Max Mara

Gabriele Colangelo

KNITTING

Antonio Marras

Fendi

Iceberg

Julien Macdonald

Knitting refers to fabric made with knitting needles. This activity dates back at least to ancient communities in the Middle East, as the abundance of surviving relics attest to. The word "knitting" comes from the Anglo-Saxon word *ketten*, itself derived from the Sanskrit *nahyat* (translated as knitting or crochet mesh). However, knitting has only been visually documented since the beginning of the 13th century, in the painting depicting Mary of Nazareth sewing a small seamless tunic using the circular system of four needles by Master Bertram of Minden in the altarpiece known as the *Visit of the Angel*, from the Buxtehude Altar, in Germany. Manual knit fabrics form part of the common wardrobe, with the only difference being that silk hose made from valuable yarns corresponded to the upper classes, while peasants wore rustic wool stockings beneath their trousers. One of the most important knitting schools, famous for its gloves made of silk and gold threads, was in Spain. Modern technology enhances this technique with contemporary solutions that dazzle us with their original micro and macro openwork effects, braids in relief and classic or ethnic motifs from many different places.

Dries Van Noten

John Galliano

Laura Biagiotti

Antonio Berardi

Prada

183

CROCHET

Anna Sui

Kenzo

Dolce & Gabbana

Missoni

Circular and concentric knit fabrics made by hand with special needles with hooks and used for ribs or wider openwork surfaces. This technique is practiced in many cultures: from Mediterranean countries to Africa to Europe to America. The crochet needle consists of a straight aluminum or steel rod covered in plastic, about 20 cm long, with a little hook at one end that takes up and guides a continuous strand of thread. In the past it was made from tortoise shell, ivory and wood. There are also 30 cm needles, suitable for Tunisian knit, a type of linear, compact and even material. In contrast to the thread needle, the crochet needle is not used to form stitches. Rather it is only used to make loops, and is held in the center to be able to grasp it better. According to the International Standard Range (ISR), the measurements of the hooks range from a diameter of 0.60 mm, for fine cotton, to 10 mm, for stouter threads. Crochet patterns are made in different materials, such as distinct qualities of perle cotton, cordonet, silk, twisted wool or mohair, linen, hemp and jute, raffia, string and soutache, and are used alone or combined with other threads to obtain unconventional results. The basic stitch with which all knitting begins is a chain stitch consisting of a knotted loop through which the thread is passed to form a soft filling chain. The work is easy to do with other basic stitches such as high stitch and low stitch, which are combined in different ways to create novelty knits, ruffled or continuous, superimpositions, in relief or knotted, cross stitch, opposing, fan, boucle loop stitch, picot, etc. Among ethnic and traditional products are crochet cloaks of African tribes, Turkish caps, three-dimensional puppets made in China and others in pre-Colombia America. Ireland specialized in crochet that imitates expensive embroidery, known as Irish embroidery, in local industries mainly in the towns of Carrickmacross and Clones. Still very famous today are the Old America bedspreads consisting of checks crocheted with different woolen yarns, invented by North American pioneers when wool was scarce. Different fashion designers have exhibited an interest in the possibilities of these techniques, among them Salvatore Ferragamo, who created magnificent raffia sandals. Crochet designs are also suitable for shawls, footwear and knit garments with "spider web" and "snowflake" effects, for parts of "nude-look" clothes or for shirt collars and cuffs with a romantic bon ton flavor.

METALLIC MESH

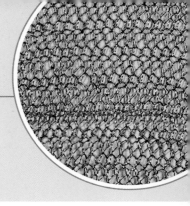

Metallic fiber consisting of materials such as iron, copper, steel, nickel and cobalt alloys. It can be spun, woven or stranded to produce a ductile fabric that adapts easily to the lines of the body. Metallic mesh can also be made of polyester and imitate old coats of mail worn by warriors in the Middle Ages to protect themselves from the blows of swords during battle. The first fashion designer to introduce garments made from this fabric was Paco Rabanne, who created dresses with scales, rings and modular metallic elements very similar to the corset worn by American actress Joan Fonda in the role of Barbarella. To make this imaginative design, he had to use pliers instead of the usual needles and thread. In 1968, Paco Rabanne designed a windbreaker with springy metal plaques, forming a tightly arranged yet springy texture, for stylish singer Franscoise Hurdy. The finest metallic mesh, however, is the invention of Gianni Versace, who, in the eighties, experimented with different applications of gold and silver that he used in garments and accessories, treating the mesh almost as if it was jersey fabric and designing printed versions as well. Today, metallic mesh appears in sinuous evening gowns, tops and asymmetrical tunics with polished or aged sheets that evoke the androgynous fascination associated with the Amazons.

House of Holland

Stella McCartney

Barbara Bui

AF Vandevorst

Barbara Bui

AF Vandevorst

Knit fabric made with two yarns with a different thread count: the reverse side is of pure re-twisted cotton thread or wool blended with other fibers and the front side is made of carded yarn, only slightly twisted, always cotton, mixed cotton or wool fibers softened by brushing. The names comes from the old French word *ferpe* or *feupe* and refers to a fabric with pile on the front, due to the extraction of the hair, and smooth on the back. Felt is made with simple mesh knitting machines and consists of a series of relatively fine background threads woven in satin that serve to support a second series of threads held in place by occasional anchoring and that run in a linear fashion. These threads, thicker than those of the background, form a springy surface, especially if brushed (Pireney felt). While smooth and soft to the touch, felt protects the body due its considerable absorbing power. It is available in different weights: the heaviest is the one preferred for winter, while in summer cotton-angora felt, a lightweight fiber blend of un-brushed cotton, is preferred. Invisible felt refers to a fabric in which two types of background threads are used with the aim of obtaining a more even reverse side. A velvety surface is used as the reverse side of the fabric in the production of clothes. The same term alludes to a kind of felt that athletes use when training. In the United States its use was consolidated in the eighties for casual unisex garments, due to its undeniable comfort and the importance physical activities such as jogging, ae-

robics and dance had come to assume in contemporary life. Hollywood stars that became spokespersons for cultural designs oriented toward modernity left us with unforgettable images of garments from those years. The masculine version was embodied in a dapper Warren Beatty with white wings and a gray tracksuit in the role of quarterback Joe Pendleton in *Heaven Can Wait*. The feminine versions run from Jill Clayburgh – in the role of a woman determined to gain complete control of her life in the movie *An Unmarried Woman* (1978) – to the characters in *Flashdance* (1983). As a result, a genuine craze for felt garments emerged, also nurtured by the contribution of Jane Fonda, who turned fitness into a lifestyle with the creation of a series of videos in which she served as an aerobic trainer for women interested in exercising at home.

Undercover

C. P. Company

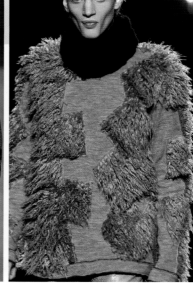

Custo Barcelona

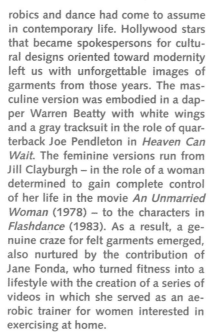

Number Nine

Jean Paul Gaultier

HEAVY FABRICS

15

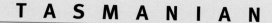

T A S M A N I A N

Tasmanian® is a registered trademark of Loro Piana, a global leader in the production of quality fabrics. It is a regular, light, plain-weave fabric, soft and smooth to the touch, originally made solely with expensive combed wool from Tasmania, an island to the southeast of Australia discovered by Dutchman Abel Tasman in 1642. The island's climate, particularly suitable for raising herds of merino sheep, allows for the production of extraordinarily fine fleece. The natural characteristics of the fabric are hygroscopicity up to 33%, permeability, thermal insulation, and optimum resistance to tearing and wrinkles. The highly twisted thread, super merino fiber with a diameter of only 17.5 microns, is especially resistant on account of its lightness, as the short fibers are eliminated with brushing. Tasmanian has a very high thread count, up to almost 4,000 weft threads per meter of fabric. The result is a material that weighs only 250 g/ml, equal to 166 g/m², which means that a dress made with Tasmanian weighs on average only around 500 grams. There are different types of the fabric, all with the same excellent basic features but intended for different times of the year: Winter Tasmanian: for the coldest days, a double chain stitch weighing 340 grams; the sophisticated Summer Tasmanian: made of wool mixed with silk, suitable for jackets, pants and dresses. A predecessor of Tasmanian was Priest Cloth, a special fabric intended for the ecclesiastical wardrobe that possessed extraordinary characteristics of fineness and comfort. The name of

Burberry Prorsum

the brand has entered into the vernacular of textile sector professionals as a synonym for garments made out of this fabric. It is highly prized for men's midseason suits. It is a medium-weight material, anti-wrinkle and especially comfortable for travelling. It is also very frequently used in the wardrobe of the professional woman, in jackets characterized by classic good taste, overcoats and tailored dresses. Finally, it is a product that answers perfectly to the demands of impeccability of modern life.

Armani Privè

Bottega Veneta

Gucci

Bottega Veneta

LIGHT WOOL

Marithé & François Girbaud

Marithé & François Girbaud

Roccobarocco

Roccobarocco

Sportmax

A lightweight fabric with a plain or twill weave consisting of several layers of combed merino wool threads. It has a tightly woven weft and a uniform surface, is dry to the touch and doesn't wrinkle. It lends itself to the production of spring-summer suits for men and women. Fresco® is a patented trademark of Cagniere, a textile company that experimented with this treatment starting with an anti-wrinkle fabric obtained by interweaving a twisted thread of three strands to produce a particularly porous surface. The expression "cool wool" entered into the common vernacular in the seventies as a generic term for relatively lightweight combed wool fabrics with a fine structure, suitable for producing midseason garments. Its construction is almost invariably simple (taffeta, twill, Batavia), based on the combination of equal threads that give the fabric a smooth feel. Currently, light wool garments are also very common in winter in climate-controlled places such as offices and hotels and are particularly in demand throughout the world by people who have a dynamic lifestyle and want to maintain an impeccable appearance even after enduring many hours of travel. A fabric similar to light wool, though lighter, is Tropical, a wool cloth formed by twisted threads with two strands, ideal for especially warm climates.

FLANNEL

A springy, resistant fabric woven out of carded wool or cotton threads with different frameworks (often diagonal). After weaving, a fulling hammer is used to make the fabric more compact. Napping produces a slightly piled surface on both sides. The layer of pile acts as thermal insulation, resulting in a warm and comfortable fabric, even if it is light. The word "flannel" derives from the Gallic term *gelane*, the name of a type of local wool. It is an emblematic fabric in the masculine wardrobe, eternalized by Gregory Peck in the movie *The Man In The Gray Flannel Suit*, based on the novel of the same name by Sloan Wilson, which tells the story of the protagonist's labor resentment after the dark years of the war. A symbol of virility, often the gray color of London fog, wool flannel is available in different weights, especially for jackets, pants, suits and overcoats with a serious, rigorous look. Gray flannel pants serve as a neutral foundation to which can be added garments of other colors and fabrics to make a "combination" suit. Flannel tends to wear with time at vulnerable chafing points. Conventionally, the term "flannel" includes all napped fabrics (cotton, rayon, etc.) made in solid colors or printed with patterns that are either produced with a shuttle or knit (pajamas and bedclothes). Cotton flannel is widely used in yarn-dyed solid shirts, with printed patterns and Scotch checks. While a classic, the flannel shirt became a prominent symbol of

Anteprima

Dsquared2

Dior

Belstaff

transgression in the "grunge" look, a favorite of musicians in the 80s and 90s such as Kurt Cobain. The brilliant and tempestuous guitarist of Nirvana often wore oversized checked or printed lumberjack shirts, and through his influence, not just musical, contributed to renewing the somewhat ungainly image of this fabric. One of the cult objects of contemporary society is thought to be made of flannel: the famous tranquilizing blanket with which Linus van Pelt, Charlie Brown's friend, never parts. In Italian the expression *far flanella* ("make flannel") refers to the attitude of allowing time to pass idly.

Julien Macdonald

Dior

Ann Demeulemeester

Bottega Veneta

Ann Demeulemeester

Hermès

Fustian is a cotton or wool fabric, woven in a diagonal (twill 3 or 4) or satin (5 or 8) weave, with a solid and compact velvety surface. Soft on the front and coarse on the reverse side, its appearance is similar to suede or chamois. Fustian is obtained with successive napping, polishing or satin treatments. There is a difference between plain fustian (without pile), also called satin fustian, and classic fustian (with the pile raised and polished to make it seem like suede). The name derives from the word *fushtan*, which referred to a type of heavy fabric with a cotton base. Fustat is a suburb of Cairo (Egypt), from where the cloth was imported. In the past it was woven with a strong line warp and a cotton weft, and was considered a valuable fabric due to this second component, more costly than other fibers given that it was imported from India. Other sources attribute the origin of the name to more remote times, claiming that the Latin term *fustis* (stick) was crossed in medieval times with the word *fustaneum* (wood) to refer to a kind of material called "wood wool". In the 13th century the most highly prized fustian was produced in Milan; the region of Chieri (Turin) specialized in the production of blue fustian, dyed with dyer's woad (isathis tinctoria), a plant from which indigo is extracted. Because of the protectionist measures of the Dukes of Savoy, it spread from Italy to the rest of Europe and America. With the drop in the price of cotton, what was once a valuable fabric became a material used for work clothes due to

Undercover

Roberto Cavalli

its characteristics of strong resistance to use. It was also known as Genoa fustian or in France as *gene*. It was also considered the ideal fabric for the pants worn by shepherds in the Meremma region of Tuscany and, in general, for all hunting and country clothes, as its initial rigidness weakens with use. In urban style, the preference is for classic fustians with a weight between 280 and 285 g/m², used in the construction of men's jackets with the unmistakable patches on the elbows. With fabric weights between 350 and 500 g/m² it is also used to make informal coats and jackets. Varieties of fustian include beaverteen, moleskin and doeskin. Attention should be paid to the reverse side of the fabric, which can be of hues with a distinctive sheen, especially in dark colors. In the past bleached fustian was also used for bedclothes and furniture covers.

C L O T H

Issey Miyake

Versace

C.P. Company

Miu Miu

Cloth is one of the oldest fabrics, known for centuries as a useful material for protection against the cold and intemperate weather. In the cities of ancient Rome, highly specialized guilds were already compressing woolen cloth, which was then subjected to a complex series of treatments. In the 12th century, the Order of Humilati in Lombardy began the organized production of wool cloth that soon spread from the monasteries, ultimately becoming a flourishing national industry. Among the varieties of locally produced cloth that have disappeared over time, orbace and bergamo are worth noting. The word "cloth" is a generic synonym for "fabric", used in this sense since antiquity. It is a fabric woven with carded thread, of pure wool or mixed with synthetic fibers. After weaving it is compressed with a fulling hammer to reduce the space between the weft and warp, with matte and condensed effects. This operation also makes it waterproof. Successive preparations include napping, to raise the fibers and obtain a side with pile, and later shearing, to cut all the pile the same size. Cloth has a uniform compact appearance that conceals the background fabric, generally taffeta, thus guaranteeing perfect technical insulation. Cloth of different weights and thicknesses are available on the market. During World War One, the cloth colors of military divisions ran from the gray of Austrian soldiers to the bluish gray of the French Army to the earthy brown tone of the Russian Army to the traditional khaki of the British troops. The blazer worn by crew members of the British Navy was made of cloth with white and blue strips. Its properties of resistance to cold and rain make it suitable for winter garments such as jackets, cloaks, capes and hoods. It is also used in decorative accessories for bedcovers, linings, filling and bedspreads.

DRAB

In Italian it is called "drap", from the Latin *drappus*, a termed used to generically indicate cloth or fabric. It is a very fine cloth, with a weight of 250-300 g/m², of pure combed wool or blended with fibers of different weights. It is also called *draplan*, a soft, silk fabric with a lustrous appearance on the front often made with elegant fibers like cashmere woven in a plain or silk weave. It undergoes a slight fulling process, napping, shearing and ironing. Often it receives a final treatment that increases the sheen of the pile. It has short, straight, directed hair, and so the direction of the pattern to the cut is obligatory. Among the different kinds of drab are *Zibeline*, with slanted and crimped pile similar to the coat of an animal; *l'édredon* with an opaque soft pile; *drap de vire*, a highly regarded fabric that has a "talking selvage", with a password consisting of four threads of three different colors (blue, red and white for the maximum quality fabric; red, yellow and white for intermediate quality material; and six beige threads and six white threads for a low quality version). Drab cloth includes all medium-weight wool fabrics, especially ones of combed yarn, used in men's clothes, while in the past, lighter woolen fabrics, reserved for ladies' garments, were called woolen goods. Nowadays, this distinction is obsolete, and drab is used indiscriminately for blazers, tailored suits and tablecloths.

Tommy Hilfiger

Aigner

Hermès

Emanuel Ungaro

Bill Blass

Resistant fabric made of thick select merino or mohair wool yarns,
carded and not scoured to make it
waterproof. Its long hair, compact
and lustrous structure is subjected to
different finishes, fulled and napped
on the reverse side and brushed and
flattened on the front in a single direction, in a way that allows drops
of water slide across it, thus increasing its resistance to water. It is often
dyed solid green, and is also found
in brown, gray, blue and black, with
medium and heavy weights for making jackets, overcoats and capes. The
origin of the word "loden" is attribu-
ted to the word "lod", which in Old
German means "bale of wool," which
was spun and woven in the Dolomi-
tes and the Tyrol in the Middle Ages.
At the time the only color used was
a vague grayish hue, typical of raw
wool, which was used to make the
cloth for peasants' clothes. Today, the
name "loden" is also applied to the
classic forest-green jacket from the
south of Tyrol, with a cape that extends past the forearm, covering it,
and with unmistakable convex leather
buttons. The shape and fabric of this
garment come from the wide hunting
cloaks favored by the nobility of the
Austro-Hungarian Empire for their natural characteristics of impermeability
and breathability. Original loden was
produced in the old Mossmer wool
shop, a factory founded in 1882 and
that has continued researching the
material, recently introducing the first
fireproof loden, capable of resisting

Marc by Marc Jacobs

Vivienne Westwood

flames. In the town of Vandoies is
a small museum devoted to loden,
where one can follow the complete
production cycle of the fabric, from
the shearing of the sheep to the production of the finished garment.

Dolce & Gabbana

Marc by Marc Jacobs

Juun.J

NUTRIA

Emanuel Ungaro

A heavy woolen cloth fabric, very soft, with a short dense flattened pile. Its especially lustrous surface recalls the fur of the beaver or nutria, an animal that lives in the rivers of South America. For reasons of survival, the fur of this rodent is adapted to its natural habitat, and for this reason is waterproof. The pile on nutria fabric has a dense soft wooly layer, with long and thick hairs, like hog's bristles, which are successively shaved to give them a uniform length in a special production process. Nutria fur is not as highly prized as beaver fur. Nutria fabric, after the pile is trimmed, is given a lustrous finish that highlights the characteristics of the base and enhances its appearance. It is identified with luxury and splendor, worn unostentatiously out of respect for nature. It is particularly suitable for winter jackets, capes and classic coats like the Chesterfield, with buttons along the chest, but also lends itself to the production of more articulated patterns, with a cut and details that emphasize warmth, sheen and softness.

Max Mara

Emanuel Ungaro

French term that indicates a traditional fabric woven in carded or semi-combed wool, with a short, springy, tight and straight pile and a soft look similar to velvet. It differs from velvet in that the hairy surface, dense and opaque, is obtained by shaving the fibers previously raised by napping instead of raising the supplementary warp and weft threads. The pile is steamed and electrified so that it remains straight. Conventionally, the best weaves for producing velour are Batavia for medium-weight cloths and satin for lightweight ones. It is less resistant and not as highly regarded as velvet. Today, the word

Frankie Morello

Carolina Herrera

"velour" is also applied to plush knit, often of cotton or synthetic materials such as polyester. Velour, in medium and semi-heavy weights, has a vast range of applications. Quality wool velour is used to make coats and capes with a shawl collar and hats of various shapes. Cotton and fiber velour is used in garments such as jackets, suits and dresses, as well as in decorative accessories in a broad spectrum of colors.

Guy Laroche

Basso & Brooke

CAMEL HAIR

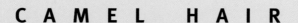

A plain weave or twill weave fabric woven with 100% camel yarn or a blended with wool, weighing between 350 and 550 g/m². The wool used to make the prestigious camel hair products, extracted from the down, a layer of fine wool that protects the epidermis of animals that live in cold climates. This wool is very soft and fine, with excellent thermal qualities, and is between 2.5 and 12.5 cm long; its color ranges from a yellowish gray-brown to sandy brown. The wool is shed naturally during the molting period and is collected in containers arranged along the route of camel caravans. This collection method is carried out in China, Mongolia, the former Soviet Union, Arab countries and Africa. The hair on the surface, of lower quality, can be up to 37.5 cm long, with a diameter between 20 and 120 microns. The more highly prized hairs, which are used to make a soft, lustrous, very warm fabric, come from Asia Minor and the Persian Gulf. It is dyed with neutral and natural dyes in colors that range from beige to reddish or darker brown, and it is carded, fulled and finished with a slightly piled appearance. The same name is used incorrectly to refer to other wool fabrics of general use that

Max Mara

only have in common with camel hair its characteristic beige color. Another use of the term refers to the men's and women's coats with a high percentage of camel hair used for the first time in the 1908 London Olympic Games. This classic design, which became popular in the 1920s, has acquired a timeless quality, adapting time after time, with infallible styles, to different fashion trends. Max Mara transformed camel hear into a signature garment of his creations, exalting it in numerous designs of more or less deconstructed garments, with enveloping or essential lines, in coats or kimonos, in nightwear with a belt or in jackets crossed with a band at the back. In an edition of *Vogue's Fashion's Night Out*, the

Aigner

Gucci

Dries Van Noten

Max Mara

Les Hommes

Max Mara

Max Mara

Tommy Hilfiger

company dedicated a photography session to these garments that depicted in all the brands's boutiques the publicity campaigns that have made it internationally famous. In the same store, a collection entitled "Max Mara The Icon" was subsequently launched, characterized precisely by the color camel.

PLAID

Chloé

Dior

Missoni

Julien Macdonald

Plaid fabric is made from heavy low-twist carded wool or expensive cashmere fiber. It is soft and particularly warm, fulled and then napped. Some plaids have warp threads of twisted cotton. It can be plain or have a novelty pattern, with a tartan or Scotch check motif. The fabric apparently comes from a garment worn by inhabitants of the Scottish mountains, where they used a large rectangle of checked wool tied to the waist with a belt to protect themselves from the harsh winters. The term "plaid" also alludes to a warm, soft blanket, of varying size, with brightly colored checks and fringes along the edges, commonly used in the United States (and today everywhere) for picnics or as shawls on trips and excursions. The types of plaid are infinite given that – while faithful to the original design – the materials are renewed with different percentages of cotton, polyester, fleece, acrylic or wool, all of which guarantee good protection against the cold and, in addition, are more resistant to washes. Plaid is suggestive of intimacy and comfort and has been one of the preferred fabrics of North American designer Ralph Lauren, a passionate cultivator of his American roots, who often presents updated designs in country-style garments such as jackets, ponchos, capes and Canada jackets with fringes at the ends, the same as on a plaid blanket.

MOLESKIN

A dense, lustrous material with an appearance similar to a heavy fur fabric. The pile on the front is very long and imitates the hair of a monkey; the reverse side is printed and napped. Traditionally, it was woven with a cotton-fiber warp and weft, but it can also be of wool or woolen blend. It is produced in a way similar to plain velvet, with a weave based on 8-Harness satin, weft effect and very tightly woven. Two wefts are inserted on the front and one on the back to create a floating effect on one side of the fabric only. In the finishing stage it is shaven and sheared. Moleskin is a fabric similar to beaverteen, though heavier. Moleskins were notepads made in France in the previous century that became famous because they were used by artists and writers such as Ernest Hemingway, Bruce Chatwin and Pablo Picasso for taking notes and making sketches. The cover was bound in varnished cotton fabric in imitation leather (i.e., moleskin). The fabric has been known since 1830 and was used in capes, coats and winter work clothes. Today, it is used in capes and coats. It lends itself to the production of the British warmer, a sporty version of the men's polo coat, and also for the classic ¾ jacket, used as a driving coat in order not to encumber the driver's movements.

Alberta Ferretti

Alberta Ferretti

Alberta Ferretti

Charlotte Ronson

CASENTINO

Louis Vuitton

Les Copains

Bottega Veneta

Marc by Marc Jacobs

A highly regarded fabric of fulled and carded wool, produced with a specific technique already documented in the Etruscan and Romen period in the region of Casentino, in the high valley of the Arno River (Tuscany). It is characterized by a distinctive piled surface, grouped in soft relief crimps obtained through medium-length hair, exposed to pressure and rubbing in a series of mechanical finishes such as carding and ratiné. The crimps constitute a double layer that grants the fabric properties of resistance to the cold and rain. Apparently, in the past the irregular appearance of casentino cloth, according to the specific rules contained in a compendium of governmental laws, was achieved by rubbing the wool with stones to produce a crimped pile. Casentino cloth, a material especially resistant to use, owes its success to the blankets, used to cover draft animals, produced in Lanificio di Stia in the last decade of 20th century and recycled by coachmen for making their own clothes. It received a definitive touch of elegance and refinement in the hands of such composers as Giuseppe Verdi and Giacomo Puccini or illustrious figures such as Baron Bettino Ricasoli, who was fond of wearing double-breasted Casetino cloth suits with a band at the back, completed with fox-fur collars. This type of clothing, ideal for hunting and horseback rising, also won over women, who used it in an unprecedented orange-red color, discovered coincidentally due to an error involving the corrosion of the alum applied to dye with chemical coloring. Over time, designers fell in love with this unique fabric, beautiful and expensive, that recurs cyclically in men's and women's fashion and is currently exported to Europe, Japan and the United States. Casentino *originale*, with its characteristic red color and orange and green tones, was very much in vogue in tailoring in the seventies. Today, many other colors have been added (the entire range from blue and beige to ice-white), chosen for ready-to-wear garments by such fashion designers as Roberto Cavalli, Pierre Cardin and Gianfranco Ferre. It is very frequently used to make brightly colored women's coats and jackets. "La Valle dei Tessuit" was created to spotlight the local textile craft trade. Held in the town of Soci, the periodical event presents an attractive showroom with samples and shows featuring the work of young Italian designers. The event is in conjunction with a national competition reserved for students and creators of fashion, clothing and design.

16

FABRICS WITH SPECIAL STRUCTURES

MESH FABRIC

A transparent fabric woven on special jacquard or raschel looms, with a gridded surface composed of small cells obtained by a series of very fine warp threads spread apart from each other (straight threads) surrounded by another series of sinuous threads arranged obliquely in relation to the first ones (curved threads). The cells can be round, square, diamond, hexagonal, orthogonal, etc. Among the meshes are bobbinet (a hexagonal mesh fabric of low or medium weight), tulle (small hexagonal mesh) and *malinas* (very fine diamond mesh made in the Belgian city of the same name). In old manufactures the mesh was accompanied by sprangs, special tense threads added to the warp, divided between even and uneven ones, and crossed by a series of wooden rods that facilitated twisting. The Egyptians and Peruvians used this technique to make sprang hats, bags and snoods. Today, mesh fabric is similar to leno fabric, obtained through inserting leno yarns into the opposing mesh with a special arrangement of the loom. The result is an openwork fabric that allows light to enter, with a loosely woven but stable and resistant texture. Mesh fabric can be used to make a series of ornamental cloths in pieces or flanges that include beads of glass, plastic, rods, tacks and sequins of varying thickness and generally separated from each other on the thread. Other openwork mesh fabrics are made using a laser-cut technique, although on a laminated or resin-coated base or with a suede effect. Mesh fabrics are used as clothing and decorative accessories, though they require special care in sewing, with reinforcements in the most tensile stitches.

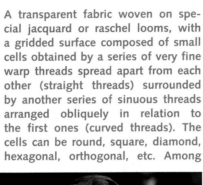

Jean Paul Gaultier

Alexander McQueen

Chanel

Burberry Prorsum

Ashish

Calvin Klein

Chanel

Jean Paul Gaultier

Dolce & Gabbana

Hervé Léger

Balenciaga

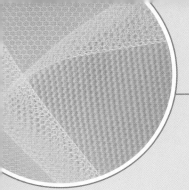

T U L L E

Dsquared2

Luisa Beccaria

Point de tulle, extremely fashionable in the court of Louis XVI, was a type of weft-knit fabric consisting of simple or double threads that formed a regular grid of fine but solid threads later embroidered with delicate floral motifs. Tulle makers from the French village of Tulle, where the annual Festival Internazionale del merletto di Tulle is still held, did this work by hand. Mechanical tulle, also called bobbinet tulle, appeared in England on the heels of the invention of the bobbinet, a modified loom for stockings, operated manually, that used bobbins to contain the weft threads, patented in Nottingham in 1809 by J. Heathcoat, who hailed from Tiverton, in the region of Devon. Tulle was made with fine twisted cotton and in reduced formats that quickly increased from 7-8 cm to 135 cm long. Both the mechanical pieces of the looms and the expensive threads were the object of contraband between French and England, until the fabric was produced industrially as a background for point lace and bobbins. Today, it is also made from viscose rayon or nylon to lower the cost. Tulle can be made in layers to give it rigidity, consistency and volume or can be used as a bridal veil, in which case it is called *tulle illusion*, from the French. It is semi-transparent when lit from the inside and opaque when hit with direct light. Among the varieties of tulle are plain and uniform fabrics with only a base twist and point d'esprit-style fabrics, with thick polka dots spread throughout the surface. There are tulles with vertical stripes, obtained from different weaves, and patterned tulle, in which mesh fabrics and different tones define a decorative motif. There is also elastic tulle, made with fibers more suitable for contouring the body. Tulle is used in many sectors, from fashion to decoration, from lace curtains to floral adornments and cloths, from theatrical scenery to ballet tutus and clothes for the theater. While common in white and black, it is also made in colors and with printed floral patterns. Rigid nylon tulle, which *opens up* and is coarser to the touch, is used to make petticoats, ribbons, headwear and veils for hats. Softer tulle is used to produce ruffles, piping and applications for elegant dresses, as well as veils and trimming for wedding gowns.

Luisa Beccaria

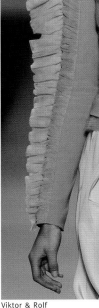

Viktor & Rolf

Stéphane Rolland

Dior

Jean Paul Gaultier

Viktor & Rolf

Alexander McQueen

Agatha Ruiz de la Prada

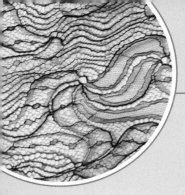

LACE

Emilio Pucci

Elie Saab

Lightweight, transparent fabric enhanced with decorative floral or geometric motifs on a mesh base and defined by the alternation of fillings and empty spaces. Lace can include woven structures, boucle (twisted or knotted) and is made with threads of all fibers, both natural ones – linen, cotton, silk, wool, hemp and raffia – and gold, silver and copper threads, as well as synthetic materials such as nylon or polyester. Mechanical lace is produced rapidly and precisely and represents the modern evolution of old needlework and bobbins work methods. It is a fabric that does not have a true thread orientation and can be made in pieces or with a limited length, using the entredeux technique or embroidered with arches in the margins. The first loom for weaving lace was based on manual bobbin lace and was invented in 1814 by J. Leavers, who perfected the bobbin loom to enable the production of novelty tulles. In 1883 power looms for weaving lace emerged thanks to the adaptation of the mechanism to a jacquard-like machine for patterned fabrics. With this system, in place for many years, it was possible to produce a long series of backgrounds and stitches with soft floating threads on the surface and many decorative effects with motifs in relief. The quality of the design permits arrangements with a high pattern repeat, with a large number of threads and constantly maintaining their tension, always in accordance with the quality of the material used. Because of their particular fineness, Leaver loom laces were the most used, even when these machines, which are no longer manufactured, were replaced in the 1950s by more up-to-date jacquard looms for weaving lace, offshoots of the raschel loom, jacquard tronic, textronic and supertextronic machines, in which the fabric was made with needle point, which produces an initially coarser lace with a more uniform background. The exquisiteness of ornamental lace is determined by the number of stitches, expressed through an encryption system, while the digitalization of the designs with the help of a computer allows for directly linking the project to the electronic management of the machines. These machines can reproduce the designs with significant precision on a sharp crotchet background, with an alveolar appearance (similar to tulle) and with a marked relief effect, with jagged lace edging like little teeth, with the difference that textronic lace is more solid and full to the touch, while supertextronic lace has richer motifs on the background and a softer feel. The expression Chantilly lace refers to a light, soft and transparent lace, very delicate and expensive, which takes it name from the eponymous French city. A sophisticated advance in the dyeing sector allows for applying to lace made from blended fibers different colors that permit obtaining, in the finishing stage, variegated and blurred effects in chiaroscuro to meet specific demands of fashion or for adapting them to diverse uses, which run from elegant clothes to adornments for decoration, net curtains, etc. Wool lace makes use at times of technologies usually associated with knitting with warp and weft threads chain-stitched together. In corsetry and intimate apparel, elastic lace, which requires preforming to obtain the desired dimensional stability, is more commonly used.

Alberta Ferretti

Dolce & Gabbana

Valentino

Alexander McQueen

Lanvin

Givenchy

Devi Kroell

Angelo Marani

NEEDLE LACE

Dolce & Gabbana

Dolce & Gabbana

Wunderkind

Ralph Lauren

Alberta Ferretti

Synonymous with lace edging, needle lace refers to work with crenellations and profiles or with triangular stitches. The old name *trine ad ago* refers to a kind of Italian craftwork produced in the early 16th century and also called *reticella* (mesh work), in which a series of geometric forms with square subdivisions are grouped together. These forms are made with thin highly twisted thread, initially of linen and later also cotton (bright piping), without using any tool other than needles. Its production requires a copy on carbon paper that reproduces the design to be replicated with specification of the outlines, motifs and linking points. The traced design is glued to rigid cardboard, perforated with small orifices separated by two millimeters, along the length of which the structure is built, which is filled in succession with festoon threads or looser ones, according to the desired effect. When the lace is finished, the template is eliminated. Old manuals devoted to female tasks provided a series of reference designs and recommended certain tricks for their correct execution. Among the varieties of needle lace is Punto in Aria (literally "point in air"), work created without fabric backing with

which skillful Venetian weavers p[roduced] figurative motifs, adornme[nt] of branches, leaves and flow[ers] known as Venetian lace. These sp[len]did creations gave rise to a genu[ine] "lace war" when in 1665, Minis[ter] Colbert decided to strengthen Fre[nch] industry through the import of spe[cia]lized textile workers. By introduc[ing] the Italian needle technique and [the] Flanders bobbin technique (carr[ied] out with pins and wooden rods), [he] founded the tradition of preci[ous] French lace. French lace knit, wh[ich] has a small mesh background, a[lso] emerged, using Alencon (Norman[dy] Argentan and Sedan knit to domin[ate] a market directed at the nobles of the courts of Europe. Starting in [the] 1930s, Salvatore Ferragamo used [a] polyester version of Tavernelle nee[dle] lace in some sandal designs. Nee[dle] lace is now used in haute coutu[re] which employs today, as in the pa[st,] the most sophisticated techniques [to] embellish proposals intended for [an] exclusive and elite public.

Vivienne Westwood Red Label

Burberry Prorsum

Anna Sui

Filet is an openwork fabric woven on special looms that imitates the traditional craftsmanship of filet lace. Filet lace consisted of loose threads knotted through the use of the *modano*, a long needle with two eyes, similar to the one that fishermen use. An embroidery needle was then used on this mesh, producing filling areas with knit work, darning stitch and *punto spirito* stitch. The result was an open-weave fabric used to embellish the white garments of the upper classes. To produce these decorations many design albums were created that contributed to spreading the iconographic repertoire. According to popular legend, filet arose out of the attempt to reproduce a thread version of "siren lace", that is, *Halimeda opuntia*, a rare form of algae that a sailor once gave to his beloved. Filet technique, common in many regions in Italy for the production of ribbons and decorative insertions in the garments of bridal trousseaus, acquires a specific identity in Tuscany, Umbria, Sicily and Sardinia, in varieties differentiated by the selection of mesh filling colors and motifs. Local traditions survive thanks to the establishment of various embroidery schools. Filet technique has deep roots in Venice, where Michelangelo Jesurum, director of a lace manufacturing company and official supplier of the Italian royal house, founded the "La scuola delle reti ricamate" (School of Embroidered Redes) and, in 1904, reached an agreement with the association Santa Caterina Sisters of Charity. Filet fabric is produced industrially nowadays, in pieces and in ribbons of different widths. It is used in intimate apparel, in an elastic version for one-pieces, corsetry, in borders with typical jagged margins that reproduce traditional designs as well as in the production of shirts, skirts, shawls and footwear. In decoration it is most frequently found in curtains woven with very fine threads.

3.1 Phillip Lim

Stella McCartney

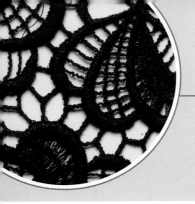

MACRAMÉ

Macramé is a knotted fabric of oriental origin woven with highly resistant opaque cotton yarn. The name comes from the fusion of two Arabic words, *mahrana* (border) and *rame* (knot), and alludes to the ornaments that sailors created on board ships interweaving and knotting by hand a series a vertical threads during long sea voyages. There are several variations of this type of work, obtained from a flat knot (half double knot, simple knot, Josephine knot, etc.) to form a heavy lace with geometric motifs finished with double borders. Also included in macramé is *escubidú*, a type of knot work typical in the Ligurian variety of Cavandoli macramé. Macramé technique, common among all communities in the Mediterranean region, with frequent and continuous varieties for cultural and commercial reasons, was developed in the 16th and 17th centuries, especially in the domestic sphere. Used as a finish for cuffs and shirt fronts in shirts with a square collar, macramè was not included in refined fashion adornments because of the excessive thickness of the knots, which prevented collecting delicate gathered material. Substituting coarse yarn with fine linen threads, macramé became a valuable lace in the interior of monasteries, while Liguria women, great specialists in its application, used it to form piping in towels. In old Genoese the term refers indiscriminately to the towel and the knotting technique. To basic knots were added others such as *ascaria* (soldier), *nexma* (star), *Musta-*

fa, Miriam and *Fatima*, which maintain the three-dimensional origin and have a common oriental source. Currently, the word "macramé" is used generically in fashion to indicate lace with borders in pronounced relief, with a refined look similar to old Venetian knit lace, not only of interwoven knots but also with devoré motifs. It is also called chemical guipur lace, since it recalls the Arab guipur technique, a lace that consists of series of interwoven motifs in relief woven with silk threads and precious metals joined with threads and bars. Like lace, it is produced mechanically, with cotton, wool, silk or laminated yarns, alternating fillings and spaces on a fabric space that is later eliminated through chemical procedures or trimming. It is used as a decorative element, in borders and insertions, accompanied at times by fringes. Fashion designer Miuccia Prada included macramé in recent collections, updating its somewhat stale image.

Gucci

Barbara Bui

Jean Paul Gaultier

Alberta Ferretti

Prada

Dolce & Gabbana

BRAIDED FABRIC

Alena Akhmadullina

Philipp Plein

through, was used to make braided fabric. The threads, which were twisted in directions more than a quarter turn in relation to the board, were interspersed with weft insertions that ended up being invisible when the weaving was completed. This system was also used to make the selvages of fabrics and striped borders of cloaks proudly worn by Germanic peoples, garments, according to Tacitus, very much admired by the Romens.

Kenzo

Braided fabric is an extendible and ductile fabric in which the material is arranged in braids. Braided material refers to almost any production that includes a diagonal intersection obtained with various series of warp thread moved obliquely. Its structure, flat or tubular, allows for producing relatively flat fabrics with strong transversal elasticity. It is used to refine edges, in the production of piping and passementerie, and in shoelaces. Made from raffia, reed, maize leaves or straw fibers, the structure of braids is one of the oldest on the face of the earth. One type is the simple rounded three-strand braid, also frequently used in hairstyles. Its interior can have filler with a core, as in the case of certain shoelaces and candlewicks. A second type, with more strands and more elements to interweave, comes

in the form of flat straps and has richer decorative motifs. Basket weave (diagonal, openwork, spiral, serpentine, with converging crosses in the center or like a fish bone, etc.) is a version that is mentioned according to the type of design obtained through superimpositions and intersections. It is used to make a wide variety objects, such as rugs, carpets, tapestries, pillows, baskets and domestic utensils, sewing the braided strips together. Braid is common in bags, hats, belts and vegetable fiber footwear. At times, a braid structure is used to make lateral edges that pass through buttonholes in the form of small crossed arches, braids or at parallel borders. In the past a small rudimentary loom, with a system of small square boards, perforated at four angles to pass four warp threads

Byblos

Y3

PLUSH

Isaac Mizrahi

Custo Barcelona

Betsey Johnson

Plush fabric is a material with a soft, light pile and thermal insulation properties that substitute those of natural hair, the aesthetic appearance of which it imitates. It is made from cotton mixed with acrylic or polyester (short polyacrylonitrile fiber); the fabric is orthogonal or knit and can be dyed a solid color or feature novelty motifs in a simple production process similar to velvet. The pile can have different qualities and lengths: flat, lustrous, curly, crimped, opaque, wooly, frise, stained, blurred and shaved. The production stages of the fabric are: thermofixation, which gives stability to the fabric by bending it toward the interior vertically; brushing the pile and cutting it to the desired length; electrification, which raises the pile and gives it sheen; application of wet chemical additives, according to the type of pile; and finally, ratine finishing treatment, calendaring or embossing with cylinders in relief to imitate the natural crimp of the fur. When the pile is inflated and voluminous, the fabric is also called "teddy bear plush". Often it is arranged in the opposite direction of the combing to facilitate its maintenance. Knit plush is produced on machines for knitting weft fabrics by feeding the needles with locks of fiber that join at the stitch and form the pile, which is then patterned with a plush effect. The knit base of the back of the finished product is reinforced with latex treatment. The color of plush is also important: it can adopt the natural tints of the animal

Custo Barcelona

Custo Barcelona

hair or be dyed bright lively colors to adapt better to the original dye of the fabric, with which it tends to be in harmony. Initially used in toys and teddy bears, plush has gained widespread use in fashion on account of the ecological conscientiousness of young people. It is also used in the decorative elements of clothes: collars, cuffs, sleeves, stoles and vests as well as in internal linings of raincoats and jackets and a wide range of sportswear. Plush is also used in the production of accessories such as hats, bags and parts of winter footwear.

Matthew Williamson   Mariella Burani

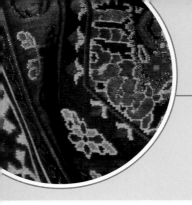

Ralph Lauren

The word "kilim" means "flat-woven carpet", that is, without knotted tufts. It is a special weaving technique performed on vertical looms with fine cotton or linen warp threads dyed a neutral color and a multicolor wool weft. It is an ethnic product, around since ancient times in very distinct cultures, including the Christian Copts of Egypt, the Indians of the North American prairies and the Incas of Peru. The technique is widespread, known in Turkey, Iran, Afghanistan, Ukraine, the Caucasus, Syria, Serbia, Romenia, Poland and Hungary. Kilim fabric emerged as a material intended for the typical floor or wall tapestries in the tents of nomadic peoples such as the yoruk (nomads) and Kurds of Anatolia, who used sheepskin and goatskin and dyed the wool by hand with vegetable substances obtained from herbs and berries. At the end of the 19th century natural dyes began to be substituted by synthetic coloring agents. Kilim is robust and resistant and lends itself well to the production of the sacks used as

containers for the transport of goods on long caravan journeys through the desert or for making cushions filled with herbs and fleece. The material is also used to make coverings for walls, seats and blankets for animals. In this sense it is a fabric intended to meet the needs of daily survival in familial and tribal environments. Precisely for this reason, the decorative elements involved contain strong symbolic value both in the motifs and colors. The motifs are always geometric and formed horizontally in the weft, with areas of contrasting color and linear or angular forms that intersect. Some kilim fabrics have a *fissure* effect; to others, "contouring" techniques are applied through diagonal interlocking of some wefts, while others are subjected to "oblique weft" operations, which require additional weft threads to create curvilinear motifs. Other warp filler techniques exist, such as soumak, cicim and sili, which use wefts that twist around the threads. Currently, kilim fabric is also produced in non-nomadic communities and large urban workshops, which sometimes act as collection and classification centers for tribal products. In fashion, kilim fabric is used in the construction of bags, footwear, belts and other leather items and especially in ornamental accessories.

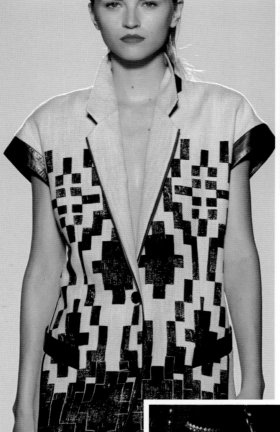

Barbara Bui

Gucci

17

FABRICS MADE FROM SPECIAL MA-
TERIALS

LAMÉ

Lamé is a laminated fabric made from different fibers produced by adding shiny metallic threads to the warp and weft. Currently, the most common lamé contains very fine inexpensive metal sheets or flexible and ductile sheets made of synthetic materials that simulate the effect of gold thread. In the past gold sheets – obtained from gold leafs produced by master *battiloros* (goldbeaters) – were used to embellish the background of patterned velvet liturgical canvases, giving them a sacred air. Another laminated effect, though of mercurial sheen, was obtained with silk threads enwrapped in spiral foils. A third effect was plaster fabric, that is, fabric enhanced by golden lights obtained through sporadic insertions of metallic thread. Lamé fabric owes its success to the idea that the light it reflects also serves as a protective shield against the exterior. In the 1920s, *femmes fatales* such as Louise Brooks and Adele Astair wore enchanting *garçon*-style hats with exotic details and wide lamé borders of gold or silver. Many admirers of Joan Crawford will recall an elegant lamé evening gown designed for her by fashion designer Adrian in 1935, which the actress wore in the movie *Live My Life*. In the late sixties, futuristic fashion, inspired by the space missions, made wide use of silver lamé not only in elegant and very feminine evening gowns, but also in fashion accessories and complements. Lamé can be rigid, soft, knit, patterned, whimsical, double and even coated, in colors that run from warm – Madeira, bronze and brass – to grayish hues such as lead and iron and the shiny satiny effects of steel. As has often been seen on the fashion runways of Thierry Mugler, lamé can assume shades of color that imitate the chrome bodywork of cars or the foil effects of candy wrappers.

Angelo Marani

Chanel

Custo Barcelona

Marc Jacobs

LUREX

Derek Lam

Marc Jacobs

Jonathan Saunders

Max Mara

Angelo Marani

Luella

Lurex is a high-tenacity polyester fiber laminate metallized through aluminum or silver vapors that provide increased sheen to the product, which is later dyed. Lurex®, a brand trademarked in the late 1940s by Dow Badishe Company, is usually woven or knit with a blend of synthetic fibers and rayon, nylon, silk or wool. There are varieties of Lurex that imitate all types of metals, from the most common such as gold and silver to bronze, pewter and copper. Mordorè Lurex, from the French *maure* (Moorish) and *dorè* (gilded), is a warm brown color with suggestive metallic-gold reflections obtained from the skillful use of basic coloring agents (suntan lotion). There are also laminated versions with faint multicolored lights and Lurex with transparent, bright, semi-bright and mother-of-pearl effects. Lurex can be flat, twisted, spiraled, frise and crimped. It is especially resistant in the weft of blue jeans; mixed with Meryl® microfiber, a multifilament with unique visual effects, it is also used in underwear, over the surface of which a shiny evanescent powder is scattered. Together with copper it is used in knit sweaters and special productions in which spots of glue are applied to an acetate fabric base according to a diagram. Later, the surface is atomized with iridescent pile that is fixed only where the glue is. The thread, which is luminous and shiny and suitable for the creation of elegant garments, is also used in decorative sewing on fur articles or as embroidery thread.

MICROFIBER

Microfiber fabric is woven with extremely thin threads of one denier or less. The types of fiber used are polyester, polyamide, polypropylene, acrylic, acetate, elastane and other materials such as viscose. Its main characteristic is the high thread count per square centimeter of fabric, given the miniaturization of the diameter of the fibers, which form a very closely woven grid. It can have an orthogonal structure, woven on a fabric loom or knit. In the case of light fabrics, microfiber threads are most frequently used in the warp and are normally interwoven with a plain weave, which creates a compact surface, though one with good drape. As for heavy fabrics, microfibers are used in the weft. Also considered microfiber fabrics are ones obtained through the blend of cotton or silk fibers with especially fine synthetic fibers. It is light and springy fabric, at times hangs well, is easy to dye, hygienic and extremely comfortable, not to mention being smooth and velvety to the touch. Moreover, it is wrinkle resistant and maintains its original shape. Microfiber is very versatile, lending itself to a variety of finishing operations such as wrinkling and thermochRometic and photosensitive effects that completely alter its appearance and qualities. In terms of performance, microfiber allows for keeping body temperature unchanged due to its anti-wind and high impermeability properties, as well as its good breathability. It is commonly used in eiderdown coverings and sports-style jackets, as well as in

Anna Sui

Bottega Veneta

Etro

Blumarine

technical garments used in extreme sports. It provides comfort in lingerie items, bath wear, knits and stockings, and is suitable for the development of seasonal fashion products. Being an easy-to-care-for material, it also lends itself to the production of fabrics for decoration. Microfiber fabrics are marketed as specific brands such as Tactel, Meryl, Diolen, Leacril, Myoliss, Trevira, Setila and Belseta, to name a few, which guarantee the quality and properties of the products on behalf of the manufacturers. These brands, in turn, are diversified in many varieties. Tactil, for example, is available in Diablo, Micro Touch, Multi Soft, HT, Acquator, Prisma, Metallic, Strata, Duo, Climat and Coloursafe, among others.

POLAR FLEECE

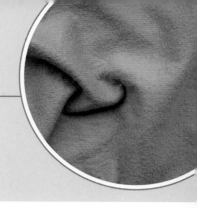

Frankie Morello

Louis Vuitton

Diane Von Furstenberg

JC de Castelbajac

A relatively new ecological fabric, polar fleece is based on an innovative material known as Polartec®, a brand trademarked in 1979 by the American company Malden Mills. It is a synthetic polyester-based fiber obtained from recycled PET (polyethylene terephthalate), a plastic material used in mineral water and soft drink bottles that is fragmented into confetti-sized flakes. For textile applications the PET flakes are transformed into little bundles similar to cotton balls, carded and joined in bunches of thread with which the fabric is woven. In addition to polyester other fibers such as polyamide, acrylic and elastane (spandex) can be added to its composition. Polar fleece, also called "pile", is obtained with a foam treatment on both sides of the material carried out on circular knitting looms. Formed in this way, with a tight and velvety pile, the surface is made voluminous and soft using raising machines. Later, the fabric is sheared, giving a springy and comfortable thermal layer, an exceptional combination of warmth and lightness capable of shielding the body from moisture and keeping the skin dry, thus providing it with insulation and protection. Polar fleece comes in a wide range of weights and styles, from silk weight polar fleece for summer to loft polar fleeces for outdoor activities in intensely cold conditions. The degree of thermal insulation of polar fleece is defined by a number: Polartec 100 for medium-weight sweaters and very light intimate garments; Polartec 200, standard fiber, warm and versatile, used in the production of the majority of commercial garments; Polartec 300, suitable for technical clothing. There is also jacquard polar fleece, a high-quality material that can be made with almost any design at the customer's request. Polar fleece is wrinkle-resistant and doesn't shrink, offers excellent breathability, is economical and easy to care for, drying quickly. Initially only used in sportswear and casual garments, it quickly gained traction in fashion due to its practical advantages, lending lends itself to a wide variety of styles and suitable for vests, pants, hats, capes, jackets, three-quarter-length jackets, windbreakers, jackets for newborns, dresses, skirts, overcoats, etc. The most advanced Polartec® technologies grant the fabric special characteristics. These can be added as parts of the fabric or be applied to already existing materials. Using silver fiber in the production of Polartec® Power Dry® fabrics grants the material permanent resistance to odors. Another production technique, combined with the application of certain polymers on the surface, results in more wind-resistant fabrics that also act as a protective screen against harmful solar radiation. Research has been done on special nylon and elastomer trim to adequately retain the heat generated by polar fleece.

STRETCH

Stretch is a mono-elastic or bi-elastic fiber that can be stretched in the direction of the weft or in both directions and is woven with yarn made up of two or more fibers. Its elasticity is due to the use of core-spun threads, which are combined with non-elastic wool, cashmere, alpaca, silk linen threads as well as blends of these fibers. The best-known commercial brands are Lycra (Invista), Elaspan (Invista), Dorlastan (Asahu), Roica (Asahi), Linel (Fillattice), RadiciSpandex (Radici Group) and Creora (Hyosung). A vast array of shuttle-loom fabrics can be woven with the combinations, including denim, gabardine, satins and velvets, in addition to knit fabrics such as jersey and chenille. Stretch fabric adheres to the body without losing its shape, increases the comfort level of clothes, offers maximum comfort and enhances the drape of garments. While resistant to washes, its maintenance requires specific attention. Created as a material intended mainly for sportswear and leisure attire, it has also adapted to more traditional styles in versions such as Noucentisme

wool-stretch, an elastic fabric used in men's suits that doesn't lose its shape or wrinkle and allows for maximum freedom of movement. Stretch fabric is very frequently used in fashion collections, characterized as a transversal material capable of meeting the demands common to all specific market niches: adaptation to a more dynamic tempo of life. Fashion designer Hervè Léger earned the nickname King of Cling when, in the late 1980s, he created an iconic "bandage" dress with strips of elastic fabric discovered by accident in a textile plant that was going to use them as scraps.

Betsey Johnson

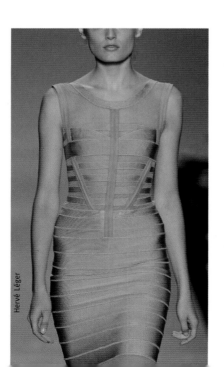

Betsey Johnson

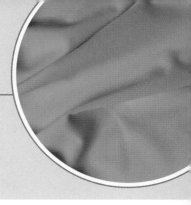

LYCRA

Ann-Sofie Back

Frankie Morello

Fisico

Lycra is a mesh fabric that takes its name from the material used in its production: a continuous segmented polyurethane elastic thread produced by the company DuPont under the trade name Lycra®. It is a synthetic fiber referred to as elastane or spandex. The thread consists of a sequence of circular section rigid multi-filaments in which flexible chains are interspersed that stretch and lengthen when under traction. The thread preserves its flexibility and can be used without coating, simple or double, coated, twisted or interwoven. Lycra is never used in a pure state, but is combined with all other types of fabric in percentages between 14 and 40%, giving rise to very different materials. It can have a shiny, transparent, dull or semi-dull appearance, thus increasing the creative potential of the material. It withstands contact with chlorinated water, and consequently is used in swimwear, corsetry and mesh undergarments. 3D Lycra, produced under rigorous quality standards in selected thread counts between 8 and 22 dtex, is used in the production of stockings and leotards, as it provides the leg with three-dimensional elasticity, broadly oriented in all directions. Lycra is a uniform material. It can be printed with vividly colored patterns in keeping with the latest fashions and produced at relatively moderate costs. This feature makes it one of the preferred materials for the production of women's garments such as dresses, boleros, one-pieces and t-shirts of all kinds. Nude is a 100% Lycra thread that, once woven, becomes totally transparent and has appeared in a Prada Sport collection.

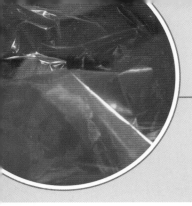

Plastic materials are obtained by polymerization, a process involving the transformation of the polymers obtained from organic compounds (petroleum derivatives). Its most prominent feature is plasticity, the capacity to be printed on or shaped at different temperatures. At the end of the 19th century, plastics were used as imitations of natural materials in the first attempts at celluloid production. In the first decade of the 20th century, Leo Bakeland patented a thermosetting product named *Bakelite* after its inventor. In the thirties and forties industrially manufactured products such as PVD and polyethylene were invented. Since then, plastic has experienced constant and progressive upgrading, to the point of being an autonomous material with enormous aesthetic and functional possibilities. Beginning in the seventies, when research was directed toward polyester, polyamide, polyurethane, polypropylene, and acrylic resin, to name a few, artists, stylists, fashion designers and draftsman witnessed a broadening of the boundaries of their creative activities. Plastic is a fascinating and expressive synthetic product capable of assuming a wide variety of appearances and consistencies in more affordable and durable objects. In the era of technology this chemical combination of polymers appears as a virtual icon transformed into an object of desire with infinite possibilities of change thanks to its ductility and flexibility and its multidimensional functionality and lightness, while at the same time inspiring a vague and poorly hidden sense of creative omnipotence.

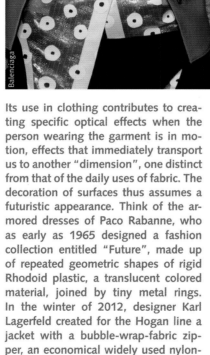

Balenciaga

Jeremy Scott

Chanel

Its use in clothing contributes to creating specific optical effects when the person wearing the garment is in motion, effects that immediately transport us to another "dimension", one distinct from that of the daily uses of fabric. The decoration of surfaces thus assumes a futuristic appearance. Think of the armored dresses of Paco Rabanne, who as early as 1965 designed a fashion collection entitled "Future", made up of repeated geometric shapes of rigid Rhodoid plastic, a translucent colored material, joined by tiny metal rings. In the winter of 2012, designer Karl Lagerfeld created for the Hogan line a jacket with a bubble-wrap-fabric zipper, an economical widely used nylon-based material employed in packaging to provide cushioning, with air balls in relief. The Lagerfeld design was indigo blue, lustrous and three-dimensional. This material lends itself to the projection of an image of fusion, the combination of luxury and urban style. Bubble wrap is available in different varie-

Tumblr

ties according to the size of the balls (small, large or micro) and the thickness of the substrate, between 35 g/m² and 150 g/m². Lightweight bubble wrap can be joined to high-density polyethylene sheets to create a three-layer bubble paper, with bubbles stuffed between two smooth layers (used to make wrappers and bags). Miu Miu has used it in Miu Miu shopping bags. It can be attached to other materials such as paper, cardboard, expanded polyethylene foam, cloth or aluminum, with the aim of adapting it to the user's needs. Bubble wrap can be substituted with undulated expanded polythene (3.5 to 4.5 mm thick), with special micro-cells that prevent the balls from bursting or deflating. Even the expanded, anti-scratch, shock-absorbent versions can be joined to films that grant uniformity to the surface. Sewing plastic requires special care and attention because the needles leave indelible marks in the orifices. Garments made with plastic don't need to be ironed.

NEOPRENE

Neoprene® is the American name for Duprene® synthetic rubber. It is composed of chloroprene or chlorobutadiene copolymers that form foam that solidifies and acquires the desired consistency. The foams are thermoplastic materials that can be shaped and sculpted as one wishes, permit a certain amount of freedom of movement and adapt well to experimental avant-garde designs. Neoprene offers excellent resistance to rusting, ozone and ageing due to heat. It has optimal chemical resistance to salts, bases, diluted acids and seawater and good resistance to oil and hydrocarbons. It is used in diving equipment and hypothermic clothing, very frequently in aquatic sports that involve contact with water for prolonged periods of time. Fashion designers experiment with the neoprene used in scuba diving, exploring its possibilities as a sophisticated textile base made springy and light through a special Japanese treatment. Neoprene was a strong presence in 2012 collections, in brilliant, energetic, anti-financial-crisis colors. Donatella Versace used it in shorts, tunics and tight-fitting tube micro-skirts printed with conch, seahorse and starfish motifs. Blumarine, for its part, redefines the leather windbreaker with its loose neoprene versions, produces tops printed with patterns of tropical flowers and pink and yellow daisies, and offers mirthful lighthearted hats a la *The Paul Street Boys*, one of the great classics of children's literature, written by Hungarian author Ferenc Molnar.

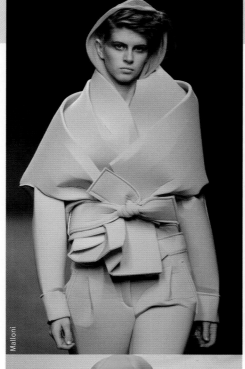

Malloni

Blumarine

Blumarine

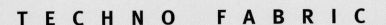

Techno fabrics are composed of very diverse materials that require the use of extremely advanced technologies. They are reflective, breathable, waterproof, high-performance materials with thermoregulation functions that allow the fabric to breathe. Initially, they were intended for applications that required a high resistance to temperatures and/or solvents, protection against UV rays and electRomegnetic waves, and control of static electricity; today, techno fabrics have entered fashion as consumer products. Luminosity is the aesthetic description of the basic concept of a surface that looks toward the future. The illumiNite Matrix process consists in the insertion by friction of millions of microscopic discs inside the fiber of the

Federico Sangalli

Versace

fabric without altering its nature; the discs act as a mirror that reflects light and illuminates the person wearing the treated garment. The process is applied to a wide range of colors and patterns, standard or personalized, on Cordura Nylon, spandex, nylon, polyester and cotton bases. Clothing and accessories produced in this way, which can even be washed in washing machines using certain accessories, remain permanently reflective, by combining the visibility and perception of the observer when determining the position and direction of movement with the identification of the entire silhouette of the person in darkness. Luminex® fabric, available in red, yellow, green, blue and white, or in intermediate tones created by

Sinha Stanic

Vivienne Westwood

the combination of the five just mentioned colors, produces light through an LED lighting system connected to rechargeable batteries. Other luminous effects are achieved through the use of new Angelina® Copper Fiber, a very fine fiber, particularly soft to the touch, that can also be combined in small percentages with cashmere, mohair, cotton or rayon to obtain metallic reflections, opalescent with composite lights, high-refraction holograms or electric colors. These fibers are used to make sparkling yarns employed in fabrics and embroideries and have been discovered to have a therapeutic effect when combined with human sweat. In fact, copper in contact with salicylic acid produces dimethyl sulfoxide (DSMO), a solvent with anti-inflammatory qualities.

GORE-TEX

Dsquared2

Y3

Byblos

Neil Barrett

Gore-Tex® fabric contains a micro-porous "gore" membrane invented in 1969 by North American W.L. Gore, a composite of carbon and fluoride molecules, 25 microns thick, that makes the material completely air- and water-resistant yet highly breathable. Its impermeability is not affected by drastic temperature shifts and it is immune to chemical agents and remains stable and unchanged over time. The membrane looks like a white translucent film and comes in different forms: sheet, that is, solidly adhered to an exterior fabric; Z-liner, or inserted independently between the exterior fabric and a lining; Gore-Tex Thermo Dry, laminated on a filling; Action, or glued to the lining by a layer of polyurethane foam. Fabric treated in this way is added to garments that require a high-degree of protection against atmospheric agents. To maintain these characteristics, sewing isn't done with needles, but is thermobonded. All Gore-Tex clothing is identified by its brand, which guarantees its authenticity and high quality. Gore-Tex is available in Top Dry, which permits attaching it with adhesives to other synthetic fabrics or leathers. This variety is used in the accessories sector to make gloves, hats and footwear. It is a technological fabric that adapts very well to the stressful demands of modern life; it is easy to care for, as it can be both machine-washed at 104 degrees Farenheit and dry-cleaned with ferric chloride.

18

EMBROIDERED FABRICS

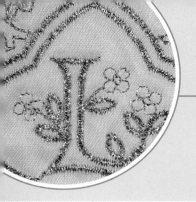

THREAD EMBROIDERY

Alexander McQueen

Dolce & Gabbana

Thread embroidery is characteristic of a fabric decorated with stitches in relief that uses multicolor threads against a pre-existing background. It is different from craft embroidery, produced with needles, and mechanical embroidery, obtained with the help of machines. In the first case, the cloth is stretched across a wooden loom, after the design to be reproduced has been copied, leaving the hands of the embroiderer totally free. In the Middle Ages artists designed professional embroidery to embellish important wardrobe garments or decorations, and specialized artisans were commissioned to produce it. Full and short stitch, often made from silk, with tight stitching that covered the entire cloth, was considered a veritable form of "painting with needles". Considered an applied art, hand embroidery, like many other artistic disciplines, was taught to adolescents in oratories and religious schools. Some stitches, such as chain stitch and flat or grass stitch, were already being practiced in the most remote antiquity, and the techniques have survived practically unchanged. Others were added later to create products of extraordinary beauty that combined fantasy and ingeniousness, materials and forms. In ethnic cultures embroidery is almost always produced traditionally, according to designs, colors and precise arrangements passed on from generation to generation, although the decorative motifs have undergone various modifications over time. The Chinese were known for Peking em-

Max Mara

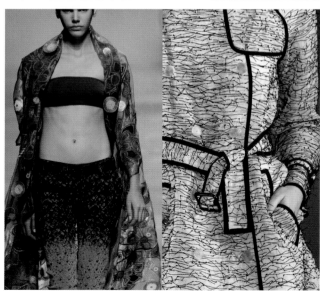

Issey Miyake

Phillip Lim

Jean Paul Gaultier

Christopher Kane

broidery, a special double-knot stitch with prominent relief, while the counted thread silk embroidery that adorned the shirts of noble courtiers in the 16th century was given the name "Holbein knit", after the artist that often painted portraits of the people who wore garments featuring it. Since the advent of the sewing machine in 1865, the company Cornely et Bonnaz patented machines with which they could produce semi-mechanical embroidery and execute elongated, satin, chain, moss and braided stitch tasks quicker than by hand. Today, all kinds of embroidery can be produced with 12-, 24- or 48-magnetic-head machines that work simultaneously with electronically controlled needles that each traces a motif. With these machines, suitable for mass production, it is possible to embroider an entire piece of fabric or transfer specific embroideries to it, omitting the design stage often carried out with CAD programs. This system is also used to produce embroidered monograms such as "CC" (Chanel), "GG" (Gucci) and "LV" (Loius Vitton), emblems used as logos of the brands.

Frankie Morello

Emilio Pucci

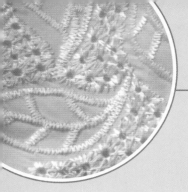

Valentino

This fabric is very similar to organza, though finer and less rigid, embroidered with small discreet repeating motifs. It is known as English or Sangallo embroidery, though in reality it is linen, cotton, wool or artificial fiber fabric that serves as a support for machine embroideries spread throughout its surface. Its distinctive feature lies in how it's made, alternating full stitch parts that delineate the decorative motif and other parts with openwork in the cloth. Its production imitates the white *English embroidery* that was made on muslins from India and used in white garments in the 18th century. An intensely naive and Romentic taste has survived from that period, one characterized by tiny flower buds, stylized daisies, star-shaped motifs, etc. A very similar type of embroidery is produced on the island of Madeira. The fabric takes its name from the Swiss city of San Gallo, where the first factories that engaged in industrial production on machines with several magnetic heads appeared. It is produced in various sizes, suitable for festoons and decorative trim. It is also used in white and pastel hues in undergarments, summer clothes and children's wear. In recent years, it has been updated by fashion designers (e.g., Yohji Yamamoto) who have used Sangallo openwork fabrics with linear and geometric motifs, both in white and less traditional tones such as black, blue and brown.

Erdem

Stella McCartney

Roberto Cavalli

Mariella Burani

Tommy Hilfiger

Luisa Beccaria

Blugirl

SMOCK STITCH

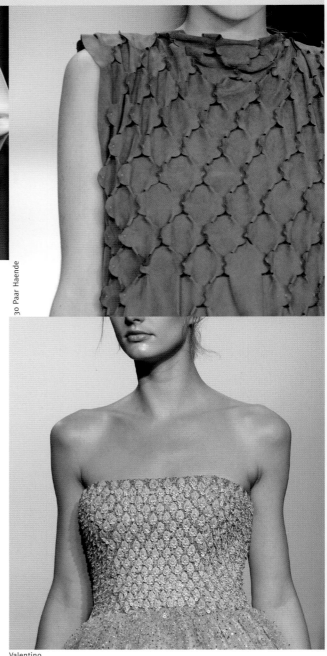

Valentino

Valentino

3o Paar Haende

The term "smock dress" literally means "loose shirt dress" and refers to garments with wide curls collected in even ribs and well-distributed pleats, made with simple chain-stitch or crimped knit yarns, or with more elaborate stitches such as diamond and Van Dyke. This type of work was very common in Northern European countries, in the Russo-Hungarian area, starting in 1600, in common shirt collars and cuffs. In England and Wales it was the most common adornment in the wardrobe of peasants in the 17th and 18th centuries. The technique allows for gathering between the pleats a width equal to three times the final breadth of the garment, alternating embroidery stitches with different tensions with the aim of obtaining different degrees of crimp. Smock stitch embroidery is found in springy collars in the form of a corolla that descends insouciantly down the shoulders with suggestive undulations on both sides, as well as in Romentic versions with puff slee-

ves or in tight-fitting bodices that harmonize well with the broad volumes of pleated fabric that hang loosely downwards. In vogue the fifties was children's clothing with a camisole, shirt front and smock stitch knit embroidery in parallel pleats or small honeycomb lozenges, worn by children from "good families" as a sign of membership in the bourgeoisie. Its production, long and complex, was substituted by regular strips obtained by machine sewing with elastic thread, used above all in industrially manufactured products. Smock stitch technique survives in the meticulous production of exclusive haute couture garments fashioned by expert hands in the realm of flawless embroidery. It is a favorite of fashion designers Maurizio Galante, Valentino Nina Ricci and Christian Lacroix, as well as the brand Miu Miu, which recently presented a collection with smock stitch embroidery on skirts and blouses.

Valentino

Mariella Burani

Mariella Burani

Openwork lace or counted thread embroidery plays with the transparency of areas in which several contiguous weft threads have been removed from the fabric to obtain an exclusively warp border in which multiple threads are then regrouped in clusters and finished with small cross stitches. Openwork is also called *entredieux* because in old bridal trousseaus it served to join two different pieces of fabric by the edges. Openwork technique emerged in different regions of Italy in the 14th century, where it was used to embroider pillow and bed sheets, as can be seen in the fresco by Simone Martini in the lower basilica of St. Francis of Assisi. Openwork is achieved preferably with fabrics of markedly wide and homogenous texture, such as linen cloth, which makes counting the threads easier. The junction points can be simple or multiple openwork weaves, combined with the use of square stitch, hemstitch and diagonal stitch to make fringes and flanges of various widths in horizontal lines. The embroiderer decides on the arrangement of the sequence of motifs in the loom. Always visible behind openwork are more or less extensive spaces in the fabric base. Among the most costly old white products are the beautiful "Sicilian yarns". Some more sophisticated versions were multicolor silk or fine metallic thread openwork that adorned works in ancient Egypt and Peru. More recent ones come from Eastern Europe. Haute couture has transformed splendid starched linen borders into veritable works of art with the use of openwork on square- and V-neck collars, cuffs and ribbed skirts. Gianfranco Ferrè, who reinterpreted openwork in contemporary versions by increasing its dimensions and turning it into an element of exploration in his historic and austere white shirts, was a big proponent of openwork.

Mariella Burani

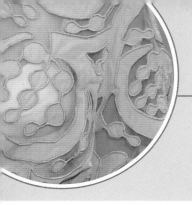

LACE EMBROIDERY

In Italian, lace technique is called *intagliatela*, as it recalls the carving or inlay work used in the decoration of caskets, wedding chests, doors and sacristy cabinets. This type of adornment, which is produced by assembling boards or other materials (marble, bone or mother-of-pearl) of different colors carved into cardboard molds, reached it apogee of refinement between 1440 and 1550. In cloth, it is made by sewing buttonhole stitches (also called festoon stitch) along all the outlines of the design and then trimming certain parts of the fabric to obtain an open-weave effect. The results vary greatly

Franck Sorbier

Vivienne Tam

Stella McCartney

Blumarine

McCartney

Mariella Burani

depending on the balance between fillings and empty spaces that create the play of light and shadow. Despite its delicate appearance lace embroidery is a resistant fabric that acquires relief and underscores outlines. In bridal trousseaus of yore, sets of bed sheets, pillowcases and white linen curtains – with tiny baroque-style openwork – as well as shirtfronts, collars and cuffs with open-weave and shaped borders, were made of lace. Some separable festoon-stitch pieces were used to combine ornamental motifs of lace fabrics. Lace is called "Renaissance" or "Richelieu stitch", depending on whether it has more or less stitching along the juncture strips. The same openwork effect can be achieved combining manual and machine or multi-magnetic head electric machine work, substituting festoon lace with chain-stitch lace, which forms a consistent and thick outline along the lines and prevents the cloth from unraveling after embroidering. The result is very elegant lace that evokes the time of our grandmothers, with openwork arranged in various ways on the bare back or along the neckline. Fashion in the eighties and nineties ritualized this work of sharply drawn outlines using silk satin and even felt and cotton jersey in vibrant fuchsia, blue, yellow and black tones.

GOLD EMBROIDERY

Fabric with gold embroidery denotes luxury and wealth, as evidenced by the clothes worn by the figures in *Adoration of the Magi*, an altarpiece painted by Gentile da Fabriano in 1423. It is of oriental origin. Linen cloths, dense fabrics opulently ornamented with gold, also appear in dowries. In the past gold was employed using the extended thread method (threads arranged on the fabric and attached with silk thread). "Gold thread", thread with a yellow silk core around which a metal sheet was enrolled, was used for this. The nue technique, also called "transparent gold", is the work of Florentine embroiderers, who used it frequently for making ornamental covers with polychrome silk threads that more or less densely covered the extended gold threads, creating areas of shadowed or blurred colors. Another very old technique is that of rolled gold, which is applied in extremely fine strips, which the highly specialized guild of goldbeaters hammered and reduced to thin sheets that were later cut. In gold embroidery today, based predominantly on Indian processes, these ancient techniques survive, although they have been simplified, and gold thread has been replaced with less prestigious and costly metals or ones more flexible and resistant such as yellow silk, silver, copper, frisottine, ganca or polyester film with iridescent reflections. Also, Canutillo gold, made with opaque, shiny or polished tempered metal in conjunction with a wide range of textures, is still used in haute couture embroidery, creating the effect of gold, silver, copper or colored filigree work. It consists in small elements of stiff thread wrapped in a spiral, twisted or curled lamellas cut in sections of the desired size, or round or square pieces applied to the thread like pearls, with flat backgrounds or filling in relief. Canutillo was used in the broderies d'apparatement of courtly dresses and decorations, guild uniforms and the velvet curtains of thrones and canopies.

Alexander McQueen

Alexander McQueen

Kenzo

Dries Van Noten

Alexander McQueen

Emilio Pucci

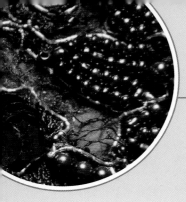

REBRODE LACE

Mariella Burani

Rebrode is a fabric with a specific production process consisting of back embroidery in relief. The technique, of French origin, is used in Parisian haute couture and is a specialty in the region of Nord-Pas de Calais, famous in the 18th century for its prestigious production of cotton mechanical tulle. The quality of rebrode fabric depends most importantly on the background material on which it is produced, normally silk or cotton lace, although synthetic as well. Rebrode can also be obtained from novelty fabrics such as previously adorned organza or tulle and from heavier fabrics such as velvet or from patterned fabrics. The embroidery work underscores the details of the design, which are placed in relief with the help of small pearls, pebbles or sequins, silk thread, raffia, ribbon, chain stitch, edging, viscose strips, etc. Rebrode fabric often outlines the border of white bridal veils and the sleeves and necklines of elegant sophisticated dresses, while its plethora of adornments contributes to creating an image of extreme luxury and wealth.

Mariella Burani

Emilio Pucci

Barbara Bui

Erdem

Dolce & Gabbana

BEADING, JAIS, QUILL

Ralph Lauren

Dolce & Gabbana.

Valentino

Barbara Bui

To produce spectacular embroidery one can use beads, small glass spheres – flat, round or in the form of teardrops – and oblong, cylindrical and faceted glass beads, which reflect opaque or iridescent light in a multitude of tones. Beadwork can be arranged in a row to accompany silk embroidery, highlighting areas or details, or can form the content of an entire motif. The sizes and weight of these elements should be adapted to the consistency of the fabric onto which they are sewn. Bohemia beads are from the Czech Republic while labeled ones such as Rocaille TAI beads are occasionally of Chinese or Indian origin. Beads from the island of Murano, known as Venetian beads, occasionally contain a fine gold powder and are highly prized throughout the world for the quality of their brightness. The material is inserted with very thin needles or using a crochet, a small hook-shaped tool used in Lunèville embroidery on tulle. This embroidery technique, at one time the specialty of the French village of Lunèville, requires great technical skill and a high degree of expertise. In the Victorian Era beads were immensely popular, arranged in graceful flo-ral compositions on silk bags, ladies' slippers, belts and other accessories. French designers, from Poiret to Ertè and Vionnet, covered their dresses with brilliant glass beads, even arranged in stripes, on designs widely worn in dance halls that fueled the dreams of women the world over. Interwoven beads of vitreous paste are used to make clothing elements (shirtfronts, skirts, loincloths, trouser legs and hairbands) in some African tribes. Among North American Indian tribes, embroidery with beads was a skill highly valued in young women. Bird of Paradise embroidery consists of shiny faceted black beads that became fashionable in Victorian England when the mourning of the queen extended to the use of dark clothing among women of the aristocracy and bourgeoisie. The material is extracted from different lignitos, derived from brown coal, and is hard, compact, bright black and very light. For this reason it is used in embroidery on luxury garments.

SEQUINS

Jean Paul Gaultier

Karl Lagerfeld

Givenchy

Sequined fabric is a material embroidered by hand or with a machine containing sequins of different colors that can be used to cover the background entirely or appear only in certain areas of the embroidery. The sequins are cut from fine polyester or cellulose-derived acetate sheets and appear as small shiny reflective plastic discs of various colors and diameters, flat and with a hole in the center. They can be transparent, iridescent, metallized or glossy, with curved forms that are more or less convex, couvette, bell-shaped instead of flat, with facets or more linear and geometric. All are sold either pre-threaded (in lines of up to 100 units) or loose in packets and with one or two holes. There are also thread bobbins that include spaced sequins, suitable for knit garments. The same material is used to embroider sequin motifs on haute couture articles and also on accessories, small costume jewelry, little boxes, etc. Sequins are applied semi-mechanically with old Cornely machines or more modern equipment that braids them with a very fine acetate strip, sewing them simultaneously to the fabric support. In the past sequins were called *lustrini* in Italian, as they add luster and splendor to the person who wears them, with evident decorative effects, whether made of precious metals, steel or rigid PVC, on their own or combined with beadwork or multicolor silk thread, studs, etc. Sequins have been present, with ups and downs, over the course of four centuries in the history of clothing and are used on evening gowns and elegant accessories produced by large fashion companies. Garments adorned with sequined fabrics require careful maintenance, especially in the case of metal sequins, although polyester sequins, washable at 860 degrees Fahrenheit in a washing machine and suitable for bathing wear and beach attire, are also available.

Alberta Ferretti

Manish Arora

Emilio Pucci

Bill Blass

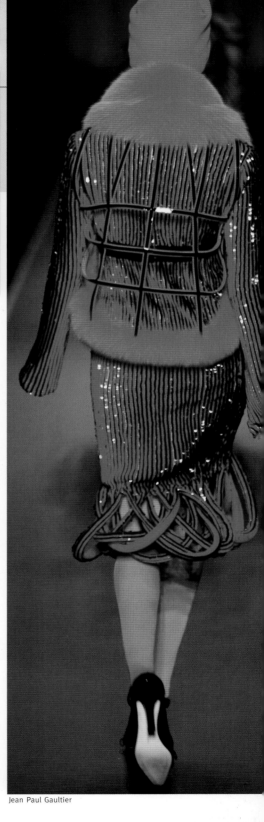

Jean Paul Gaultier

243

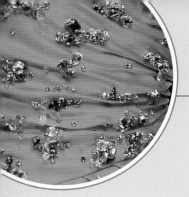

STONE EMBROIDERY

Isaac Mizrahi

Antonio Berardi

The application of carved glass stones and precious Bohemia crystal, large and small pearls, teardrops and cabochons recalls the lavish luxury of another time, evoking the splendor of *The Book of a Thousand and One Nights*, of magical Oriental fortresses and coffers from the cave of Ali Baba or the Byzantine court so well depicted in the mosaics of Sant Apollonare Nuovo Church in Ravenna. Queen Theodora wore dresses, accessories and hairstyles literally covered with precious stones, which underscored the power of her rank and wealth. Stone embroidery, especially when sewn on silky supports such as crinkly iridescent taffeta and fluid shiny satin, gives off a multitude of glints and flashes and reverberates diffuse light in its facets, enveloping the person in a very special aura. It has always been a favorite of dressmakers and top designers due to its capacity to transform a woman into a queen, although today, as in other times, it is not uncommon for men to wear a garment adorned with stones for special occasions. Among the most commonly used in embroidery are Swarovski crystal, a brand that offers a wide range of elements also employed in costume jewelry, in white crystal or colors and with iridescent or diaphanous effects, and in various shapes and sizes. Rounded stones are divided into rose and strass crystal. Rose stones are small, with a flat base and crosswise setting below, and are available in Swarovski and Bohemian crystal. Strass crystal

Alberta Ferretti

Dolce & Gabbana

Jean Paul Gaultier

Dolce & Gabbana

Dolce & Gabbana

is carved in the shape of a diamond (conical background). There are other types of classic set stones such as bead, naveta, orthogonal, etc. Stones for embroidery (glass or plastic) can have two holes. While not as pretty as glass ones, plastic stones are lighter, not to mention less expensive, making them suitable for using on lighter fabrics and in larger pieces. Glass stones are from the Czech Republic, while acrylic stones come from Hong Kong. The Swarovski line includes Stretch Banding, for elastic garments, and Diamond Transfer. As substitutes for stones, heat-sealed strass and Flat Backs Hitfix are also used in many different sizes and colors and can easily be fixed to the fabric with an iron or a hot-melt applicator.

Versace

APPLIQUE EMBROIDERY

Valentino

The name refers to an "added" adornment, with bulging relief, obtained through the application of diverse elements (edgings, strips, ribbons, piping, fillings, etc.) fixed with embroidery stitches that personalize garments. It is a technique of humble origin that emerged to reinforce light or worn-out materials and that ultimately became a form of ornamentation. Known worldwide, it is used in different ways in ethnic and non-ethnic products. North American Indians used remnants of leather for tent decorations, trouser legs and saddles. Applique technique, carried out with trimming procedures, is used to make *molas* (on shirts or dresses), rectangular panels that adorn the clothes of the Kuna Indians of the island of San Blas, in Panama. With successive layers of pieces of cotton fabric of contrasting colors cut into scraps and sewn without seams, the Kuna create complex motifs inspired by nature and popular legends. The linear and geometric lines have their origin in decorative elements that were once painted on the body. In the world of seventies fashion, dresses with skillfully crafted floral and geometric chiaroscuro were made through the application, in "shadow stitch" on organza and batiste, of delicate watercolor tones. Moschino is a fashion designer that has used this technique in ironic code, even including it as a decorative element in accessories. Today, applique embroidery lends itself to interesting experiments in the realm of ethically conscientious fashion that

Gattinoni

Emma Cook

supports recycling material (organic and non-organic) through the use of second-hand clothing. Designer Natalie Chanin, for instance, uses simple cotton t-shirts, skillfully recycled as scraps, to form a layer of color fabrics superimposed with decorative grass-knit and cord stitch in her highly original creations. Using this technique she designs refined handmade embroidery produced by sewers, a group of 200 talented artisans based in the Appalachian Mountains who combine applique traditions with stencil prints and biological materials. The designer created the "Alabama Project", a company specializing in limited-edition products.

Bora Aksu

Kenzo

Oscar de la Renta

PATCHWORK

This decorative fabric pattern is obtained by assembling patches of different kinds of cloth to form a single-layer surface. The technique, often completed with quilting, is also called "quilt". It arose from the practical need to recycle scraps of old clothing and the desire to organize social gatherings in the small European immigrant communities in the United States. The amalgam of very disparate fabrics, apparently arranged at random but tastefully combined according to the rules of contrast and juxtaposition, produces an overall rich and varied effect. Patchwork

Antonio Marras

Antonio Marras

is used in the construction of typical suits in a variety of countries. These are usually craft products (single, original and unrepeatable pieces) that sometimes involve detailed study of possible chrometic and material combinations and the weight and consistency of the fabrics. In patchwork, the seams can be invisible or delineated, with a wide repertoire of embroidery stitches with polychrome threads, regular highlights or superimposed decorative motifs. In current fashion, machine-produced ready-to-use patchwork fabrics are available. They are used in decoration but also appear in clothes, with surprising combination effects. An uncountable number of fashion designers have crafted mag-

Barbara Bui

Custo Barcelona

Hermès

Miu Miu

Agatha Ruiz de la Prada

nificent patchwork creations. During several seasons (1979-81) Yves St. Laurent presented long, broad, domed skirts decorated with closely arranged patchwork that radiated out from the hem upwards, gradually becoming denser. Christian Lacroix has made patchwork a warhorse of his style, characterized by the skillful combination of materials that evoke the atmosphere of Provence, the gold of Baroque stuccowork, the transparency of intricate macramé and the opulence of Spanish passementerie. Valentino, the prince of feminine sobriety, created a bolero jacket whose surface was covered with "crazy quilt" patchwork in homage to the almost casual mastery apparent in the lively masterpieces of the pioneers. Antonio Marras, a recherché and elitist artistic genius, combines beautiful damasks woven in gold and rustic tweeds, fine embroidery and tartan checks, creating a perfect blend of masculine and feminine that fuses drama and mystery. John Galliano, a modern interpreter of the historic Dior maison couture, seems to find inspiration in a kind of patchwork "code" that recycles technological and industrial materials. His shows feature an abundance of futuristic women who don't scorn tulle and glitter in combination with a whirlwind of embedded pieces and colors. Among up and coming designers, the gleeful patchwork of Ágata Ruiz de la Prada and Manish Arora are worth mentioning.

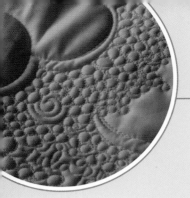

QUILTED FABRIC

This warm protective sometime waterproof fabric consists of one or more layers crossed by a series of seams that serve the practical purpose of keeping the layers together and the decorative function of delineating a motif. Machine-made quilted fabric is produced quickly and is even and resistant, while handmade quilted material is more versatile and allows for closer attention to detail. The production of quilted fabric prospered in Florence, where Florentine quilting, also known as *lavoro impuntit*, had two variants. The first kind was without stuffing and ribbed, with a sewing effect achieved by the relief of a rib inserted between two parallel seams throughout the length of the design. The second was known as Florentine trapunto quilting or "stuffed technique" and had areas in relief characterized by seams and stuffing. This type of work was also done in England starting in the 16th century and was highly regarded in Europe in the centuries that followed, used in clothing and decorative accessories. With the arrival of the first pioneers it spread to America, where even today the Amish community is famous for its quilts, magnificent bedspreads and tapestries with large geometric sections of contrasting colors, accentuated by the intermittent movement of the threads, which follow lines that trace "invisible" patterns on the entire surface. Today, sewn and quilted fabrics are available by the yard and in many different widths. Quilted fabric that

Etro

Louise Goldin

Giles

Angelo Marani

Giles

Dolce & Gabbana

Kenzo

contains the least number of seams provides better insulation compared with quilted fabrics with a large number of seams. This is because the sewing lines cause a decrease in the degree of insulation. Quilted fabrics are used frequently in the production of clothing and accessories as well as in decoration, particularly in the lightweight coverings, made with expanded nylon fabric, with internal polyester stuffing, such as the Husky, a kind of equestrian jacket with a corduroy collar and outlines. There is also a vest-like sleeveless version with metallic pressure buttons, aesthetically akin to the horse rugs used at the racetrack.

19

FABRICS WITH FINISH

WATERPROOFED

Iceberg

Paul Smith

Dsquared2

Waterproofed fabric is treated with water-repellant molecular substances that make it impermeable to water, which is unable to penetrate the material thanks to capillarity and slides across its surface without leaving any trace of moisture. Waterproof fabric also possesses the technical requirements to be certified as wind resistant, due to the insertion of induction below its surface, which is to say, covering with a paste or liquid (for example, aluminum salts or paraffin emulsions) or a membrane, a very fine polymer film (polyurethane, polyester or PTFE) between 5 and 25 microns applied to give it high performance in terms of waterproofness and breathability. Breathable induction offers the advantage of allowing water vapor to pass through (breathable nature). Both effects can be applied to fabrics suitable for the production of quality waterproof articles that must pass laboratory tests in which the fabric is exposed to a system that simulates rain or bathes the material. The quicker the water slides, the more waterproof the fabric. Generally, all garments used for sports or outdoors are waterproofed, not only through the use of water-resistant fabrics but also by applying

Dior

Alberto Biani

Marc by Marc Jacobs

waterproof seals or special solutions such as waterproof strips and adhesives at critical points within the seams to make them one hundred percent watertight (heat-sealed seams). The degree of exposure in the tests depends on the garment's intended use: skiing, snowboarding, mountain climbing, boating, sailing, fishing, etc. Nova-dry technology is a treatment that distributes water-repellant molecules perpendicularly to the fabric; with time, use and water in large quantities, the molecules weaken and the water-repellant capacity of the fabric diminishes. Nonetheless, this water-resistant feature can be reactivated through ironing at 284 degrees Fahrenheit or by applying an aerosol spray.

Burberry Prorsum

OILSKIN

Oilskin consists of a taffeta framework base with very dense threads soaked with a waterproof substance spread across its surface. The base support is made with simple, inexpensive fabrics (cotton, linen, wool, hemp or other natural fibers with high absorbent capacity). The waxing consists in the formation of a thin layer of special wax-, tar- or linseed-oil-based resin that penetrates the structure and sets and solidifies in the fabric. There are oilskin fabrics of different thicknesses, colors and consistencies with a particularly compact, oily and slippery appearance. Before the discovery of rubber, plastic and nylon, waxing the fabric was the only way to ensure protection against the cold and moisture. It was used in the pro-

duction of masks worn in World War I and other military supplies and stores. Waxed material is especially used in trench coats, windbreakers and raincoats, often equipped with capes and hoods that shield the wearer from the cold and rain as well as atmospheric turbulence without needing to wear a hat. One of the most widespread garments is the English stormproof shooting jacket of oiled cotton, more commonly called the Barbour jacket, used initially by English peasants and later adopted by hunters. Belstaff motorcycle jackets are always made with oiled surfaces. Nowadays, rubber, silicone and other chemical products are used in waterproofing. An oilskin jacket, made of colorful waterproof fabric obtained through the applica-

Gaetano Navarra

Dirk Bikkembergs

Undercover

tion of a layer of rubber, silicone or varnish, is a garment used specifically in nautical activities and sports. It is combined with overall-style pants stuffed into boots and with sailors' rucksacks. Oilskin fabric was used in coats and three-quarter coats, work clothes, jackets and motorcycle jackets, automobile hoods and truck and boat covers.

Costume National

Number Nine

Antonio Berardi

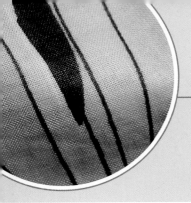

CHINTZ

The term "chintz" derives from the word *chit* or *chitta* whose common root refers to *chiazzato* (heathered) or *macchiato* (stained). In the past this fabric was handcrafted in India with coarse, robust and resistant cotton thread, which was then painted or wood-engraved with pigments of very bright natural colors that diluted easily in successive washes, creating irreparable stains in the fabric. There was an authentic tradition of calico painted with designs that reproduced Indian motifs of the tree of life,

Jonathan Saunders

Calvin Klein

Cantao

adorned with flowers and leaves and with flowery borders like frames. These fabrics were used in quilted bedcovers or shawls. The Dutch East India Company introduced them as an import product for the homes of European bourgeoisie, where they became very popular from the 16th to the 18th century. To repel dust and avoid stains during long sea transports, chintz materials were covered with a thin layer of starch or resin similar to wax that gave them a shiny, luminous appearance. Given that it was moderately priced, the dissemination of chintz posed a threat to French and English textile manufacturers, who, in turn, imposed protectionist tariffs that virtually blackballed its sale until it began to be produced locally in Marseilles. A specific type of chintz became famous in France under the name *toile de jouy* fabric, produced starting in 1759 in the city of Jouy-en-Josas (Versailles) and characterized by monochrome designs with thin, sharply defied outlines, with medallions containing bucolic scenes, historic figures and landscapes printed in red terracotta, sky blue or indigo against a white or ecru background. Today, it is a stout cotton or blended plain-weave or satin-weave fabric, solid and resistant in appearance, that can be plain or printed, finished with a special calendaring that rubberizes the material and makes it shiny and smooth to the touch. This special surface covering is also obtained through the application of silicone products that make it practically waterproof. In the name of tradition, chintz often contains very vivid floral motifs against a clear background.

Comme des Garçons

Anglomania

Joop!

COATED

Coated material is a backing fabric on which a finish has been applied consisting of a patina of plastic material, such as PVC, polyurethane, poly-acrylic or synthetic resin, with the aim of altering its appearance and consistency. The coating can give the material a smoother feel or make

Cerruti

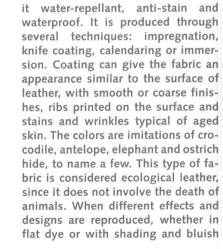

Michalsky

it water-repellant, anti-stain and waterproof. It is produced through several techniques: impregnation, knife coating, calendaring or immersion. Coating can give the fabric an appearance similar to the surface of leather, with smooth or coarse finishes, ribs printed on the surface and stains and wrinkles typical of aged skin. The colors are imitations of crocodile, antelope, elephant and ostrich hide, to name a few. This type of fabric is considered ecological leather, since it does not involve the death of animals. When different effects and designs are reproduced, whether in flat dye or with shading and bluish

Jason Wu

Angelo Marani

white toning, metallized, iridescent, printed or over-printed with decorations, it is called imitation leather; it is a material much in demand for the production of accessories such as shoes, boots, purses, bags, bags with shoulder straps, covers and suitcases in keeping with fashion trends. Coated fabric is easy to sew but is coarse and not very slick to the touch, with very little breathability. In clothes it is suitable for economical skirts and pants as well as coats and jackets, lending them its waterproof feature.

Byblos

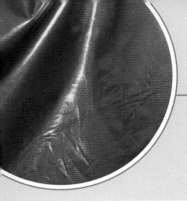

CIRÉ

Aquascutum

Fabric treated with ciré has a compact, polished and lustrous surface, obtained by coating the material with shiny synthetic resin or rubberized wax. The name comes from the verb *cirer*, which means, "to wax". It is also called vinyl, a special varnish made from organic compounds such as polyvinyl chloride (PVC) or vinyl acetate (Vinavil) that give it a shiny, "bathed" appearance and make it waterproof. The word "vinyl" recalls the world of music, given its association with the material used to make 45 rpm singles and 33 rpm discs, modern versions of the old 78 rpm shellac records. The black support, typical of record albums in the sixties, was emulated in the eye-catching ciré raincoats worn by young people in the swinging London of the same period that frequented the boutiques on Carnaby Street. This famous street, a meeting place for innovative artists and musicians, contributed to spreading the philosophy of moving and learning in which aesthetic manifestations such as art, music and fashion assumed a protest value and became statements of rupture with the past throughout the world. Today, ciré is used primarily in accessories such as bags, footwear, hats and waterproof jackets, as well as in audacious, transgressing garments that embody the fashion launched by the urban tribe known as the "mods", an abbreviation of the word "modern".

Dsquared2

Cantao

Agatha Ruiz de la Prada

Rubberized fabric is coated with a thin layer of rubber derived from certain sugars, glycosides and hydrocarbons that can give rise to solutions with high viscosity or elastic masses. Rubber or textile rubber is a natural polyisoprene fiber obtained from latex, liquid, paste and elastic, scorched in a process invented by Macintosh in 1923 to waterproof wool with rubber and elasticized through chemical treatments. Rubber guarantees optimal characteristics of elasticity and resistance to use, cuts and lacerations, and acids and alkaline of medium concentration. Stretched by traction, rubberized fabric increases up to three times its initial length (this length is recovered once the force of traction is eliminated). Fabric coated in natural rubber tends to offer little resistance to ageing and heat; for this reason, nowadays, synthetic materials are always used in its place. It is usually used in protective work clothing, with anti-abrasive coating. Synthetic rubber has diverse consistencies, hard and soft, and thicknesses between 0.2 mm and 1 cm. It protects the body with a strong but lightweight layer distributed uniformly throughout the body and maintains a certain amount of heat. Rubberized fabric can have different compositions: cotton with acrylonitrile rubber, suitable for the constructions of membranes; nylon with hypalon rubber on one side and neoprene on the other; glass fiber with polychloroprene (neoprene) with flameproof properties; glass fiber with silicone rubber coating on both surfaces and with a transparent anti-abrasive film on one side. The high-tech collections of Corpo Nove often consist of coated cotton fabric, siliconized and slightly rubberized. Rubber can be cut into silky thin strips and woven like knit or can enwrap the irregular structure and contain it, as in the case of the accessories designed by Luisa Cevese, with colored selvages and abraded textile materials that become interesting when they appear floating inside a layer of milky rubber.

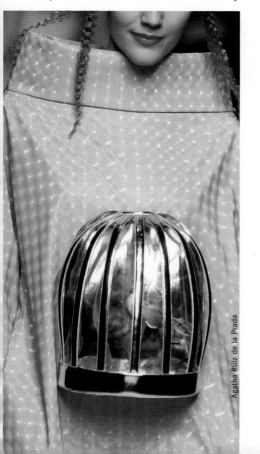

Agatha Ruiz de la Prada

Ports 1961

Iceberg

"Rubbermania" has recently spread to finished garments, some of whose parts are rubberized (for example, shoulders, elbows or kneepads), with ad hoc coatings that serve as reinforcements or simply play a decorative role.

Antonio Berardi

PATTERNED

Blumarine

Alexander McQueen

Carlos Miele

Patterned fabric features multicolor designs on only one side of the material. The patterns are obtained through the application of a coloring agent in paste form that penetrates the textile fibers, permanently fixing them to the cloth in such a way that they are resistant to contact with light and repeated washes. Patterning is carried out with different techniques; the colors are applied one by one according to the instructions on a sketch that reproduces an exact diagram of the composition. The arrangements of the designs are varied: positional printing, according to a precise order reproduced in one or more pattern repeat, or integral printing, which occupies the entire textile surface uniformly. The quality of a patterned fabric is recognized in the solidity of the

dyes, the number of colors used, the outlines and sharpness of the designs, and the type of textile support used as a base. The techniques are divided into traditional and industrial, and are chosen depending on the type of product and the desired effects. The coloring agent can be acid, base, direct, reactive, in tank, cationic, disperse, fluorescent, pre-metallized or enhanced through the use of mordants. The most common process is direct printing, wherein the coloring substances already contain the fixers and mordant dyes needed to transfer the dye to the fabric permanently. In technical manuals the pattern is printed in several passes using block matrixes, stamps or stencil masks; in mechanical processes the color is supplied from the interior of revolving nickel

Cacharel

Etro

Emilio Pucci

Suzanna Peric

cylinders that contain the motifs of the design. Another system consists in spreading the color with a spatula in the interior of special serigraphic frames, with light-sensitive gelatin polyester cloth supports arranged on a mobile cart according to the pattern repeat along the length of the printing table across the top of which the piece is stretched. Other techniques are indirect or mordant-dye printing (the pattern is transferred to the textile base before being immersed in a dye bath so that the latter adheres only to the points delimited by the mordant dye); reserve printing (a layer of wax or another material waterproofs the fabric in certain places to prevent the penetration of color); corrosion printing (discoloring agents eliminate part of the background color of the already

dyed fabric, creating a motif by subtraction); and pigment printing (involving the use of abrasion-resistant and wash-resistant colored, metalized or lacquered substances). Other techniques include transfer printing (the pattern is heat-transferred directly to the synthetic fibers of the cloth from a continuous paper matrix under the action of a press) and inkjet printing (applied to fabric prepared with a thickening agent through the injection of drops of ink cast at high speed through computer-controlled plotters that permit the direct transfer of the pattern to the fabric, with the advantage that photographic images can be reproduced with a certain degree of faithfulness).

263

POSITIONAL PRINTING

Frankie Morello

Etro

Moschino Cheap & Chic

Paul & Joe

Issey Miyake

Versace

Marni

O V E R - D Y E

Etro

Oscar de la Renta

Sportmax

Custo Barcelona

The superimposition of several shades of colors, which can be different, produces an over-dye effect applied to directly to the piece of fabric or the already produced individual garment. The result is a variegated dye, with heterogeneous borders that seem to be the result of the irregular random absorption of colors. In reality, it is a treatment involving calculated and purposeful study. The preexisting dye base has a significant impact on the final effect of the cloth, in accordance also with the percentages of the surfaces and the number of colorant passes carried out. Very specific shading effects, with progressive blurring of one color into another, are achieved with the use of fibers of varied material compositions that behave differently with the respect to the absorption of a determined paint bath. Similarly, the effects can be diversified and stratified applying chemically distinct coloring agents to a single fabric. Some young fashion designers have experimented with colorants, combining traditional craft techniques – such as reserve dyeing with clay, mildew, leather or wax – with modern digital printing systems. Over-dye technique can also be applied to a fabric base printed with any color design, which is subjected to a superimposed application of color dye, muting the sheen of the printed colors to obtain a homogeneous, almost aged look.

Jason Wu

Kenzo

Miss Sixty

Sprayed fabric consists of a preexisting knit or woven base on which various types of substances are sprayed only on one side in aerosol applications with a compressed air pistol similar to the kind used in aerography or with a spatula. The intensity and flow speed of the diffuser regulates the desired effect, obtained with silicone, synthetic resin, polyvinyl, metallic, etc. Among the most innovative treatments are a cotton-polyester fabric with a surface like plaster and a salt finish, a copolymer polyurethane-

Valentino

Halston

Chanel

based treatment that gives the fabric the appearance of a cloth subjected to a water and salt bath and then dried in the sun. In China, an organza or knit fabric, sprinkled with gold, silver or brightly colored powder, is produced. A recent version of sprayed fabric is "spray-on fabric", a substance made up of cotton fiber, polymers and solvents sprayed directly onto the body of the person with a spray jar or a simple pistol and permits creating, in just 15 minutes, a fabric capable of adap-

ting perfectly to the person's anatomy. The procedure – invented by Spanish designer Manuel Torres, a Ph.D in the Department of Chemical Engineering at the Imperial College of London –, which revitalized the artistic technique of body painting practiced in the West since the 1960s as an outgrowth of the liberation from social customs, is still in an experimental phase. Conceptually, patina sprayed on the body recalls felt.It becomes elastic quickly, adhering perfectly to the skin. The

Betsey Johnson

Jason Wu

fiber layers, tighter or looser, permit designing clothes such as bath wear, t-shirts, bodices, pants or dresses that, when finished, can be reused and re-modeled according to one's tastes and exhibit good drape without having to be sewn. The compound can be lique-fied and reused to make new pieces or repair old ones, in addition to being washable and easy to personalize with aerosol coloring agents and perfumed substances selected according to the user's preference. Torres founded Fa-brican Ltd., a factory that has collabo-rated in the complete development of spray-on technology over the last ten years with Paul Luckham, a professor of particle technology who currently is working on a somewhat less adherent fabric for possible future applications.

B. Jackson

FLOCKING

Comme des Garçons

Bora Aksu

Bill Blass

Flocked fabric has a velvety uniform surface or one with decorative motifs characterized by a short tight pile consisting of tiny fibers, chamois-like in appearance. Flock printing is applied to a base sprayed beforehand with adhesive. The procedure consists in exposing the fabric to an electrostatic field applied between the fiber dispensers and the surface to be flocked, in such a way that thin, very short viscose, rayon, cotton or polya-mide fibers (between a few tenths of a millimeter and several millimeters), arranged perpendicularly to the fabric, adhere to the textile substrate. The uniform distribution of the fibers is achieved by having them pass through a sieve. Then, they are pressure-fixed by a series of cylinders and presses. The fibers remain fixed due to the polymerization of the adhesive, with a thickness in the millimeter range, and can have an infinite variety of colors. The excess material that is not fixed to the base is later eliminated. The process of flocking is carried out indistinctly on natural and synthetic fibers and is applied to the entire surface or to create varied effects with a high aesthetic content that personalizes garments according to pre-established designs.

Just Cavalli

Marc by Marc Jacobs

Betsey Johnson

271

MOIRE

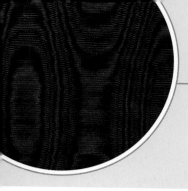

Moire is a medium-weight monochrome silk or synthetic fabric characterized by its stiffness and solidity. It has a lustrous silky appearance, with a finely ribbed surface, like *faille*, and a crimped pattern with small variations in tone and streaks of shifting reflections that create the impression of movement, like concentric or irregular ocean waves or the grains in

Bottega Veneta

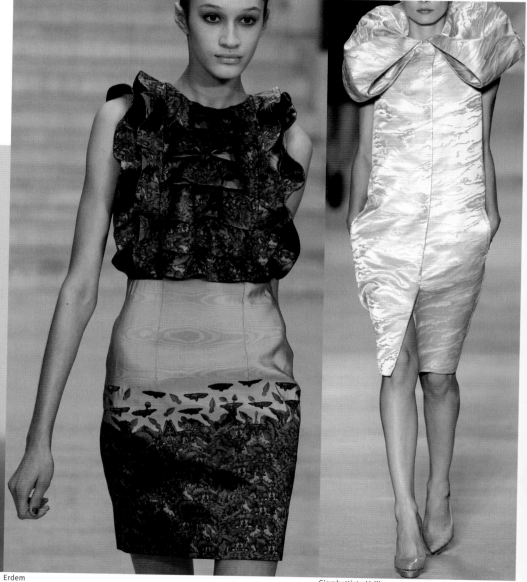

Erdem

Giambattista Valli

wood or marble. It is also available in acetate or viscose, and even in cotton, though the sheen and duration of the effect are different. In Italian it is called *moerro* and in French *moire*. There are four types of moire: old, characterized by large open undulations; French, with shapes like lentils; intermediate; and embossed or by incision. Authentic moire is obtained by a traditional craft procedure and is an expensive product used in elegant high-end garments on account of its special sheen. The fabric slides across a surface scored by extremely fine boards with the aim of slightly stretching the weft threads. The best results are obtained with materials that already contain small ribs. Then, the fabric is subjected to wet calendaring, passing between two cylinders, one made of steel heated to 160-180 degrees Celcius and another made of rubber that contains the motif to be printed in relief. The calendar presses two superimposed layers of fabric (folded in two longitudinally) and the pressing movement prints thin staggered striations. The pressing of certain areas, which crushes some threads and leaves others in tact, produces the typical moire effect, with its sinuous undulations visible in shifting chiaroscuro by the effect of the diverse refractions of light. The variations in pressure and heat influence the final sheen of the fabric. Moire requires careful maintenance and must be dry-cleaned. It is used in dresses, overcoats, footwear and very chic handbags, occasionally enriched

Nicole Farhi

Christian Lacroix

Roccobarocco

with embroidery. It is also used as lining in luxury fur items, in ecclesiastical attire and in coverings for period decorations, as well as in ornamental ribbons.

Pleated fabric receives a specific finish that leaves it semi-permanently pleated. The treatment can be applied to very light silk, cotton, wool and synthetic fiber bases or to leather, straw or other material supports. Pleating is done by hand, with stencils or a machine, involving various types of preparations to obtain what can be very special results. It is possible to obtain multiple chiaroscuro effects, which range from the tiny vertical and horizontal ribs the Egyptians used to produce through the pressu-

Federico Sangalli

Gianfranco Ferré

Jean Paul Gaultier

re of wet fabric on ribbed blocks of woods to scenic productions with foil, spirals, fans, large shells and baskets, produced industrially through thermo-adhesion and with sophisticated machinery that intersect and interrupt the direction of the pleats to form subtle patterns in relief. One of the most original innovators in the field of pleats was Mariano Fortuny, who, after many experiments in his workshop in Venice, patented the technique and its use in large Delfi tunics, linear and sculptural dresses inspired by the Charioteer of Delphi that

caressed the figures of charismatic non-conformist women such as Isadora Duncan, Eleonora Duse and Peggy Guggenheim. In the 1930s, Ms. Gres achieved great notoriety with her creations of statuesque peplos dresses sculpted with fabric directly on the body, which made Marlene Dietrich and Grace Kelly seem like stunning and graceful goddesses. It's impossible to forget the scene of a seductive Marilyn Monroe in her undulating plisse soleil dress in *Some Like It Hot*, which became an icon in the collective imagination. Roberto Ca-

Byblos

Issey Miyake

Jean Paul Gaultier

...ucci exercises skillful and meticulous virtuosity in his majestic sculptures of pleated fabric that find an ideal place in design museums. In 1983, Krizia presented a futuristic collection of silver-pleated metallic acetate coats that recreated the shiny and faceted surfaces of the Chrysler Building in New York, embodying the hedonism of the eighties. Issey Miyake is considered the grand master of contemporary pleats, thanks to an ingenious revision of the technique that involves the contribution of the culture of Japanese origami and polyester thermo-plastic technique. His modernity lies in his having revolutionized the fabric/dress dynamic, sewing the form first and then inserting the movement of the pleats. His "Minaret" designs, similar to small Japanese paper lanterns, and his poetic renditions of natural forms possess an impalpable and ethereal elegance.

EMBOSSING

Burberry Prorsum

Issey Miyake

Armani Privè

Erdem

Federico Sangalli

Embossed fabric is characterized by a surface that is in relief (gauffre) and that contains a sculpted image or ornamental motif (dessin gaufre or dessin a carreau), obtained artificially by hot stamping or through a finish that causes shrinkage in desired areas. The technique can be applied to fabrics, paper, cardboard, sheet metal, rubber, plastic materials, leather, fur, etc. Hot stamping for embossing can be done in several ways: using tools with special red-hot metal points or by having the material pass through the calendar of a goffer, a machine with etched and heated steel rotary cylinders that compress the fabric. The pre-fixed motifs, in relief or etched, are transferred from the matrixes to the receiver support of the embossing, spread out on a cylinder with a larger diameter and covered with cotton, paper or elastic rubber. A third cylinder (cold) cools the large cylinder eliminating the prints that remain on it once the embossing is complete, leaving it in a position to receive a fresh amount of fabric. Embossing applied to synthetic fibers is permanent, given the fact that these are thermoplastic, while natural fibers receive the addition of reticulate resin that fixes the embossing and makes it wash-resistant. In Italian, embossing (*goffrato*) is also called *bugnato* ("padding") due to its similarity to a wall covering technique known since antiquity. Padding consists in blocks of ribbed stone arranged in a way that they project out from the wall, creating projections whose surface is faceted with carved squares, *baguet*

te molding and diamond shapes with softened points reproduced throughout the embossing. During weaving, natural embossing can be obtained through different tensions of the warp and weft threads, arranged according to a special pattern of the warp that the French call *gaufrage*. Another embossing technique on fabric involves sewing the material very tightly with elastic thread on special mechanical embroidery looms. It is a fabric widely appreciated in fashion, used by Giorgio Armani to make sophisticated, elegant short jackets for women, as well as sport coats and accessories with tasteful three-dimensional touches such as men's ties and shoes.

Giorgio Armani

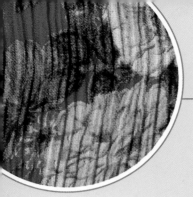

WRINKLED

Froissé in French, this type of fabric has a wrinkled and folded look, full of irregular pleats more or less close together and directed, similar to vertical and horizontal lines with slight relief like tree bark. Chemically altering the flat structure of the fabric through a special semi-permanent finish, in alkaline solution, and calendaring with etched cylinders produces wrinkling which tends to disappear after repeated washes unless it is thermofixed. A prior requirement of products that receive this treatment is that not only the base fabric but the linings, complementary materials and sewing thread be resistant to the pleats and maintain their shape. Slightly exaggerated wrinkling, more natural to

Custo Barcelona

Issey Miyake

Jil Sander

the touch, obtained perhaps without thermofixing but with thread and weaving techniques, is used above all in casual wear for the construction of shirts that evoke the Anglo-American style of outdoor garments. Its intentionally pleated surface forms a "wash and wear" fabric for easy-to-maintain clothes that dry quickly after washing and don't need to be ironed to recover their original shape. Wrinkled fabric is most frequently used in fashion in dresses and ladies' footwear, as in the case of designer Nanni Strada in her collection "Le cortecce", presented in 1986-1987, with the prototypical "dress-cloth", the fruit of innovative experimentation with textiles. The design, conceived as an essential form, of dyed linen or silk jersey, with irregular permanent pleats with a "tree bark" effect, became a must-have garment that could be rolled up and placed in a suitcase, taking up minimal space. Practical for travel but also a conceptual and refined garment, suitable for diverse occasions and seasons, it was followed in 1989 by the "wrinkled rice paper" designs and in 1990 by the "new wrinkled" creations, collections in which traditional Indian and Japanese techniques were united with machine wrinkling techniques that provide an elastic feel that increases the comfort of the garments.

Juun J.

Prada

SHAPE-MEMORY

Angelo Marani

Issey Miyake

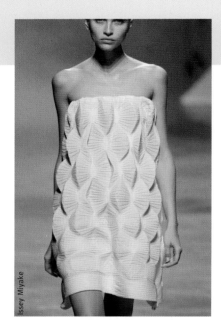

Vivienne Westwood

Donna Karan

Shape-memory allows for the creation of fabric with a surprising wrinkled coating look. The resulting fabric has a strong plastic effect, one that places emphasis on wrinkles, crimps and pleats that the textile surface assumes naturally in response to the movements of the body and that leave their sculptural print on the fabric only to disappear with the next movement. Wrinkled material with shape memory is often taffeta or very solid reps and is produced combining textile fibers with metallic fibers in the fabric. The metal is converted into spherical section threads, flexible and ductile, in such a way that it can be spun or woven alternating it with insertions of normal weft threads. The thread count per cm/m² of the inserted metal wefts determines the degree of stiffness or softness of the surface and influences the degree of shape memory of the fabric. Brass, copper,

aluminum or stainless steel thread can also be varnished to adapt any color and be twisted with other threads (cotton, viscose, cashmere or silk) to form novelty yarns. The fabric, on top of being much more resistant to use, highlights the passage of light and its reflections, mixing the pleasantly changing effects of the metal, which acquires and spreads the colored dye, with the lightness and transparency of a thin fabric. This cloth is produced in widths between 25 and 2,400 mm and was initially used experimentally by artists and decorators in scenic decorations on account of its ductile characteristics. Soon, however, these fabrics flamed the ardent imaginations of designers, and today they appear in their own right in the aesthetics of fashion and dress. Another fabric uses metal alloys that have the capacity to undergo a mechanical transformation in response to shape memory through

280

Krizia

thermal control. In other words, they are sensitive to a *single-effect* structural change that causes plastic deformations in the presence of low temperatures and regains its original shape with a simple re-heating. For example, the fabric can be wrinkled up into a ball, yet exposing it to a gust of hot air, the material expands and recovers its original appearance. A double memory or reversible effect is sometimes mentioned when the fabric, subjected to thermomechanical treatments, is capable of alternating its reversibility between two stable shapes. This is the case of the Oricalco jacket, a highly advanced technological garment, whose collar automatically lifts when the wind blows, while the sleeves are programed to shorten on their own as soon as the temperature rises and surpasses a predetermined value. The material used in the production of this garment is a light cloth composed of 50% interwoven titanium with an orthogonal structure.

Alexander McQueen

RATINE FABRIC

Bill Blass

Matthew Williamson

Betsey Johnson

Ratine is a very nappy fabric to which ratine technique has been applied: a finish used in certain types of carded wool consisting of a series of operations in which the fabric is mildly fulled, napped (rollers with metallic needles raise a dense pile from the surface of the fabric) and sheared (this last process makes the ratine fabric homogeneous). Additionally, rubbing with circular movements and brushing in various directions group the pile in the form of tufts, fringes, small knots and crimped agglomerations. With pressure, the pile is united with the aim of imitating the appearance of animal fur. In the past, this type of effect was achieved by rubbing stones on the surface of the wool. Some Sumerian and Scythian communities wore long ribbed skirts and shawls made from goat and ram hair called *kunakes*, at times with long locks of hair similar to those found on edging or with acorn-shaped crimp. Today, ratine fabric is produced on ratine machines that work with the assistance of an iron. Regulating the movement of the ratine machine, the fabric can be subjected to various types of ratine techniques, depending on the desired aesthetic. The different effects on the fabric are distinguished by the sizes of the locks of hair and the direction and crimp they adopt. The most requested ratines are ratine with curl effects, a typical Casentio cloth production; armourè, which leaves the background weave visible; *frisé*, with undulating curls; *floconè*, consisting of tufts similar to snowflakes; *perlinè*, with a highly visible cluster effect; and *moutonnè*, which mimics fleece. This production is suitable for overcoats, especially capes, coats and jackets with a primitive and nomadic look, garments often dyed vivid colors that are very popular in fashion.

Lorenzo Riva

Francesco Scognamiglio

Emporio Armani

Pollini

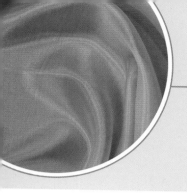

Habutai (or habotai) silk is a silky fabric with flat smooth structure, one of the most basic known. It is rather light, similar to crepe de Chine but more consistent, and formed by continuous, fine, shiny fiber threads which are slightly twisted, hairy and soft. It is made up of treated silk, that is, silk which has been degummed. The word "habutai" is from Japan, where this cloth was traditionally woven and where it is still used today for making judges' robes. In Japanese, it means "soft hair", in allusion to the character of the fabric. Today, the majority of habutai is woven and produced in China. Habutai silk is smoother and springier than common mulberry silk and has a slick texture like lining. This feature is due to a particular finish that the material receives during a wash process with sand, which softens the surface

Gucci

and gives it an especially fluid and opulent peach- or suede-like feel. The negative side of this treatment is that during production, in order to make the fabric soft, some of the fibers break, resulting in a less durable fabric. The fabric lends itself easily to piece dyeing in a vast array of colors; visually it demonstrates a light whitish patina that gives it a dusty look, especially in dark tones. This type of silk is often used in women's garments such as t-shirts, drape blouses, wide pants and dresses, and in elegant lingerie, pajamas and unisex nightshirts. Because of its smooth and springy quality, habutai fabric can be used to make luxury silk bedding, an anallergic material preferred by a growing number of people throughout the world. Its reflections and sheen especially highlight the figure in movement and grant elegance to foulards, shoes, beach wraps and hand-painted decorative panels using batik tie-dye and shibori techniques. The 2011 SS collection, presented by Diane Von Furstenberg in collaboration with designer Yvan Mispelaere, celebrates an adamant, resolute femininity, giving priority to habutai silk dresses that are fluid, loose, extremely lightweight and drape softly on the body, dyed in colors ranging from mint green, jade and lilac to warm orange and intense red.

Alviero Martini

Antonio Marras

Chapurin

BOILED WOOL

Boiled wool is pleasant to the touch, warm and comfortable. It is a product with high insulation and protection properties given that it has a thick surface made of spun wool that has been infiltrated. The knit piece is infiltrated using special machines called Links-Links, through fulling that causes nearly 30% shrinkage but does not alter the elasticity of the fiber. In a mechanical process that combines the action of heat, moisture pressure and rubbing, the fibers are compressed, which tangle with each other as a re-

Céline

Emporio Armani

sult of their layered structure. Fulling lasts for at least thirty minutes and a maximum of twelve hours. The product is then subjected to flat drying to allow the fabric fibers to settle naturally. Boiled wool is similar to felt and cloth. It differs from the former in that felt is made from carded wool and from the latter in that while woolen cloth undergoes the same fulling treatment, it is produced on a loom. The fabric guarantees a high heat-retention and moisture-absorbing capacity. Traditionally, boiled wool is produced in mountainous regions in Central and Northern Europe, in particular Austria, where it is used in the construction of hats, vests and comfortable slippers native to the alpine area as well as in the production

of typical Tyrolean jackets. This unique garment with metal buttons and large wool herringbone fringes seems to have been inspired directly by the classic short jackets of Coco Chanel. In recent years other designers have taken an interest in this product and updated its traditional image. Prada, for instance, a great experimenter with fabric effects, presented mohair boiled wool cardigan, hot-hammered and externally covered with a plasticizer that leaves it shiny and silky on the outside while remaining soft and warm in contact with the skin.

DECONSTRUCTED

Deconstructed fabric is characterized by the deconstruction of the elements that make it up (warp and weft) in certain areas. The name is composed of the privative prefix "de-" followed by the adjective derived from the Latin verb *struere*, "to build". Deconstructed fabric is produced with chemical procedures that corrode some of the threads and leave others floating. The technique is applied to simulate the wear and tear of time and is highly regarded in fashion linked to seasonal trends. Deconstructed denim was launched in the nineties by conceptual fashion designer Martin Margiela, whose collections are noteworthy not only for the deconstruction of the fabric but also of the garment itself through a different arrangement of its components. There is a craft-produced clothing line called "O", by Margiela, Paris, made completely by hand with old fabrics and recycled out-of-fashion dresses. In clothing, deconstruction is a response to the idea of taking a tailored piece of clothing and rethinking its structure completely in terms of form and volume. Deconstructed fabric is an ideal material for transmitting the notion of rupture with tradition. The fashion of slashed garments, that is, clothes full of cuts – slits so large that the fabrics of the clothes worn underneath are visible – was introduced around the year 1500 in the clothing of the Lansquenetes, a mercenary army that, in turn, had inherited the style from the

Aquascutum

Dolce & Gab

Betsey Johnson

Central Saint Martins

Vivienne Westwood

Dolce & Gabbana

"knifed" attire of Swiss peasants. Later, it spread among the upper classes, which slashed expensive satin or velvet fabrics to further underscore their economic power. The arrangement of the cuts followed a precise pattern, which could be diagonal, crossed, starred, fish tail, etc., according to personal taste and the dictates of fashion. In 1982, designer Rei Kawakubo presented a collection of white cotton dresses characterized by asymmetrical cuts, hanging strips and holes produced by open stitching, under the motto "bag lady post Hiroshima look", in opposition to the reigning hedonism of those times. The structure of the Japanese designer's knit garments was riddled with holes, which she envisioned as a kind of contemporary lace. The deconstruction of the fabric with personalized rips and tears became a iconic feature of *grunge style*, which adopted a studied look consisting of apparently random superimpositions of clothes such as torn shirts of variable length, jeans frayed at the borders and open sweat shirts, all arranged with feigned indifference.

A G E D

Aged fabric features structural wear and tear effects or depletion of color in certain areas that give the material an impoverished look. Often it is treated with enzymes that cause the surface layers to corrode, thereby altering the texture. In other cases, aged fabric evidences alterations in the weft through abrasion with paper, rubbing with pumice, expanded perlite-based treatments or through "sandwashing", a technique used to age denim consisting in using sand and silicone to abrade the fabric. Subsequent modifications can be made through discoloration and fading of colors, making the material look as if it has been slightly consumed by time, or through localized, scratched and rubbed ageing according to the design, using abrasive brushes with diamond tips, air pistols for chlorine derivatives or directed laser beams. Examples of natural substances used in the ageing of fabrics are salt, which softens the fabric, tea, which gives it a yellowish antiquated patina, and the "wine bath", which through rusting gives the material an iridescent sheen. The "vagabond" finish is a specific ageing process for cellulose fibers involving four stages: cationization with Indosol, dye with adequate coloring agents, enzyme wash and silicone treatment. Artificial ageing technique can be applied to a piece of fabric. However, it is also frequently applied to the end garment as a finish that gives a worn second-hand look to luxurious clothes taken directly from the shop windows of Christian

Unique

Custo Barcelona

Dior or Louis Vuitton that tell us a story and transmit an emotion. The aged appearance of cotton, velvet and leather is linked to vintage style, a trend that evokes the atmospheres of previous decades through the reuse of aged or obsolete accessories and clothes found in grandma's closet or in specialized boutiques.

Central Saint Martins

Dirk Bikkembergs

Wunderkind

LASER

Fabric exposed to electRomegnetic radiation emitted by laser, a luminous beam of constant frequency that spreads its rays in one direction. The device, which takes its name from the definition "light amplification by stimulated emission of radiation", synthesizes a focalization process of the laser source of various strengths in a beam transported via a system of flat refraction mirrors. The fabric is spread out on a plane and is completely crossed by a software-controlled ray. The system is based on low-environmental-impact technology and for this reason is very frequently used in the textile industry for the preparation of dyes and finishes. Laser treatment allows for obtaining fabrics that are pierced superficially or perforated at the same time, laminated fabrics that are then pierced or cut through *laser design*, with crow's foot, cloud or wood effects, etc. Laser cutting can be carried out on taffeta, silk satin, special fabrics like microfiber or Lurex, suede, leather and fur, and is considered indispensable in fashion garments and accessories. Australian designer Mark Liu has researched innovative cutting techniques applying a renewed concept of the puzzle to a simple rectangle of fabric. This technique produces very structured and elaborate creations, with intricate three-dimensional beveled and stratified motifs. His collection "On the Cutting Edge", with a strong ecological bent, was conceived in such a way that, above all, the fabric is what influences the cut of the garment,

Blumarine

Jonathan Saunders

Marni

handmade with heat-sealed borders to avoid fraying. The designer is among the creators of new concepts that place special weight on art and economics, given that the method allows for making use of fabric that would have been considered scrap in traditional production, that is, up to 15% of the total material used.

Giambattista Valli

Jonathan Saunders

Marithé & François Girbaud

Unique

This treatment is used to give the fabric a shiny, luminous and burnished look, with the aim of increasing the capacity of the textile surface to reflect luminous beams of light. The technique used is calendaring, a process in which the fabric is passed under cylinders that press and compress it. The material is flattened and polished by the combined effect of pressure and high temperatures. The heat and pressure produce such effects as bright/dull, a silky finish, etc. Another system consists of preparing the fabric with the help of filler substances and reticulate resins that polymerize and neutralize the microporosity of the fibers and the irregularity resulting from the twisting of the threads. As a result the surface is smoother, and the polishing effect lasts longer. Later, the fabric is submerged in a bath of polishing substances and dried in stenter machines. Natural or synthetic waxes emulsified in solvents or in hydrocarbons such as paraffin are used for polishing. The result depends on the nature of the thread, the characteristics of the fiber and the type of fabric weave. For example, continuous yarns are notably smoother and more regular than others, and the structure of satin is smoother than diagonal fibers. Apart from the silk effect, which imitates the sheen of this fabric, one of the preferred polishing treatments in fashion is the glacé effect (literally, "frozen"), which creates a slippery surface like ice on the fabric. Other treatments requested by designers are "glossy-iridescent"

Armani Privè

and "clear-sheeny" resinous effects and the "glossy-under-stained-glass" shading effect. In 2000, designer Laura Pellati launched a line of summer bags that recreated a traditional fabric like linen with a "vitrified patina" obtained with chemical treatments. In the same season Guillermo Mariotto proposed lacquered linen dresses with a practically liquid look, including openings finished with Meryl.

Alberta Ferretti

NONWOVEN BONDED FABRIC

Comme des Garçons

Bottega Veneta

The structure of nonwoven fabric doesn't have its foundation in the interweaving of fibers (hence the name). Rather, fiber layers are consolidated and joined through mechanical processes (e.g., with needles), chemical adhesives or thermal processes. The fibers used can be natural or chemical, often polyester, and come in the form of continuous thread or tufts. The orientation of the fibers can be random or directed according to the desired final effect. The first nonwoven textile was a product obtained through a special paper production method with the aim of having a practical and economical substitute to make disposable clothes and objects. The material is used in clothing primarily in linings and fillings, as it is soft to the touch, water-repellent and resistant to high temperatures. It is also used in clothing destined for professional uses such as sterile surgical garments, liners and single-use shoe covers for beauty centers and gyms, due to its protective capacity against liquids and dust infiltration. Splenditex is a nonwoven fabric invented in Japan consisting of 50% polyester and 50% polyamide, with 10,000 fibers per cm² and an absorptive capacity in the interstices of a percentage of water greater than that of a sponge. The material is used to produce Splendy, a bathrobe with an indefinite duration, weighs less than a pound and that lightly and comfortably massages the skin when worn.

Anne Valérie Hash

Alcantara is made from composite material, formed by very fine polyester and polyurethane fibers combined by means of textile and chemical processes that make it similar to suede, with a characteristic opaqueness and a softness that endures even after numerous washes. These qualities make it similar to leather. It has a light, soft surface, is pleasant to the touch, has a variable thickness (0.40-1.20 mm), weighs around 200 or 270 g/m² and, despite this, is particularly resistant. The innovative production cycle of this type of fabric involves high technological content and low environmental impact (no carbon impact), the fruit of Japanese scientific research. The technology is protected under patents registered in 1970 by Miyoshi Okamoto, a researcher at Toray Industries, Inc. The name of the fabric corresponds to the registered trademark of Alcantara Spa, a company with headquarters in Italy that has marketed the product worldwide since 1981. The word is Spanish, of Arabic origin, and referred to a breed of sheep. It is a versatile material that offers fashion designers infinite expressive possibilities and interpretations: for example, a flat, regular surface; perforated openwork designs; trendy printed patterns; folded with polymeric film on the back; in heavy or pasha versions (0.10 mm thick and 30 g/m²) and thermolight or stretch versions. The Incanto de Alcantara line uses special treatments such as brushing, pleating and wrinkling. It comes in many colors and shades. In fashion it is used in coats, robes and vests and is also added as patches and reinforcements to knit garments. Alcantara can also be draped as though it were a silk fabric and is used in novelty designs, wide and fluid, crafted with sharp point needles. Alcantara is also used in a wide range of accessories such as gloves, belts, bags, bags with shoulder straps and seams, briefcases, boots and sandals. In other areas, it is used to line car seats and as a covering for armchairs and sofas.

Byblos

Bill Blass

Anne Valérie Hash

PAPER

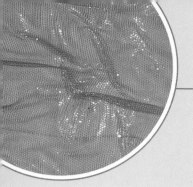

Rue du Mail

This type of fabric is visually very similar to paper, a response to the practical and dynamic notion of "disposable" clothing. In 1966, the company Scott Paper launched the first Dura-Weve dress, a paper fabric reinforced by rayon that, until then, had only been used in medical and protective products. The idea enjoyed unsuspected success, lending itself to the development of a multitude of decorative variations and many colors. In the late sixties, designer Harry Gordon introduced a line of "poster dresses", a linear tube dress (one of which was the "paper caper" dress) enriched with an enormous photographic print. Since then, pleated paper garments have also been popular with the public. Paper fabric is produced with Tyvek®, a matted polyethylene-fiber-based (PLP) material manufactured by DuPont in the form of nonwoven polyolefin sheets (Spunbonded Olefin). The fibers are assembled and heat-soldered to form a surface resistant to cutting and tearing. It is a lightweight, fine, flexible, waterproof material that doesn't deteriorate even when exposed to atmospheric agents for a long period of time. Because of its resistance properties and versatility, it can function as common paper and be used in packaging, in safety garments and in places that require a certain degree of sterilization, such as hospitals and laboratories. In knit fabrics, novelty yarns (polyester and polyamide) are used that imitate the appearance, thickness and relief of paper. In the nineties, Rei Kawakubo experimented with paper, a highly regarded material in Japanese fashion, in openwork designs similar to the

Paul Smith

Paul Smith

Rodarte

rosette lace and lace circles used to make long cape-like-coats. Hussein Chalayan and Mark Eisen also belong to the generation of fashion designers that created wrinkled-paper dresses (paper-look) from nonwoven materials. Paper fabric was the object of study at "Tokyo Fiber '09 Sensewer", an exhibition devoted to showing the possibilities of new materials developed with Japanese technology through the production of articles obtained from Smash, a spunbond nonwoven polyester fabric with long fibers manufactured by Asahi Kasei Fibers Corporation that can be transformed through a hot-press process.

Cantao

FELT

Gaetano Navarra

Gaetano Navarra

Armand Basi

Felt is the result of the chemical reaction between an acid (wool) and a base (soap). It is produced by bathing carded sheep fleece fibers, or the fleece or hair of other animals (goat, hare, rabbit, nutria or camel), impregnated with soap in hot water. Through a modification obtained by rubbing and pressure to create several stratified layers, the fibers adhere to each other and become entangled. The friction combines with the heat, hardening and compressing the fabric, which, in turn, turns into felt. Felt is light, ductile yet compact, and good insulation against the cold and noise. It is highly water resistant, making it suitable for indoor and outdoor use. Given that it doesn't fray, complex treatments for edges aren't necessary. Designers such as Christine Birkle have reassessed the material through experiments, either dyeing the fleece in multicolored strata before the agglomeration process or hardening it subsequently to form bodices-corsets in the natural color of the hair used. The techniques applied to these special felts allow for the production of material using a fabric felting technique called nuno felting. This entails the inclusion of felt only in certain areas of silk, linen or cotton clothing assembled exclusively with basic stitching and that later acquires the desired shape substituting pleats and cuts for the control of the inserted felt fabric. Felt is used in coats and capes, and especially in accessories such as bags and hats. Noteworthy among felt hats are the fedora, which goes well with all kinds of garments, the trilby,

a North American version without lining, and the Borsalino, manufactured in Alexandria since 1857. Felt is also used in jewelry boxes and musical instrument cases. It is a fabric as old as sheep breeding, handcrafted before primitive peoples shifted from nomadism to an agricultural way of life. Felt decorated with applications and polychrome silk lace is used to make such objects as the saddles, tent coverings and clothing elements of the communities that lived in the Altai Mountains, in Siberia, vestiges of which survive in the tombs of the Pazyryk. The name "felt" is thought to come from the city of Feltre, a municipality of the Romen Empire famous for the fulling of wool and for trade in felt fabrics.

John Galliano

Stella McCartney

Agatha Ruiz de la Prada

Roccobarocco

Cantao

This fine lightweight yet resistant cloth is obtained through the felting of fibers. Traditionally, it is made from carded sheep's wool or goat hairs. Lacking both a weft and warp, it doesn't fray when cut and is easy to work with since it doesn't require sewing hems. The term "Lenci cloth" has its origin in the famous Lenci factory in Turin, founded in 1919 by Enrico and Elena Scavini, where the fabric was used in the construction of valuable artistic dolls made entirely of cloth, which are now collector's items. The name was created from the acronym of Elena's motto: *Ludus est nobis costanter industria* (Play is our constant labor). The Lenci studio, where the dolls were made along with wooden toy objects and furniture, was a factory of ideas open to collaboration with many artists of the period. To craft the heads

Agatha Ruiz de la Prada

of the dolls, the cloth was pressed in stamping dies, the faces were painted and the little dresses were faithfully reproduced with all the luxury of details and accessories. Lenci devoted itself to experimenting with the production of semi-washable dolls, covering the cloth with fine muslin and sprinkling velvet powder on it to imitate a velvety skin. Disjoined from its original use, today Lenci cloth is still manufactured and sold as a very ductile and versatile hobby material used to make small adornments such as flower bouquets, broaches, jewelry, and cloth dolls. It is also used in the green cloth of card tables and, especially, in the production of vividly colored Carnival dresses.

GUINEA CLOTH

Guinea fabric is a raw cream-colored or white cotton fabric with a plain weave that is very economical and used in tailoring to make test garments before cutting more expensive fabrics. The test garment serves to verify the fit of the cut, ensure that the chosen style adapts to the figure and contribute possible changes to particularly complex patterns. Typically, the Guinea fabric chosen is very similar to the definitive fabric in terms of weight, consistency and drape. Many types exist, including 100% linen Guinea fabric, Guinea fabric with a fine short weft and medium-weight Guinea fabric. The material is essential in the *moulage* technique that allows the fashion designer to immediately see what he or she has created. The fabric is fit directly on the dressmaker dummy or model with the help of pins to produce a kind of "mold" of the garment to be crafted. The pins define the cloth and hold the form, which the designer gradually molds with her hands, making the fabric the living element of a free and instinctive architectural structure that can be changed or rebuilt at any time. Once the design is outlined with all its details, the subsequent marking takes place, followed first by the transfer to the cloth, then to the pattern and finally to the original fabric. The French word *moulage* indicates a three-dimensional form throughout the production process, whether craft or industrial. The technique is frequently used in haute couture. From the 1920s to the 1940s it was the technique preferred

Antonio Marras

Giorgio Armani

Gaspard Yurkievich

by Madeleine Vionnet, who experimented with the infinite potential of drape with bias-cut fabrics. In the eighties French pattern designer Janine Niepceron introduced *moulage* technique in Brazil, expanding the horizons of the burgeoning fashion industry in that country. Blue Guinea fabric originally came from India and constituted the primary object of exchange in commercial transactions involving rubber, produced in Senegal and exported to France through the ports of Marseilles and Bordeaux.

Guinea fabrics were also manufactured in France and Switzerland and were considered a rather ordinary product, used to make bed sheets, robes and shirts of low quality. Traveling salesman from the Florence ghetto visited houses and the countryside with a bundle on their back that contained Guinea cloth, Dutch cloth and Aleppo and Cambri kerchiefs to sell in installments for assembling trousseaus. Africans were not as fond of European cloths as they were Indian products, recognizable for their feel and smell

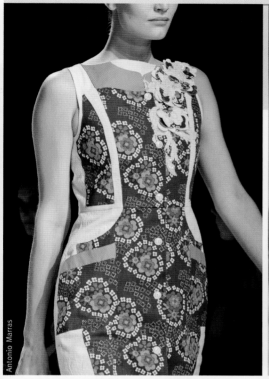

Antonio Marras

Antonio Marras

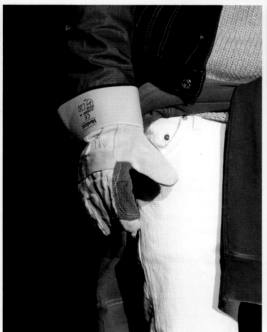

Dsquared2

Antonio Marras

C.P. Company

even when they were being unloaded at night from ships. Thus, the English, who had colonized India, acquired, in 1784, the right to sell Guinea cloth at a very favorable price, continuing to do business with rubber owners in the port of Portendick. The name comes from Guinea, the country that exported the fabric.

INTERFACING

Interfacing is a compact, light- or medium-weight fabric that serves to reinforce a lighter fabric avoiding possible transparencies and making the construction and seams invisible while reinforcing them at the same time. It is a genuine duplication applied to the reverse side of the cloth and the inside of the garment or only in parts exposed to more tension. Interfacing isn't visible in the finished garment. Becoming indistinguishable from the fabric it is applied to and sandwiched between the lining and the cloth. It fulfills multiple functions: holding the design from the inside contributing to the formation of volume; controlling the movement of the exterior fabric during ironing and washing; granting resistance to deformations caused by use (for example, in shirt front pockets). Interfacing fabric can be made from various fibers. Still, it needs to harmonize with the composition of the raw materials of the fabric, as well as with its weight and color selection. It can be muslin, batiste or light knit fabric: any material that has been appropriately stiffened or reinforced to achieve the desired result. When choosing interfacing, it must kept in mind that interfacing cut in the direction of the thread has the elasticity of knit, while if cut on the cross, it becomes weaker and prevents the material from hanging well. Knit interfacing has all or almost all the elasticity of a cloth; crepe fabric, for its part, is good for granting tone and body to the production of the design. Developing the concept of internal interfacing, French

Colcci

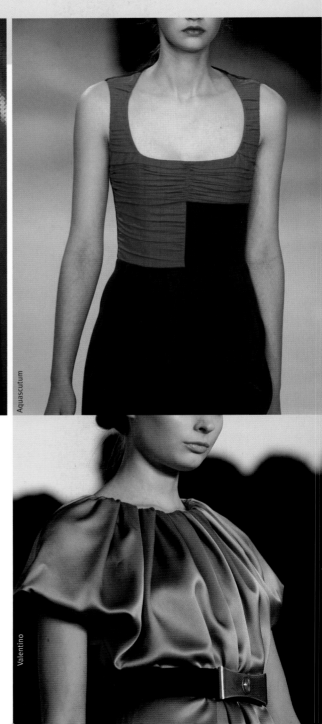

Aquascutum

Valentino

designer Paul Gaultier has created clothing from shiny acetate or opaque polyester, cut in more abundant sizes than the actual measurements of the external fabric, which seem like sculptures in motion. Its form undulates with each step the person wearing the garment takes, forming large pleats the volume of which is fed in several directions from the interior. The garment appeared on the fashion runway in the SS 2003 collection.

REINFORCING CLOTH

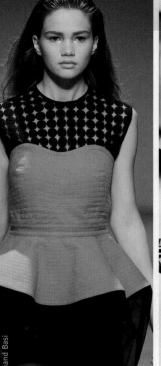

Armand Basi

Fendi

John Varvatos

Dries Van Noten

Kenzo

The use of reinforcing interlining prevents the outer fabric from stretching. It is used in collars, cuffs, pocket flaps, loops, along necklines, in openings and edgings. It can be made of cotton or rayon, sometimes mixed with other synthetic fibers. It is woven on a loom or knit, and comes in light, medium and heavy weights; it can be sewn in the traditional manner or joined by an adhesive covering on one or both sides. A good interlining shouldn't constrict the cloth. Pressed interlinings, which lack thread direction, generally are more elastic than fabrics woven on the loom, which, however, are more binding and better shape the form. Japanese designers Yohji Yamamoto and Kawakubo along with Martin Margiela, one of the six enfants terribles of the Antwerp school, proposed an unconventional use of reinforcement interlining. These designers privileged ingenious tailoring techniques and special creative craft solutions, joined on the basis of a concept of re-creating the traditional style. In an attempt to shed light on the construction of the garment and grant value to its intrinsic content, they brought simple coarse cotton to the outside of the garment and transformed it into a decorative-structural element of central interest, highlighting its unfinished quality with tack-downs and visible seams.

THERMOADHESIVE

Roland Mouret

Adhesive interfacing can be heat-sealed to other fabrics, thereby joining them. It is glued to the reverse side of the fabric with a special press at medium temperature; the resin flows in the fabric reducing the application time. Currently, it is the method most used in mass production for both economic and functional reasons. It is formed by a support fabric (knit or nonwoven textile) sprayed on one side with a thermoplastic-resin-based adhesive that is softened (liquefies) by the effect of heat. The adhesive can also be distributed with a film or with a geometric arrangement of more or less dense stitches. The parameters of time, pressure and temperature are the determining factors for the success of the operation. The application of hot-pressed interfacings slightly alters the characteristics of the fabric, grants it consistency and occasionally tends to make it stiffer. It is not suitable for slippery or rubbery materials, but is used to reinforce embroidered fabrics. Sometimes a double adhesive strip is used to construct the border between two fabrics without having to use a sewing machine that hides stitches, especially in low-cost productions.

Hussein Chalayan

Balenciaga

Roland Mouret

Valentino

Sonia Rykiel

HORSEHAIR

Costume National

Horsehair is a fiber with a structure similar to wool but obtained from the manes and tails of horses, donkeys, mules, etc. and used to make a medium-weight reinforcement sewn on the back of the fabric: in the lower part of jackets, in the shoulders and in collars, with long and slack transversal stitches to give the garment form and stability. Generally, a man's jacket needs 0.40 m. It is possible to make two pieces, thinner in the upper part and wider and rounder in the bottom, positioned in the area between the shoulder and armhole and until the waist. Horsehair contains a plain-woven taffeta fabric and a structure of twisted cotton threads (or cotton and polyester) in the warp and 100% equine horsehair or synthetic horsehair in the weft. Animal horsehair is the *non plus ultra* in interlinings. It has a very highly prized natural consistency and feel that favor the broadness of chest without making it too stiff. It used in men's outerwear of the most prestigious Italian companies, generally in the construction of the chest or turnback cuffs. Animal horsehair fabrics are woven on special rapier looms of limited height (40-45 cm), according to the length of the hair used. It weighs 130 and 180 g/m². Normally it receives a special finish that, through a mechanical-chemical procedure, permits securing the horsehair, thereby preventing it from coming loose. In the early years of the 20th century, horsehair was either pure horsehair or a blend, woven on a manual loom and used in coverings for cushions in train

Christian Lacroix

Antonio Berardi

cars. In the twenties coats emerged as a novelty in the history of fashion and gradually replaced old winter capes. The evolution of the jacket, adopted by women with the pantsuit fashion, made clear the need for more adequate interlinings. The search for new products led to diversification in the use of horsehairs to that of other animals, with a preference for goat hair or blends. Synthetic horsehairs were developed in the seventies as an alterative to natural hairs. They have a viscose weft or one blended with hair, imitate the natural fall of a horse's tail, weigh between 180 and 250 g/m², are 150-160 cm wide, and, thus, adapted to the characteristics and cut of industrial productions. An intermediate type of horsehair, soft and fluid to the touch, uses gimped weft threads with a rayon and cotton core on which horsehairs are interwoven with a special machine.

Fatima Lopes

CAMEL HAIR

Camel hair interlining is sometimes identified with sackcloth, hemp, rustic hemp cloth or linen fabrics of little value but very suitable, thanks to their coarse fibers, for "scaffolding" functions with the purpose of completely reinforcing the front part of jackets. Camel hair is woven with 100% cotton or 100% wool or wool-viscose warp and a weft of animal fibers, such as wool or goat hair (hair blend) with artificial fibers (100% viscose). It weighs between 180 and 250 g/m². The finish of camel hair fabric is of special importance. In addition to ensuring the right feel (soft or coarse, but always elastic), the finish must also grant perfect dimensional stability since before sewing lining into the front part, the fabric is submerged in water for several hours to "reshape" it. For a time, the coat (long and coarse) of camelids was used (hence the eventual name of the fabric). Both the two-hump camel, which lives in Central Asia, and the dromedary (single-hump Arab camel) have hair that reaches 37.5 cm long, with a diameter between 20 and 120 microns, and is used in the textile industry. Currently, due to its high cost, camel hair is often substituted by other interlining fa-

Gucci

Les Hommes

Aquascutum

Burberry Prorsum

brics. Camel hair serves a permanent fastening role in the garment, is the soul of the article or, so to speak, the invisible trunk that sustains the details of its external image. Camel hair interlining is softer than horsehair interlining and has more width.

JC de Castelbajac

LINING

Jean Paul Gaultier

Emporio Armani

The Italian word for lining, *fodera*, comes from the French *fourrer*, itself derived from the German *fodr*, which means "sword holster". It can be made of silk fibers, viscose, cupro, or pure or mixed acetate, all more highly regarded than polyamide or polyester lining destined for more economical sectors of the market. It is used for insulating and protecting the fabric from direct contact with the body and for improving the fit of the garment, in addition to making it heavier, warmer and more comfortable. It facilitates removal of the garment, which slides easily across the body. For this reason lining is often made with silky fabrics of varying weights depending on the intended use. It is attached to the garment solely by seams and is unencumbered at other points to facilitate movement. Noteworthy among classic linings are: very light, also called "feather" lining; light (taffeta) for summer outerwear; medium weight (twill) for winter clothes; and heavy (satin) for coats and fur-lined jackets. They can also be flannel or knit, stuffed or padded. The brand Bemberg®, created in Germany at the end of the 19th century and applied industrially starting in 1911, is identified by the production of artificial silk obtained from cotton fibers treated with copper rayon. While less resistant to large tears and use, it is a valid alternative to silk lining. *Silene* is an organically produced thread, obtained through the dissolution of cellulose diacetate *flakes* (process that uses soft wood, acetone and water), using linings that respond flexibly to the different demands of fashion and that guarantee considerable breathability, softness and dimensional stability. Other threads used in the construction of linings are: situssa (74% acetate-26% polyamide) and silfresh from Novaceta for sports clothes. Very sensitive, it is a particularly lightweight microfiber

Carolina Herrera

Etro

Etro

Cynthia Steffe

30 Paar Haende

and Lycra lining used to make complete garments in direct contact with the skin, resistant to chlorine and intended for beach and sports attire. Tecnosan lining, manufactured with tecnosan technology, incorporates special silver and carbon fiber wefts, inserted alternately and at predetermined distances in the interior of a textile base of any kind; it has a "screen" effect vis-à-vis electRomegnetic waves of 60% and avoids absorption of radiation from radio-television and mobile telephone emissions. The color of linings can match the tone of the external fabric or can be in contrast to its color, structure or design. Lining can serve as a complement the piece or be an independent autonomous element that personalizes the garment. Such is the case of iridescent linings or jacquard fabric linings, with designs that reproduce the logo and name of the most important brands. The same applies to the printed silk linings in Gucci gabardines and blazers, which recall equestrian elements such as stirrups or bridles, a tradition that identifies Florentine companies.

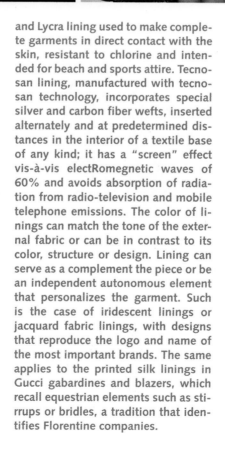

Alberta Ferretti

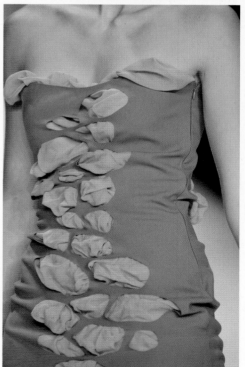

30 Paar Haende

WEBBING

Its name in Italian, *fettuccia*, is the diminutive of *fetta*, a fine piece of fabric between 5 mm and several centimeters wide. It is not cut from a piece of cloth but rather manufactured with the required width, such that its edges, corresponding to the selvages, are consistent and well defined. Webbing

Dries Van Noten

Christopher Kane

is essentially a strip of cheap cotton or synthetic fibers produced in the direction of the thread or on the cross, with different technical characteristics according to its use. Generally, it is used for reinforcement or internal fastening, for refinement applications or joining, as well as for purely decorative purposes. The structure can be of cotton threads with a plain or herringbone weave (to enhance hems), with a diagonal cut of diverse widths (to soften the hems of outerwear), with transparent mesh (for reinforcing shoulders in knit fabrics), with elastic thread fabrics (elastan) or be of Latex (for strapless dresses), etc. Other varieties exist on the market: with folded hems; ribbon finish to cover the edges of the fabric or seam; to be used as hems... In tailored garments webbing increases the resistance of the seams, which tend to break in lighter fabrics, highlight the undulation and softness of the hang and pleats from the inside, or reinforce the construction of the design near the pleats. It is also used around borders to add consistency and weight to the cloth and to enhance the way the material falls, or as a protective element in classic men's pants to prevent the fabric from wearing down due to chafing.

Louis Vuitton

Barbara Bui

Jean Paul Gaultier

Vivienne Westwood

Erdem

Dior

Fatima Lopes

BATTING

Batting is a kind of layered insulation included in the group of interlinings because it provides high thermal insulation to garments without increasing their weight, creating a dry and warm microclimate between the skin and the exterior. Light and soft, batting consists of discontinuous fibers, layers of stuffing or wool fiber filling (microfiber or polyester), with high insulation properties. The stuffing is joined through special connection techniques such as needle technique. On the other hand, batting can be stiffened with nebulized resins, with the fibers intercrossed to obtain maximum stability. Often the fibers are strati-

fied so that batting includes a large quantity of air, useful in guaranteeing good insulation. The microfiber version is much finer but provides more insulation than thicker layers of other materials. Batting is inserted in the interlining before lining the garment. It is only applied in certain areas, such as the torso and shoulders of jackets and coats, to give more body to the piece by increasing the volume of the areas in question. Batting (and also rubber foam) is used to make shoulder pads,

Hiroko Koshino

Blugirl

Agatha Ruiz de la Prada

Issey Miyake

Giles

Giles

316

shapeable and removable pads very common in women's garments in the eighties. The fashion of large shoulder pads took firm hold, as had occurred in the 1930s and 1940s, in periods when women were seeking to assert themselves socially and gain a more significant role in the workplace. In other cases, batting interlining is sewn to the garment and constitutes an inseparable internal layer. Some avant-garde designers such as Rei Kawakubo have used it to dilate and deform the anatomical curves of the dress, creating intentionally filled relief, almost as if it were a soft prosthesis added to the body. Batting is flexible and compressible material that lends itself to the "shock-resistant" digressions of contemporary fashion. It is used in the production of stuffed fabrics, in the interior of which is introduced one or more layers with the aim of increasing its thickness. The external fabric must be tight and dense to prevent the stuffing from coming to the surface. Thermore synthetic insulation is used in the manufacturing of comforters, anoraks and ski jackets with zippers and hoods. In its 2003 summer collection, the brand Allegri launched a men's line with waterproof thermolight materials, fabrics consisting of two layers of nylon and another of thermal batting. For its part, Biovalthem is a nonwoven biological textile with an alveolar structure of differentiated density made of polyester microfiber, viscose rayon and copper fiber. This particular composition gives this type of batting antistatic and antibacterial properties, in addition to the

Jean Paul Gaultier

ability to act as a shield against electRomegnetic radiation and external agents, the main causes of emotional stress and tension. Use and washing don't affect its thermal effect, its resistance to deformation or its specific features.

Comme des Garçons

VELCRO

Velcro is a protected trademark, an acronym made up of the first three letters of the words "velvet" and "crochet". It is a special material consisting entirely of nylon fiber and formed by two different parts on rigid supports that come together perfectly to form a closing system. Velcro was invented by accident in the 1950s by

Givenchy

Betsey Johnson

Dsquared2

Georges de Mestral when he observed through a microscope the tiny burrs that had used their small hooks to grab on to the pile of his jacket while he walking through the country. Velcro is made up of a strip of hairy fabric (similar to uncut velvet or a sponge) called a loop, arranged on a stiff base from which emerge small rings of hair and a second strip of fabric with tiny flexible hooks made of hard material. The two strips can be sewn or glued on either side of the opening of the garment to close it. When the two parts come into contact, the hooks grab firmly to the loop, forming a well-sealed closure. To open Velcro requires the application of a slight amount force, pulling the two strips in opposite directions. Velcro, which

is also the name of the company that produces the material, is used in the technical equipment of NASA astronauts during space voyages. It is available in different colors and is sold by the yard or already prepared in shapes that respond to the most disparate requirements. It is very common in sports clothes for fastening cuffs, collars and pockets on jackets as well as for hoods and hats. It is also used, always for fastening purposes, on shoes, bags, handbags, toilet bags, cases and backpacks.

FABRICS FOR DECORATIVE EFFECT

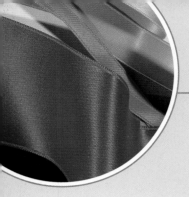

Antonio Marras

A strip of indeterminate length, more or less fine and flat, of flexible material with a width no greater than 20 cm, finished with a kind of selvage on the sides to give it more solidity and prevent fraying. Its name in Italian, *nastro*, comes from the Greek word *anastole* and the Latin anastula, which means, "to gather up the hair". Also, the Gothic term *nastilo*, which means ribbon or tie, suggests the practical function of this element

of refinement in custom-made and industrially produced garments. Ribbons are used in collars, bows, outlines and adornments. As independent elements they can act as little belts or fringe, though they are also interwoven to form new autonomous structures or rosette and cockade designs. The lateral reinforcement contains at times a fine metal thread that helps maintain the shape of the adornment. Ribbon can be woven on special automatic looms for ribbons, which allow for simultaneous production of several ribbons up to a maximum of forty units. Ribbons are made with silk thread (often substituted by polyester, which is more economical), cotton, viscose, acetate, polyamide, plastic or paper, and come in different colors and novelty designs. The weaves are those of plain fabrics or more common derivatives: stiff taffeta and shiny satin, soft and slick to the touch and occasionally double sided. Of a more consistent weight are canete and grosgrain, the vertical ribs of reps, smooth velvets, plain or

Hervé Léger

Luella

Christopher Kane

John Rocha

double striped with several warps, with jacquard patterns, with more or less elaborated edges with motifs in low relief, as well as lame, maure, velvet or printed effects, which are used in different areas as elegant, sophisticated and graceful accessories. More economical ribbons are also made by cutting pieces of fabric from synthetic fibers and sealing the edges with heat to avoid fraying. Rhythmic gymnastics with ribbons, one of the most beautiful and elegant athletic disciplines, consists in a choreographic exhibition set to music in which the athlete grasps a

fine textile ribbon, of heavy silk (35 g, 5 or 6 cm long), and keeps it in constant motion. A big fan of "love knot" ribbons, made with ribbons with two levels and two bands, was Jeanne Antoinette Poisson, Marquise of Pompadour, the favorite lover of King Loius XV and one of the most elegant and powerful women in the 18th century. In the Rococo period, during which a style that prioritized the superabundance of adornments took hold, fashion interest in ribbons found fertile ground, to the point that women transformed into "screens filled with ribbons". Rose Bertin, personal stylist of Queen Marie Antoinette, once observed that women "spent all that money only to look ridiculous." The first Universal Exhibition in 1851 was an important showroom for industrial textile ribbons, with the participation of important English textile manufacturers such as Collard & Co., Cox & Co., J.C. Ratcliff, M. Clack, C. Bray and Redmayne & Son. This consolidated industrial production during the Victorian period, when fashion required ribbons for all kinds of garments, from dresses and accessories to elaborate lingerie.

Jean Paul Gaultier

G I M P E D

The term "gimped" refers to a smooth, flat or rounded strip, around 15 mm wide, woven diagonally and with a zigzag pattern like a fishbone or knit on two-sided, compact, highly resistant material. It is used to highlight cuffs and borders, as well as for defining cuts and openings on clothes.

Gucci

Betsey Johnson

Bensoni

Gimped silk piping is used to make *alamares* (a word derived from the Arabic *al-amara*, that is, cord, lace, string), an interwoven material typical of military uniforms with double button holes into which elongated bone buttons are inserted, very similar to the ones on the well-known Montgomery coats. Today, *alamares* come in many varieties, including plain gimped material and lace or more elaborate creations consisting of silk passementerie, which are added to three-quarter-coats, overcoats and coats that evoke the look of *Doctor Zhivago*, a classic movie set in the Russia of the October Revolution and inspired by a novel by

Alberta Ferretti

Alberta Ferretti

Jean Paul Gaultier

Boris Leonidovich Pasternak. *Alamares* are also applied to elegant dresses, shirts, jackets and knit cardigans. In the language of fashion, gimped material is also called *soutache*. The name is a transposition of the term sujtas, or, "little braid", a decorative element in the *dolman*, a garment worn in Hungary. It is a fine braid, flat and flexible with two ribs, of silk, viscose, rayon or other materials, and used to make elegant eyelet closures, passementerie and decorative relief motifs for adornments.

Jean Paul Gaultier

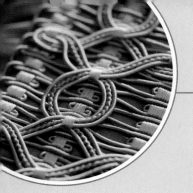

Gucci

Betsey Johnson

Betsey Johnson

Passementerie is an ornamental edging or trimming of one or various colors with festooned and jagged borders. It is sold by the yard. The same word alludes to the set of ribbons, braid, lace overlay and ribs used to adorn clothing and tapestries. It can be made from a wide variety of materials: silk with metallic threads, wool with plastic, polyester with cotton and rayon, raffia with strips of leather, with precious stone and sequins for decoration. The consistency and stiffness of passementerie are varying, as are its color combinations and widths. The name comes from the French word *passement*, or ornamental braid. Passementerie uses the textures typical of all other textile products and is made employing diverse techniques, depending on whether it is a flat fabric weave, a braided weave, a knit weave or a bonded structure. It is woven on special looms, on jacquard or crochet machines. Occasionally a single piece of passementerie contains different fabrics and techniques, embellished with finishing effects such as printing or embroidery. Gallons are ribbons with an especially soft braid, with or without patterns, similar to ones that adorn the visors and epaulets of military uniforms, flags and standards, livery and regional suits. The diameter of the cords is between 1mm and several centimeters. There are different kinds of passementerie (tooled, agreman, Polish perle and jagged) used in jewelry and costume jewelry as accessory adornments or borders on garments.

Alexander Wang

Blumarine

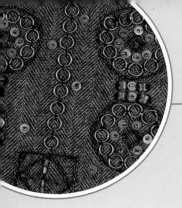

R I V E T S

Tacks, jagged borders, little chains, brooches, stickpins and abundant zippers and other metallic elements used to cover fabrics and parts of garments in keeping with the style of urban street trends. In the seventies, black leather became an anti-fashion symbol of transgression and the favorite of punk groups such as the Sex Pistols. The look caught on in London through the store Let It Rock, a point of reference in the punk music scene, owned by Malcolm McLaren and his partner Vivienne Westwood, who soon would become a famous designer. Imitating their idols, and as a sign of protest against the dominant culture, the first English squatters and ravers applied the culture of "Do it yourself" to their flight jackets, adding distinctive featu-

Antonio Berardi

Malloni

Emilio Pucci

Viktor & Rolf

Frankie Morello

Proenza Schouler

John Richmond

res and sayings surrounded by spikes and tacks, wearing leather pants and fetish accessories, and tearing their shirts and sewing them back with staples and safety pins. The phenomenon was enhanced by the arrival of body piercing, the fashion of perforating one's ear lobes, nose, lips and other less visible parts of the body with rings and pins of all kinds. These metallic accessories represented, to paraphrase the title of a book by George McKay, "foolish acts of beauty", exhibited by young people as if they were trophies of tests of bravery. The style, which became firmly entrenched thanks to the movie *The Punk Rock Movie*, moved onto ready-to-wear fashion runways, reinterpreted by designers such as Moschino, Dolce & Gabbana or John Ritchmnd and emptied of their original symbolism.

Ann Demeulemeester

Burberry Prorsum

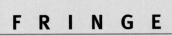

Fringe is an adornment similar to passementerie trimming but characterized by the presence of threads that hang like beards, dancing freely and undulating together at the slightest movement of the body. It is sold by the yard and sewn along the edges of the garment. Fringes add a notable decorative effect accentuated by the beauty of the yarn of which they are made and the length of the hanging threads. Technically, fringe is made from wool, silk or viscose fibers, technological fibers or nonwoven textile, which are left free and floating at one end; fringes are kept together by another series of threads that crosses them horizontally to prevent the floating threads from slipping and the border from coming undone. Its structure can be woven, knotted, braided or sewn for structural or merely ornamental purposes. It is used to decorate borders to highlight the gracefulness of the wearer's gait, such as finishing on shoe and adornments on shawls that drape sensually over the arms and shoulders. Fringe is added to belts, collars and cuffs as an attractive detail. The floating fringes of Josephine Baker, one of the first cabaret dancers, who embraced the style to emphasize her dynamic performances, are unforgettable. Fringes are the characteristic adornment on Charleston-style dance dresses, formed entirely by a succession of strips between 20 and 30 cm long that fall one over the other producing a rich waterfall effect. The image of the alarming dress with long fringes is linked to the intriguing power

Alessandro Dell'Acqua

Basso & Brooke

Hermès

Matthew Williamson

of seduction, masterfully embodied by Dolores del Rio, dame of erotic fascination, in the 1935 movie *In Caliente*. The AW 2011 fashion runway reintroduced this highly regarded trend to add a touch of refinement to dresses, skirts, jackets, capes, coats, boots and bags, all featuring fringes.

Jean Paul Gaultier

FEATHERS

Lanvin

Givenchy

Burberry Prorsum

The custom of using feathers to adorn people, weapons and rooms can be observed at all levels of cultural development, from primitive hunters to contemporary civilization that still seeks out exotic avian feathers to decorate dresses and fashion accessories. Bird plumage consists of various types of feathers that cover the animal's skin and protect it. The color of the plumage depends on the natural pigmentation of each species and the age and gender of the animals, the season of the year and specific climate and environmental conditions. A feather is made of a quill or calamus, the hollow axial part of the shaft of the feather, and two other parts known as the vane, which consist of barbs. Bird feathers are differentiated from each other by their form and structure, which, in turn, perform different functions. A pre-feather is an embryonic feather that falls out periodically and is regenerated in subsequent molting. Filoplumes are the first feathers of young birds; they have a small stem with a long, fine axis ending in three or four short barbs. In some species, young plumage remains unchanged in both sexes throughout the animal's lifetime. Feathers as such are called contour feathers because they form the covering of the bird's mantle and give consistency to the figure and form of its body. In some species the plumage of adult males and females is very different. In general, males have longer, more colorful feathers, which are accentuated in mating season and form the so-called "nuptial plumage". Downy feathers are made up of soft, light feathers without any rigid elements, in such a way that the barbs remain separate without forming a consistent mantle but act together to provide thermal insulation. The art of working with plumage consists of arranging the feathers to make clothes, adornments and accessories and has its origin in the atavistic need to mark social differences. Feathers, applied according to determined aesthetic conventions, acquire symbolic value and respond to a precise code of clothing. Production techniques demand careful classification of the material in terms of stiff or soft feathers or by criteria of length or color. The combination and alternation of two or more colors create patterns and tones that constitute the inherent characteristics of each species. To prepare the feathers for production and decoration essentially three methods are used: threading the quill, sometimes artificially enlarged, in a base material that serves as a support; gluing light or small feathers to a smooth base (flexible or inflexible); and knotting the feathers to the stem, individually or in plumes, with cords

Valentino

Alberta Ferretti

Emilio Pucci

Alexander McQueen

Bill Blass

and then interweaving them in nets or sewing them to fabrics or other materials. Another method is the art of applying the entire bird's skin along with its plumage to a base. Feathers, an element that has always been held in high regard by the most prestigious Italian and French haute couture fashion houses, are ductile and can be worked with in different ways: cut, sculpted, brushed, gilded, printed and dyed in bright fashionable tones. Heron, duck, swan, emu, pheasant, guinea-fowl, crane, turkey, partridge, tragopan and peacock-pheasant feathers are used for all kinds of adornments. Feathers are also used in the world of accessories for sheer cockades on hats and shoes or arranged in long airy rooster, turkey, peacock, Marabou stork or ostrich plumes. These are feathers for full dresses that lend themselves to elegant traditional designs or inspirations with a primitive air, simultaneously tribal and chic. Antonio Marras has used bright feathers, coated in a bath, in a Kenzo collection set in the Amazon forest and inspired by the movie *Fitzcarraldo*. The ingenious Alexander McQueen created a suggestive scenario in his SS 2008 collection, featuring a phantasmagoric "bird woman" fitted out with wings made of actual feathers. Dutch designer Lidewij Edelkoort has dusted off the theme of birds' feathers and birds' nests in trees or among the bamboo along the shores of lakes in recent creations, featuring intense and deep animal colors such as olive brown, ochre and dark blue illuminated by the gold and silver glimmers of the water. To be "feathered" has more than one meaning. In reference to birds it means "to grow feathers; when referring to a hat, it means, "to adorn with feathers".

BIBLIOGRAPHY

A.A.V.v. *Au royaume du signe. Appliqués sur toile des Kuba, Zaire*, 1988, Adam Biro, Parls

A.A.V.v. *Bathik, simboli magici e tradizione femminile a Giava*, cat. expo Palazzo Isimbardi, Milan, edited by S. FELDBAUER, 1988, Electa, Milan

A.A.V.v. *Blu Blue-jeans, il Blu Popolare*, cat. exposición, 1989, Electa, Milan

A.A.V.v. *Emilio Pucci*, cat. expo *Il Tempo e la Moda*, Biennale di Florence, edited by G. CELANT, L. SETTEMBRINI, I. SISCHY, 1996, Skira, Milan

A.A.V.v. *Guida alle fibre Man Made*, 1996, Editoriale Alfa, Sesto S.G. (MI)

A.A.V.v. *Il cinema. Grande storia illustrata*, 1982, Istituto Geografico de Agostini, Novara

A.A.V.v. *Il linguaggio della moda*, edited by L. DIODATO, 2000, Rubbettino, Catanzaro

A.A.V.v. *Il motore della moda*, cat. expo, 1998, *The Monacelli Press*, New York

A.A.V.v. *Il velo*, cat. expo edited by A. BUSTO, 2007, Silvana Editoriale, Milan

A.A.V.v. *La Moda Italiana*, I y II, 1987, Electa, Milan

A.A.V.v. *Quaderni di tecnologia tessile, La nobilitazione*, 2006, Collane Fondazione Acimit, Milan

A.A.V.v. *Quaderni di tecnologia tessile, La tessitura*, 2000, Collane Fondazione Acimit, Milan

A.A.V.v. *Le microfibre sintetiche*. Congresso of studies on the evolution of textile for clothing and chemical fibers, 1992, Assofibre

A.A.V.v. *Mariano Fortuny*, cat. expo, 1999, Marsilio, Venice

A.A.V.v. *Musée de l'impression sur étoffe de Mulhouse*, nn. 761-4 del *Bulletin Trimestriel de la Società Industrielle de Mulhouse*, 1975, Mulhouse

A.A.V.v. *Museo del lino: le collezioni, gli strumenti, i manufatti*, edited by F. MERISI, 1999, Museo del Lino editions, Pescarolo ed Uniti, Cremona

A.a.V.v. *Paris Couture - Années Trente*, cat. expo, 1987, Musée de la Mode et du Costume, Palais Galliera, Paris

A.A.V.v. *Per una storia della moda pronta, Problemi e ricerche*, Minutes of the Fifth International Congress of the CISST. Milan 26-28 febrero 1991, Edifir, Florence

A.A.V.v. *Robes du soir*, 1850-1990, cat. expo, 1990, Paris Musees editions, Paris

A.A.V.v. *Seconda Pelle*, edited by K. DUNSEATH, 2001, Feltrinelli, Turin

A.A.V.v. *Seta. Il Novecento a Como*, cat. expo edited by C. BUSS, 2001, Silvana, Milan

A.A.V.v. *Tecnologia dell'abbigliamento: dalla fibra all'abito*, 2001, Ascontex, Milan

A.A.V.v. *Tessuti antichi nelle chiese di Arona*, cat. expo edited by D. DEVOTI y G. ROMENO, 1981, Musei civici di Torino Editori, Turin

A.A.V.v. *Una moda mondiale*, 1990, Editrice Consumatori, Bologna

A.A.V.v. *Velluto. Fortune, tecniche, mode*, edited by F. DE' MARINIS, 1993, Idea Books, Milan

A.A.V.v. *100 anni di tintura e stampa*, edited by A. Tagliabue, 2003, Pro.No.Tex, Milan

NO ESPECIFICADO, *Zegna Baruffa Lane Borgosesia*, s.d.

NO ESPECIFICADO, *Elementi di Tecnologia Tessile*, 1961, I.N.A.P.L.I.

NO ESPECIFICADO, *Le filet brodè*, Boucherit, Paris

NO ESPECIFICADO, *Trattato di confezione moderna, la moda maschile*, La moda maschile editore, Milan

AMATO F. BOTTERO A. TOMASINI E. y M. *Dal foderame alla fodera*, 1989, Edizioni Emmetiemme, Manifattura Tessuti, Milan

ANDREW A. *Il Punto Smock*, 1990, Mondadori, Milan

ASPESI N. *Il lusso & l'autarchia*, 1982, Rizzoli, Milan

BARBERIS G. *Omaggio al cappello, La Borsalino di Teresio Usuelli*, 1989, Scheiwiller, Milan

BARDINI BARBAFIERA L. MORONI A. *Elementi di tecnica tessile*, 2009, Trevisini Libri, Milan

BARICCO A. *Seta*, 1999, Rizzoli, Milan

BARNARD N. *La Passion des Tissus*, 1989, Éditions du Chene, Paris

BARTES R. *Sistema della Moda*, 1970, Einaudi, Turin

BARTES R. *Il senso della Moda*, edited by G. Marrone, 2002, Einaudi, Turin

BEANEY J. *Stitches: New Approaches*, 1985, B.T. Batsford Ltd, London

BELLEZZA ROSINA, CATALDI M. GALLO M. *Cotoni stampati e Mezzari, dalle Indie all'Europa*, 1993, Sagep, Genoa

BELTRAME G. *La decorazione su stoffa*, 1989, Editorial Paradigma

BERGAMASCHI G. *Fior di Lino*, 1985, Idealibri, Milan

BIANCHI E. *Dizionario Internazionale dei tessuti*, 1997, Tessile di Como

Black J.A. Garland M. *Storia della Moda*, 1984, Istituto Geografico De Agostini, Novara

BLIGNAUT H. POPOVA L. *Maschile, femminile e altro. Le mutazioni dell'identità nella moda dal 1900 ad oggi*, 2005, Franco Angeli, Milan

BOCCHERINI T. MARABELLI P. *Atlante di Storia del Tessuto*, 1995, M. Cristina de Montemayor, Florence

BONA M. ISNARDI F.A. STRANEO S.L. *Manuale di Tecnologia Tessile*, 1981, Edizioni Scientifiche A. Cremonese, Rome

BONAMI F. FRISA M.L. TRONCHI S. *Uniforme. Ordine e disordine*, cat. expo, 2000, Charta, Milan

BOURRIAUD N. *Estetica relazionale*, 2010, Postmedia, Milan

BRADDOCK S.E. O'MAHONY M. *Techno Textiles. Tessuti rivoluzionari per la moda e il design*, 2002, Ascontex, Milan

BRADLEY Q. *Textile Designers, at the cutting edge*, 2009, Laurence King Publishing, London

BROWN S. *Ecomoda*, 2010, Logos, Modena

BOUCHER F. *Histoire du costume en occidente de l'antiquité a nos jours*, 1965, Flammarion, Paris

BUHLER E. *Tingere la lana con erbe, foglie, fiori*, 1978, Fabbri, Milan

CALEFATO P. *Lusso*, 2003, Meltemi, Rome

CALEFATO P. *Moda, corpo, mito*, 1999, Castelvecchi, Rome

CERRI M. *La tintura*, 1995, Arnaldo Caprai gruppo tessile S.p.A. Foligno (PG)

CERRI M. *Dal ricamo al merletto*, 1995, Arnaldo Caprai gruppo tessile S.p.A. Foligno (PG)

CERULLI E. *Vestirsi, spogliarsi, travestirsi*, 1981, Sellerio, Palermo

CHAILLE F. *La grande histoire de la cravate*, 1994, Flammarion, Paris

CLARCKE S. *Disegnatore tessile*, 2009, Logos, Modena

COLCHESTER C. *Textiles today*, 2007, Thames & Hudson, London

COLE D. *Textiles now*, 2008, Laurence King Publishing, London

DAVANZO POLI D. *Tessuti del Novecento*, 2007, Skira, Milan

DE BUZZACCAMINI V. *Giacche da uomo*, 1994, Zanfi, Modena

DE BUZZACCAMINI V. *Pantaloni & Co*, 1989, Zanfi, Modena

DE BUZZACCAMINI V. DAVANZO POLI D. *L'abito da sposa*, 1989, Zanfi, Modena

DE DILLMONT T. *Encyclopédie des ouvrages de dames*, 1909, T. De Dillmont, Dornach

DE LA HAYE A. *Mode '900*, 1988, Istituto Geografico De Agostini, Novara

DEMARIA M.D. GOLETTI A.V. PACE C. *Moda & Dintorni*, 2008, Hoepli, Milan

DHAMIJA J. JAIN J. *Handwoven Fabrics of India*, 1989, Mapin Publishing Pvt. Ltd. Ahmedabad

DEVOTI D. *L'arte del tessuto in Europa*, 1974, Bramante, Milan

DUBIN L.S. *Histoire des Perles*, 1988, Nathan Image, Paris

EARNSHAW P. *Identification of Lace*, 1980, Shire publications Ltd, London

EARNSHAW P. *Lace machines and machine laces*, vol I-II, 1995, Gorse publications, Guildford

FANELLI G. E R. *Il tessuto moderno*, 1976, Vallecchi, Florence

FAUQUE C. *La Dentelle*, 1995, Syros, Paris

FAZZIOLI E. *La moda nella storia della Cina*, 1991 Mondadori, Milan

FOLLEDORE G. *Il cappello da uomo*, 1988, Zanfi, Modena

FRACASSI GUILAVOGUI M. *Pittura su corteccia degli Aborigeni australiani*, 1996, tesis doctoral, Nuova Accademia di Belle Arti, Milan

FRANCONETTI V.A. *Elementi di Tecnologia Tessile*, 1995, Padus, Cremona

GANDELLI E. *C'è tessuto e tessuto*, 2009, Lampi di stampa, Milan
GAROFOLI M. *Le fibre intelligenti*, 1991, Electa, Milan
GHISALBERTI A. *Elementi di tessitura*, 1968, San Marco, Trescore Balneario (BG)
GIBELLINI L. TOMASI C. *Il disegno per la moda*, vol. I e II, 2004, Clitt, Rome
GLYNN P. *Pelle a Pelle, l'erotismo nell'abbigliamento*, 1982, Gremese, Rome
GOSTELOW M. *Le livre de la broderie*, 1978, Dessain et Tolra, Paris
GROSSINI G. *Firme in passerella*, 1986, Dedalo, Bari
GRANA C. *Tecnologia e Merceologia Tessile*, vol. I e II, 2005, San Marco, Trescore Balneario (BG)
GRANA C. *Tecnologia del taglio industriale nel tessile*, 2010, San Marco, Trescore Balneario (BG)

HAGENEY W. *Tartans*, 1987, Belvedere co. Ltd, Rome
Harris, J. *5000 years of textiles*, 1993, British Museum Press, London
KLEIN N. *No logo*, 2000, Baldini & Castoldi, Milan
KOREN L. *New Fashion Japan*, 1984, Kodansha International Ltd
KRAATZ A. *Merletti*, 1988, Mondadori, Milan

LAMBERT P. STAEPELAERE B. FRY M.G. *Color and Fibres*, 1986, Schiffer Pub. Ltd, West Chester, Pensilvania
LEE S. *Fashioning the future*, 2005, Thames & Hudson, London
Lehnert, G. *Storia della Moda del XX secolo*, 2000, Koenemann Verlagsgesellschaft mbH, Colonia
LEMOINE-LUCCIONI E. *Psicoanalisi della moda*, 2002, Bruno Mondadori, Milan
LEMON J. *Metal Thread Embroidery*, 1987, B.T. Batsford Ltd, London
LEVI PISETZKY R. *Il costume e la moda nella società italiana*, 1978, Einaudi, Turin
LUNDELL L. *Le livre du tissage*, 1978, Dessain et Tolra, Paris
LUNGHI M.D. PESSA L. *Macramé, l'arte del pizzo a nodi nei paesi mediterranei*, 1996, Sagep, Genoa
LUZZATO L. POMPAS R. *I colori del vestire*, 1997, Hoepli, Milan

MALOSSI G. *La regola estrosa*, 1995, Electa, Milan
MANCINELLI A. *Moda!* 2006, Sperling & Kupfer, Milan
MARIANO B. *Psicologia dell'abbigliamento*, 1993, A. Pontecorboli, Florence
MENDICINI G. *L'eleganza maschile*, 1996, Mondadori, Milan
MIZZAU T. *Cambiamenti strutturali in corso nel mercato e nella lavorazione dei cascami di seta di filanda* in *La Seta*, 1993, Bollettino ufficiale della Stazione Sperimentale della Seta di Como XLVII-N.2-3
MONTAGU A. *Il tatto*, 1975, Garzanti, Milan
MORACE F. *Real Fashion Trend*, 2007, Scheiwiller, Milan
MORESCHI G. *Tecnologia tessile*, 1989, San Marco, Trescore Balneario (BG)
MORINI E. *Storia della Moda XVIII-XX secolo*, 2000, Skira, Milan
MORRIS D. *Il comportamento intimo*, 1972, Mondadori, Milan
MOSCONI D. VILLAROSA R. *188 nodi da collo. Cravatte e colletti: tecniche, storia, immagini*, 1984, Idealibri, Milan
NEBREDA L. E. *Atlante della Moda*, 2009, Logos, Modena
NUVOLETTI G. *Elogio della cravatta*, 1982, Idealibri, Milan

ORLANDI R. *Punti ai ferri, collezione 3000 punti*, 1987, Zanfi, Modena
ORSI LANDINI R. *Seta, Potere e glamour*, 2006, Silvana Editoriale, Milan
ORSI LANDINI R. *I tessuti Lisio: il broccato Desdemona in Jacquard* n. 8, 1990, boletín trimestral de la Fondazione Arte della Seta Lisio, Florence

PAINE M. *Tessuti Classici*, 1991, Rizzoli, Milan
Pastoureau, M. *I colori dei nostri ricordi*, 2010, Ponte alle Grazie, Milan
PASTOUREAU M. *La stoffa del diavolo*, 1993, Il melangolo, Genoa
PASTOUREAU M. *L'uomo e il colore*, in *Storia e Dossier* n. 5, marzo 1987, Giunti, Florence
PEACOCK J. *Gli accessori del XX secolo*, 2001, Mondadori, Milan
PIFFERI E. *Il mondo della lana*, 1994, E.P.I., Milan
POMPAS R. *Textile Design*, 1994, Hoepli, Milan
PULITI M. *Disegno tecnico tessile*, 1990, Media, Florence

RICCI S. *Materiali per la fantasia*, cat. mostra, 1997, Museo Salvatore Ferragamo, Florence
RICCI BITTI P. E. CATERINA R. a cura di, *Moda, relazioni sociali e comunicazione*, 1995, Zanichelli, Bologna
ROBINSON K. *Il guardaroba perfetto*, 1988, Sperling & Kupfer, Milan
ROETZEL B. *Il Gentleman. Manuale dell'eleganza maschile*, 1999, Koenemann Verlagsgesellschaft mbH, Colonia

SACCHI C. *Fabbricazione delle stoffe lisce ed operate*, 1931, Hoepli, Milan
SAINT-AUBIN C. G. *The Art of Embroidered, designer to the king*, 1770, translation and commentary by N. SCHEUER 1983, Los Angeles County Museum of Art
SAN MARTIN M. *Materiali innovativi per la moda*, 2010, Logos, Modena
SEILER-BALDINGER A. *Textiles, a classification of techniques*, 1994, Crawford House Press, Liverpool
SCHOENHOLZER T. SILVESTRI I. *La collezione Gandini. Merletti, Ricami e Galloni dal XV al XIX secolo*, 2002, Franco Cosimo Panini, Modena
SCHOESER M. *Tessuti del mondo*, 2003, Skira, Milan
SCOTT P. *Il libro della Seta*, 1993, Garzanti, Milan
Seeling C. *Moda, il secolo degli stilisti, 1900-1999*, Koenemann Verlagsgesellschaft mbH, Cologne
SGARBI V. *Roberta di Camerino, i disegni: 1955-1975*, cat. mostra, 1985, Marsilio, Venice
SILVER M. SOMARÈ M. *Moda di celluloide, il cinema, la donna, la sua immagine*, 1988, Idealibri, Milan
SINISCALCO SPINOSA M. GRANDJEAN S. KING M. GONZALES PALACIOS A. *Gli Arazzi, i quaderni dell'antiquariato*, 1981, Fabbri, Milan
SOLI P. *Il genio antipatico*, cat. mostra, 1984, Mondadori, Milan
SPADONI M. *Le fibre tessili artificiali in Italia dai primi del Novecento alla seconda guerra mondiale*, 1999-2000, tesi di Dottorato in Storia Economica, Università degli Studi di Pisa
SPOSITO S. *Manufatti ricamati a crochet nella moda del XVIII e XIX secolo*, 1999, tesi di Laurea, N.A.B.A., Milan
SPOSITO S. *Mariano Fortuny: un artista inventore*, in *Notiziario tecnico tessile*, Ass. ex-allievi del setificio P. Carcano di Como. Anno LXII, 2012 Il prato, Saonara (PD)
SPOSITO S. *Bosna Quilt-tempo-cucito* in *Filoforme* n. 11, 2004, Il prato, Saonara (PD)
SPOSITO S. *La globalizzazione di Ynka Shonibare* in *Filoforme* n. 5, 2002, Il prato, Saonara (PD)
SPOSITO S. *Tessuti e Filati (Estetica della Sensorialità)* in *Mood* n. 18, 2001, Ventisei, Milan
UDALE J. *Design di tessuti per la moda*, 2010, Zanichelli, Bologna
VANNINI L. *Il lavoro impuntito, raccolta di disegni*, s.d.
VENIER A. *Elementi di tintura e analisi delle fibre sintetiche*, 1966, San Marco, Trescore Balneario (BG)
VILLAROSA R. SCHIAFFINO M. *Uomini & Calze*, 1991, Idealibri, Milan
VOLBACH W.F. *Il tessuto nell'arte antica*, 1966, Fabbri, Milan
VOLLI U. *Contro la moda*, 1990, Feltrinelli, Milan
White P. Lesage *Maitre Brodeur de la Haute Couture*, 1988, Éditions du Chene, Paris
WIDMANN C. *Il significato dei colori*, 2000, Scientifiche Magi, Rome
WILSON J. *Classic and modern fabrics*, 2010, Thames & Hudson, London
WOLTERS N. *Les Perles*, 1996, Syros, Paris
ZISCHKA A. *La Guerra segreta per il cotone*, 1935, Bompiani, Milan

CONTENTS